# Discrimination and Delegation

T0347607

# Discrimination and Delegation

*Explaining State Responses to Refugees*

LAMIS ELMY ABDELAATY

OXFORD
UNIVERSITY PRESS

# OXFORD
## UNIVERSITY PRESS

Oxford University Press is a department of the University of Oxford. It furthers
the University's objective of excellence in research, scholarship, and education
by publishing worldwide. Oxford is a registered trade mark of Oxford University
Press in the UK and certain other countries.

Published in the United States of America by Oxford University Press
198 Madison Avenue, New York, NY 10016, United States of America.

© Oxford University Press 2021

First issued as an Oxford University Press paperback, 2023

All rights reserved. No part of this publication may be reproduced, stored in
a retrieval system, or transmitted, in any form or by any means, without the
prior permission in writing of Oxford University Press, or as expressly permitted
by law, by license, or under terms agreed with the appropriate reproduction
rights organization. Inquiries concerning reproduction outside the scope of the
above should be sent to the Rights Department, Oxford University Press, at the
address above.

You must not circulate this work in any other form
and you must impose this same condition on any acquirer.

Library of Congress Cataloging-in-Publication Data
Names: Abdelaaty, Lamis Elmy, author. | Selective sovereignty
Title: Discrimination and delegation : explaining state responses to refugees /
Lamis Elmy Abdelaaty.
Description: New York, NY : Oxford University Press, [2021] |
Revision of author's thesis (doctoral)—Princeton University, 2014,
titled Selective sovereignty : foreign policy, ethnic identity, and the politics of asylum. |
Includes bibliographical references and index.
Identifiers: LCCN 2020030369 (print) | LCCN 2020030370 (ebook) |
ISBN 9780197530061 (hardback) | ISBN 9780197753385 (paperback) |
ISBN 9780197530085 (epub)
Subjects: LCSH: Refugees—Government policy. |
Emigration and immigration—Government policy. |
Emigration and immigration—Political aspects. |
Emigration and immigration—Social aspects. | International agencies. | Sovereignty.
Classification: LCC JV6346 .A43 2021 (print) |
LCC JV6346 (ebook) | DDC 325/.21—dc23
LC record available at https://lccn.loc.gov/2020030369
LC ebook record available at https://lccn.loc.gov/2020030370

DOI: 10.1093/oso/9780197530061.001.0001

Paperback printed by Integrated Books International, United States of America

*For Papa*

# Contents

# Contents

# Acknowledgments

This book is based on my doctoral dissertation, so I begin with my committee—Robert Keohane, Evan Lieberman, Christina Davis, and Amaney Jamal. I could not have asked for more thoughtful guidance, more careful critiques, or steadier support. I distinctly remember first seeing Bob's name as an undergraduate at the American University in Cairo. I knew I wanted to pursue a PhD, but I never imagined I would meet him in person. Being Bob's advisee was an extraordinary privilege, and I could not be more grateful to have such an exceptional mentor.

For their constructive comments and their firm encouragement, I am also indebted to Anar Ahmadov, Gary Bass, Galya Ben-Arieh, Alexander Betts, Sarah Bush, Stephen Chaudoin, Tom Christensen, Bess Davis, Rex Douglass, Andrea Everett, Sarah El-Kazaz, Alexandra Escobar, Andrea Everett, Luara Ferracioli, Joanna Gowa, Tom Hale, Rebecca Hamlin, Marina Henke, David Hsu, Kip Kendall, Julius Lagodny, Alex Lanoszka, Helen Morris, Alex Ovodenko, Sarah Parkinson, Maggie Peters, Kris Ramsay, Tom Scherer, Anna Schrimpf, Jake Shapiro, Christine Shenouda, Justin Simeone, Erin Snider, Liza Steele, Timo Thoms, Jaquilyn Waddell Boie, Chris Way, Beth Whitaker, Meredith Wilf, Keren Yarhi-Milo, and many many others. For their comments at my manuscript workshop, I am grateful to Michael Barnett and Jim Hollifield. My colleagues at Syracuse University and at the University of California-Santa Cruz have been particularly supportive, especially Neda Atanasoski, Matt Cleary, Elizabeth Cohen, Kent Eaton, Chris Faricy, Shana Gadarian, Dimitar Georgiev, Seth Jolly, Audie Klotz, Ronnie Lipschutz, Mark Massoud, Dean Mathiowetz, Dan McDowell, Eleonora Pasotti, Rebecca Peters, Catherine Ramírez, Ben Read, Cecilia Rivas, Roger Schoenman, Jessica Taft, Brian Taylor, Emily Thorson, Simon Weschle, and Dan Wirls.

Numerous people went out of their way to help with my research—what follows is a very incomplete list. In Egypt, Lina Attalah, Maysa Ayoub, Sherif Elsayed-Ali, Barbara Harrell-Bond, Naseem Hashim, Greg Hoadley, Amr Ismail, Ray Jureidini, Doaa Mohie, Heba Morayef, Jasmine Moussa, Sara Sadek, Hania Sholkamy, Mai Taha, and the staff at the Center for Migration and Refugee Studies at the American University in Cairo were more than generous with their advice, contacts, and documents. My fieldwork in Kenya would not have been possible without the support of Yara Bayoumy, Raymond Hopkins, Riva Jalipa, Eva Kaye-Zwiebel, Anna Lindley, James Milner, Olive Munene, Mahiri Mwita, Hélène Thiollet, Rene Vollenbroich, Jennifer Widner, and the staff at the British

Institute in Eastern Africa. For their assistance with my research trip to Turkey, I want to thank Kristen Biehl, Ali Çağlar, Özlen Çelebi, Jennifer Dixon, Ahmet İçduygu, Kemal Kirişci, Mohamed Moussa, Deniz Sert, Bertan Tokuzlu, Şirin Turkay, Başak Ural, Kadir Yildirim, the staff of the Migration Research Program at Koç University, and the staff at the American Research Institute in Turkey (Ankara and Istanbul research centers). Thank you to Heather Faulkner, Anna Haward, and Iordanis Ronganakis at the UNHCR Archives for going above and beyond. Outstanding research assistance was provided by Jonathan Fu, Pınar Gibbon, Mallika Palecanda, and Robert Spoden; Turkish-language interpretation by Marc Saurina and Uğur Yıldız; and German-language translation by Elli Homolko.

To fund my fieldwork and archival research, I am fortunate to have received a Franklin Research Grant from the American Philosophical Society, a National Science Foundation (NSF) Doctoral Dissertation Improvement Grant, an Appleby-Mosher Faculty Research Grant from the Maxwell School at Syracuse University, a Princeton Institute for International and Regional Studies Dissertation Research Grant, and a Mamdouha S. Bobst Center for Peace and Justice Research Grant. When I was finishing up my dissertation, the Graduate Fellows program at the Princeton Institute for International and Regional Studies provided me with crucial time, space, and finances.

I had many excellent opportunities to present parts of my research and receive valuable feedback: the Annual Convention of the International Studies Association (February 2017 and April 2013), the Department of Government Workshop at Cornell University (October 2016), the International Affairs Workshop at Texas A&M University (March 2015), the Workshop on Refugee Protection Outside of the International Legal Framework at Northwestern University (May 2014), the Annual Conference of the Institute for Middle East Studies at George Washington University (April 2014), the Stanford-Berkeley Immigration Conference (February 2014), the Workshop on the Ethics and Politics of the Global Refugee Regime at Princeton University (March 2013), the Migration Research Program Seminar at Koç University (February 2012), the Annual Meeting of the American Political Science Association (September 2011), the Annual Conference of the Canadian Association for Refugee and Forced Migration Studies (May 2011), the Annual National Conference of the Midwest Political Science Association (March–April 2011), and the Annual Symposium on Arab World Diasporas and Migrations at the Georgetown University Center for Contemporary Arab Studies (March 2011). I am also grateful to the participants at Syracuse University's Migration and Citizenship reading group and the Moynihan Research Workshop, as well as Princeton University's International Relations Graduate Research Seminar, the Workshop on Arab Political Development Graduate Student Colloquium, the Center for

Migration and Development Works-in-Progress Series, the Program in African Studies' Indaba, Thingira: Graduate students working on Africa and the African diaspora, the Princeton Institute for International and Regional Studies Graduate Fellows Seminar, and the Neihaus Center for Globalization and Governance "Pizza and Politics" group.

Thank you to the fantastic staff at SU's Political Science Department, the Campbell Public Affairs Institute, UCSC's Department of Politics, and Princeton's Department of Politics. The inimitable and remarkably resourceful Bobbie Zlotnik assisted with every aspect related to my NSF grant, application, travel planning, reimbursement, paperwork, and so much else. Oscar Torres-Reyna was a great help in guiding my quantitative analysis.

I am grateful to Angela Chnapko at Oxford University Press for her guidance and patience, and to Suganya Elango and Leslie Johnson for shepherding the book through the production process. Superb developmental editor Patricia Heinicke Jr. helped clarify the direction of this book early on. Mark Jason Aludino, Brid Nowlan, and Katharine Russell saved me from many typos.

My father is not here, but his memory pushes me forward. I am grateful to have my mother, Amina Elhusseiny, and my brother, Ahmed Abdel-Aaty. Most of all, I am thankful for Omar Cheta—his love and support have made me a better scholar and person. And to M: thank you for driving me crazy and for keeping me sane.

# Abbreviations

| | |
|---|---|
| AKP | Justice and Development Party |
| CBO | Cross Border Operation |
| COW | Correlates of War |
| EAC | East African Community |
| EPR | Ethnic Power Relations dataset |
| EU | European Union |
| ExCom | Executive Committee of the High Commissioner's Programme |
| FORD-K | Forum for the Restoration of Democracy-Kenya |
| GDP | Gross domestic product |
| ICTR | International Criminal Tribunal for Rwanda |
| IDP | Internally displaced person |
| IOM | International Organization for Migration |
| JRS | Jesuit Refugee Service |
| KANU | Kenya African National Union party |
| MAR | Minorities at Risk dataset |
| MoU | Memorandum of Understanding |
| NARC | National Rainbow Coalition party, Kenya |
| NATO | North Atlantic Treaty Organization |
| NEC | National Eligibility Committee, Kenya |
| NEP | North Eastern Province, Kenya |
| NGO | Non-governmental organization |
| NRS | National Refugee Secretariat, Kenya |
| OAU | Organization of African Unity |
| OECD | Organization for Economic Cooperation and Development |
| PICK | Party of Independent Candidates of Kenya |
| PITF | Political Instability Task Force |
| PFLP | Popular Front for the Liberation of Palestine |
| PKK | Kurdistan Workers' Party |
| PLO | Palestine Liberation Organization |
| PWT | Penn World Table |
| RCK | Refugee Consortium of Kenya |
| RPF | Rwandan Patriotic Front |
| RSD | Refugee status determination |
| SPLA | Sudan People's Liberation Army |
| TAC | Temporary Accommodation Center |

UN          United Nations
UNDP        United Nations Development Programme
UNHCR       Office of the UN High Commissioner for Refugees
UNRWA       UN Relief and Works Agency for Palestinian Refugees in the Near East
USCRI       US Committee for Refugees and Immigrants

# 1

# Selective Sovereignty and the Refugee Regime

Hamid's family had lived on the outskirts of Homs for generations.[1] So when war broke out in March 2011, he was determined to stay in Syria. His family dug a hole in the ground so they could shelter from the nightly bombings. The heaviest fighting sometimes drove them to one of the neighboring villages, but they would always go back home. Then a cousin and three uncles, along with 23 members of Hamid's extended family, were killed in an attack. Two years into the conflict and his house was still standing, but he knew it was time to leave.

He sold the goats his family had herded and paid smugglers to take his entire family to Jordan, at a cost of 25,000 Syrian lira (US$250) per person. They travelled at night in two dump trucks with their lights turned off. The journey south was long and harrowing. Hamid could hear machine guns firing in the darkness. His children watched as explosions lit up the night sky.

When Hamid finally crossed the border, he joined hundreds of thousands of other Syrians who had been admitted into Jordan. He and his family were taken to Za'atari refugee camp, in sheer size Jordan's fourth largest city. There, they became the responsibility of the United Nations Refugee Agency (UNHCR).[2] UNHCR staff would register them and provide documentation. Any services they received—food, medical care, education—would be administered by UNHCR's partners and overseen by an Agency official nicknamed "the mayor of Za'atari."[3]

For Samir, the decision to leave Dara'a came after his wife was injured by a sniper.[4] But unlike Hamid, Samir was Palestinian. He was able to cross the border using another man's Syrian passport, but he feared deportation if he was found out by Jordanian authorities. He stayed home to avoid being seen by Syrian neighbors who knew he was Palestinian. Samir's situation became even more precarious once the passport's owner himself arrived in Jordan.

---

[1] This account is described in Beals 2013.
[2] The organization is formally called the Office of the United Nations High Commissioner for Refugees, but its materials also call it the UN Refugee Agency for short.
[3] UNHCR 2013.
[4] This account is described in Human Rights Watch 2014.

*Discrimination and Delegation.* Lamis Elmy Abdelaaty, Oxford University Press (2021). © Oxford University Press.
DOI: 10.1093/oso/9780197530061.003.0001

Palestinians from Syria like Samir were not allowed to enter Jordan. Without Syrian identity documents, they were turned back at official border crossings. Those who managed to cross the border illegally could not live in refugee camps. And if authorities found them, they could be held indefinitely in a detention facility or returned to Syria. As far as the Jordanian government was concerned, Palestinians ought to stay in the war zone.[5]

As I write, the Syrian refugee crisis has entered its ninth year. Over five million people, nearly half of them children, have fled to neighboring countries like Turkey and Jordan. In Lebanon, one in five people is a Syrian refugee. Elsewhere, the Rohingya have crossed Bangladeshi borders by the hundreds of thousands. On the other side of the globe, tens of thousands of people are struggling to escape deadly violence in Central America.

Depending on how other states respond, these refugees may be allowed to escape persecution and violence in their country, or they may be forced back. They may be permitted to live where they wish, earn an income, pursue an education, and access medical treatment. Or they may be confined to a camp, forced to rely on aid, and denied basic services. What explains state responses to the refugees they receive?

Following a brief discussion of the links between refugee rights and international relations, I describe two puzzling patterns in state responses to refugees: states open their borders to some refugee groups while blocking others (what I call the "discrimination puzzle"), and a number of countries have given the United Nations (UN) control of asylum procedures and refugee camps on their territory (what I call the "delegation puzzle"). States do not consistently wield their capacity for control, nor do they jealously guard their authority to regulate. These observations lead to this book's central question: why do states sometimes assert their sovereignty vis-à-vis refugee rights and at other times seemingly cede it?

To explain this selective exercise of sovereignty, I develop a two-part theoretical framework in which policymakers in refugee-receiving countries weigh international and domestic concerns. At the international level, policymakers consider relations with the refugee-sending country. At the domestic level, policymakers consider political competition among ethnic groups. When these international and domestic incentives conflict, shifting responsibility to the UN allows policymakers to placate both refugee-sending countries and domestic constituencies. In short, foreign policy and ethnic identity shape states' reactions to refugees.

---

[5] Ibid.

## State Sovereignty and Refugee Rights

Refugees and asylum-seekers have a close and clear link to international relations because they cross international borders. They can bring up issues of sovereignty and border control in the country that receives them. They are also subject to a well-developed body of international law on refugee rights. However, the relationship between refugee rights and sovereignty is more complex than one trumping the other. States may sometimes assert control to deny refugee rights, they may exercise their sovereignty to ensure that refugees are protected, or they may delegate refugee protection to an international organization altogether.

Refugee migration brings to the fore questions related to the exercise, persistence, and effects of sovereignty under globalization. The very label, "refugee," is defined by sovereignty: a refugee is an individual who was forced to leave the state in which she was a citizen due to persecution or violence and who has sought refuge on the territory of another state. At the same time, control of borders is considered the sine qua non of sovereignty: it is the state's prerogative to determine who enters and remains on its territory. As a result, refugees are sometimes seen as a challenge to sovereignty. States on the receiving end of refugee influxes may come under pressure to forgo their sovereign right to determine access to and membership in their political community. Globalization has made these dynamics more pronounced, since human movement, in general, has become easier due to travel technologies, improvements in communication, and the rise of transnational human smuggling networks.

Refugees also highlight the tension between sovereignty and international human rights norms. For instance, Article 14 of the Universal Declaration of Human Rights sets out a right to seek asylum from persecution. However, it does not mention the right to receive or be granted asylum. Thus, while people, in general, have the right to leave their country, they do not have the right to enter any *particular* country. Exercising one right but not the other seems impossible.

The 1951 Refugee Convention and its 1967 Protocol focus on identifying who is a refugee and setting out standards of treatment. For instance, refugees should not be punished for illegal entry into a country, because they may find that they have no other way of seeking asylum. These treaties also set out the principle of non-refoulement, now considered a principle of customary international law, that states may not return a person to any country where they might be at risk of persecution (except under a very limited set of circumstances). Refugees also have rights under general human rights treaties relating to, for instance, civil and political rights, racial discrimination, torture, and the rights of children.

The global refugee regime lacks enforcement provisions, however, and displaced individuals may be mistreated at their destination despite being entitled to certain universal rights and freedoms. Multiple destination countries have introduced measures that make it difficult to access their territories. Even if they are somehow able to enter the country, a refugee might be returned against their wishes to their home country, where their life, liberty, or security may be threatened. For example, refugees may be detained for extended periods. Or they may be confined to camps and refused access to courts and legal aid. They might not be permitted to work to earn a living. In some countries, xenophobic and racist aggression have refugees living in constant fear.

Still, some scholars contend that the global human rights regime has driven states to grant "postnational" membership rights to migrants, challenging traditional models of citizenship and sovereignty.[6] A related argument is that transnational networks and the forces of globalization have diminished the state's capacity to control its borders.[7] In contrast, another strand of the writing on this topic claims that globalization has actually resulted in the closing down of borders.[8]

In contrast, I argue that the desire for control and the exercise of sovereignty are not uniform, even for a single state. With regard to refugees at least, countries are *selective* in their appeals to, and exercise of, sovereignty. A country may assert its sovereign prerogative to control borders, turning away refugees and restricting their rights. Or it may welcome displacees and extend to them hospitable treatment. Finally, a government could hand over decision-making to international organizations, empowering them to admit and assist refugees.

## The Discrimination and Delegation Puzzles

Despite appearances to the contrary, countries' asylum policies are not all trending in the same direction. We are not witnessing the "end of asylum," whereby countries invariably reject refugees or violate their rights to physical safety (though these abuses occur often enough).[9] On the flipside, it is not the case that states are "losing control" of their borders due to the forces of globalization and the international human rights regime.[10]

There are significant differences between countries in their responses to refugees. Each country also discriminates among refugee groups, welcoming some and excluding others. In addition, countries sometimes delegate policies, like

---

[6] Soysal 1994; Jacobson 1996.

[7] Sassen 1996.

[8] Dauvergne 2008, 47, claims that "in the face of globalizing forces, migration is increasingly being transformed into the last bastion of sovereignty."

[9] Rutinwa 1999.

[10] Sassen 1996.

approving asylum applications or managing refugee camps, to the UN. This within-country variation is both puzzling and understudied.

## Variation across Countries

Countries have responded to refugees in substantially varied ways. For instance, in 1999, Macedonia alternated three times between closing and opening its borders to refugees escaping Kosovo.[11] In Malaysia, asylum-seekers had access to a refugee status determination (RSD) process conducted by UNHCR, but in 2003 police started arresting Indonesians outside UNHCR's office before they could make appointments.[12] While Niger allowed refugees to settle and travel wherever they choose, Ethiopia required Eritrean, Sudanese, and Somali refugees to live in camps and to acquire permits to leave temporarily. Similarly, refugees could operate businesses with no more restrictions than nationals in Niger, while Ethiopia generally does not allow refugees to work.[13] There are numerous other examples.

Figure 1.1 illustrates the cross-national variation in refugee rights, using data from the *World Refugee Survey*.[14] In 2009, the US Committee for Refugees and Immigrants (USCRI) assigned countries letter grades to reflect the extent to which refugee groups enjoyed four rights: refoulement (i.e., forcible return to a country where they would be in danger) and physical protection; detention and access to courts; freedom of movement and residence; and the right to earn a livelihood. In Figure 1.1, I combine these grades into a single refugee rights score for each country, ranging from a minimum of 0 to a maximum of 4.[15]

Clearly, countries vary widely in their respect for refugee rights. At one end of the spectrum, Brazil scored points for having established an effective asylum system. Refugees had similar rights to work and to public assistance as nationals, and they enjoyed freedom of movement and residence. On the other end of the spectrum, Thailand fared poorly. It had detained and assaulted Rohingya asylum-seekers from Myanmar, then abandoned them on unseaworthy boats without supplies. Laotian Hmong refugees were confined and forcibly returned as well.[16]

---

[11] Williams and Zeager 2004.

[12] Hathaway 2005.

[13] USCRI 2009.

[14] Ibid.

[15] In countries exhibiting differences in rights across refugee groups, USCRI rated that country based on the treatment of the least-favored refugee group. USCRI assigned a letter grade for each right, and I weight them equally for illustrative purposes. The letter grades were assigned numerical scores (A=4, B=3, C=2, D=1, and F=0) and used to calculate a "grade-point average" or GPA.

[16] USCRI 2009, 1, 5.

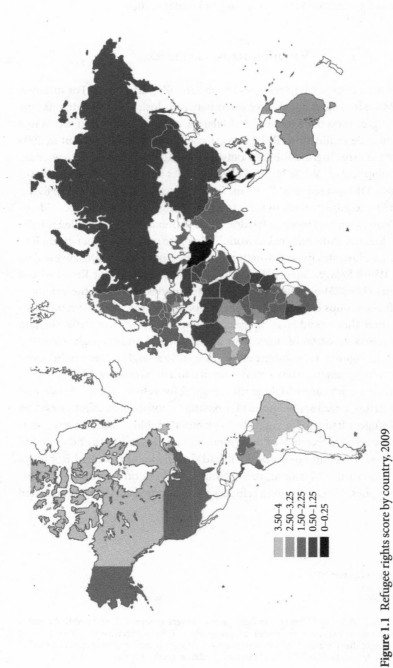

**Figure 1.1** Refugee rights score by country, 2009

Note: Data obtained from the USCRI publication *World Refugee Survey*. The latest available data was used for the following countries: Angola (2008), Australia (2008), Azerbaijan(2005), Benin (2008), Central African Republic (2008), Colombia (2005), Gabon (2008), Gambia (2008), Liberia (2008), Mali (2008), Namibia (2007), Papua New Guinea (2008), Sierra Leone (2008), Uzbekistan (2006), and Vietnam (2008). Countries in white were lacking data.

This variation across countries still needs more unpacking, though. While Figure 1.1 demonstrates that there are significant differences between countries, it masks the considerable variation within countries. A serious consideration of refugee rights must go further to recognize that each government will vary its responses across refugee groups.

## Discrimination

The modern refugee regime has been described as a "non-entrée regime," in which states use domestic restrictions and extraterritorial controls to contain refugee crises and keep most refugees out and away.[17] However, governments around the world have welcomed some refugee groups, even while blocking others or treating them poorly.

Perhaps the most familiar and well-researched example of this is the so-called Haitian-Cuban syndrome. During the Cold War, the United States saw fit to extend a warm reception to Cuban refugees but not to Haitians.[18] This differential treatment of refugees is not unique to the United States. For instance, at least until the early 1990s, India gave Tibetan refugees more expansive rights than those it provided to Sri Lankan Tamils and Bangladeshi Chakma refugees.[19] Moreover, there were stark differences in the treatment of Salvadoran and Nicaraguan refugees in Costa Rica during the 1980s.[20]

Why do governments vary their reception and policies across refugee groups? In 2019, countries received asylum-seekers and refugees from 26 different origins on average.[21] But the literature on migration often loses sight of the fact that states discriminate between these groups of putative migrants, including some and excluding others. Put differently, much of the existing scholarship on states' asylum policies tends to paint them with a broad brush, eliding discrimination among refugees.[22] As a result, we lack a well-developed theoretical argument for why countries discriminate among refugees that has been investigated across countries and regions.

Many factors that are commonly thought to influence the reception of refugees—like resources, security, regional concerns, and public opinion—would suggest that countries will adopt a "one size fits all" policy. For instance, if the material costs of hosting refugees determined state responses, then poorer

---

[17] Hathaway 1992.
[18] Zolberg, Suhrke, and Aguayo 1986; Loescher 1989; Zucker and Zucker 1987.
[19] Chimni 1994.
[20] Basok 1990.
[21] UNHCR n.d.
[22] In a notable exception, Shanks shows that debates over whether and whom to exclude have shaped conceptions of sovereignty in the United States. Shanks 2001.

states would shun all refugees. Countries that experience domestic unrest or terrorism may be more fearful of refugees in general. If a country emulated its neighbors' restrictive policies so as not to attract refugees, then it would uniformly close its borders. Finally, if publics were generally resistant to refugees, then democracies may be less welcoming overall.

## Delegation

Delegation to UNHCR is also a key feature of many countries' asylum policies. Around the world, the Agency is functioning as a "surrogate state," registering and documenting refugees, providing food and shelter, administering social services, managing camps the size of small cities, and establishing policing and justice mechanisms.[23]

Particularly striking is the delegation of RSD—the process that examines whether an applicant for asylum is indeed a genuine refugee. An individual may assert that she is fleeing persecution, but her claim must be evaluated to determine whether it is credible. RSD procedures decide who is eligible for the rights and protections that are tied to refugee status.

The conventional wisdom would expect countries to aggressively assert their sovereignty when it comes to population flows. However, a number of countries are essentially allowing an international organization to determine which individuals to include or exclude. As shown in Figure 1.2, UNHCR shared responsibility for RSD with the national government in 23 countries in 2011 (see Appendix I). In another 54 countries, UNHCR had sole responsibility for RSD.[24] The Agency was involved in these procedures in countries that continuously invoke state sovereignty (like China) as well as Organization for Economic Cooperation and Development (OECD) members (like Israel).

Why have these countries given the UN control of asylum procedures on their territory? This question has not been systematically studied. Moreover, the literature on delegation to international organizations lacks a persuasive answer. Existing principal-agent explanations have connected delegation to specialization gains, managing coordination and collaboration, agenda-setting for collective decision-making, dispute arbitration, enforcement and credibility, or ensuring lock-in of policy bias.[25] However, as I detail in chapter 2, it is not obvious that delegating asylum policy functions to UNHCR fits any of these accounts squarely.

[23] Slaughter and Crisp 2008; Kagan 2011.
[24] Annex to UNHCR 2012.
[25] Hawkins et al. 2006, 13–20.

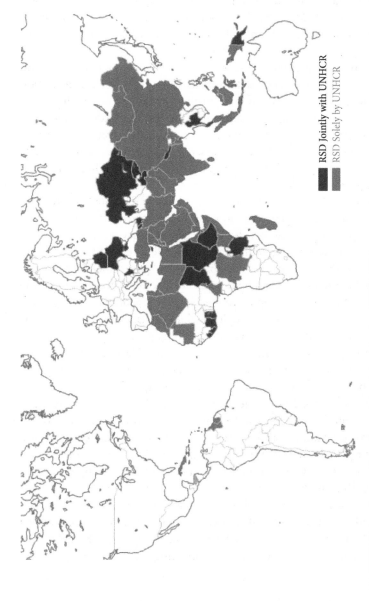

**Figure 1.2** UNHCR involvement in refugee status determination (RSD), 2011

Note: Data obtained from the UNHCR publication *Global Trends 2011*.

■ RSD Jointly with UNHCR

RSD Solely by UNHCR

## Solving the Puzzles

The key to solving the discrimination and delegation puzzles is recognizing that the two phenomena are linked. In responding to refugees, each state chooses from the options presented by discrimination and delegation. For each refugee group, a state can respond with an asylum policy of inclusion, restriction, or delegation.

I define asylum policy as the measures used to regulate the entry, exit, and conditions of residence of foreign asylum-seekers and refugees. This definition covers not only the decision to admit or turn away asylum-seekers, but other facets of the refugee experience as well. Drawing on the standards set out in the 1951 Refugee Convention, I define asylum policy to include freedom of movement, physical safety, access to social services, and other refugee rights. Both de jure laws and de facto practices constitute a country's asylum policy, which can vary over time and by refugee group.

I argue that asylum policies are shaped by interstate relations and transnational ethnic affinities. Policymakers can use refugees to reassure international allies and exert pressure on rivals. Adopting a generous asylum policy can encourage citizens of the sending country to flee, while a restrictive policy may dissuade them, with consequences for the sending government's stability.[26] Moreover, the flight of citizens can be used as evidence that people are "voting with their feet," which imposes reputational costs on the sending country in the eyes of the world as well as its own people. Asylum policies can also enable refugees to engage in activities that oppose the sending government, like participating in an insurgency or engaging in cross-border guerilla activities.

At the same time, policymakers have domestic political incentives to favor refugee groups who share their ethnic identity (i.e., language, race, and/or religion). To maintain their hold on power, leaders accommodate their constituency's desires by welcoming ethnic kin and treating others poorly. Generous asylum policies toward ethnic kin can also increase the size of the leader's constituency, while restrictive policies toward others can ensure that his constituency's relative size is maintained. Finally, asylum policies can help foster in-group favoritism and encourage ethnic mobilization.

Thus, policymakers will adopt generous policies when refugees are fleeing a hostile state and share the policymaker's ethnic identity. They will adopt restrictive policies when refugees are fleeing a friendly state and do not share the policymaker's ethnic identity. When they face conflicting incentives and pressures

---

[26] I use the terms "sending country" and "country of origin" interchangeably to mean the refugee's home country. Meanwhile, "receiving country," "host country," or "country of refuge" mean the country where the refugee seeks refuge.

at the international and domestic levels, policymakers shift responsibility to the UN. Delegation allows policymakers to avoid antagonizing refugee-sending countries or domestic constituencies by claiming that a neutral international organization is in charge of asylum policymaking. At the same time, the UNHCR is fairly easy to sanction and may self-censor to safeguard its continued presence in the country.

In a sense, this argument emphasizes the international sources of domestic politics. At the same time, it shows that policies regulating refugee access and treatment can be a foreign policy tool. Though refugees are clearly at the intersection of domestic and international politics, research that combines both levels of analysis in this way has been surprisingly rare.[27]

I substantiate this argument using a "three-stage, multi-level" research design in which each successive step corroborates and elaborates the findings of the preceding stage. Taken together, the evidence indicates that my argument is more persuasive than alternative explanations that emphasize commitment to humanitarian ideals, the desirability of skilled or wealthy refugees, the size of refugee flows, and the arbitrariness of low-level asylum decision-making.

The first stage, presented in chapter 3, involves statistical analysis of asylum admissions worldwide. I analyze when countries are likely to delegate decision-making on asylum applications to the UN Refugee Agency and why countries accept or reject asylum applications when they retain these decision-making functions themselves. The results give a general indication that my theoretical framework applies across countries and over time and merits further in-depth examination.

The second stage shifts from admissions decisions to consider refugee treatment, more broadly conceived, in two side-by-side country case studies. Egypt is broadly representative of most refugee recipients, while Turkey is an outlier that has limited the geographic application of the 1951 Refugee Convention. Drawing on elite interviews as well as archival sources and unpublished materials, chapter 4 analyzes and compares Egypt's post-WWII policies toward six refugee groups: Palestinians, Sudanese, Iraqis, Somalis, Eritreans, and Ethiopians. Chapter 5 similarly draws on a range of sources to examine how Turkey responded to Bulgarians, Iraqis, Iranians, Bosnians and Kosovars, and refugees from Soviet and post-Soviet states. In both countries, the fluctuation in policies over time and their variation by refugee group is consistent with my theoretical framework.

The third stage examines the mechanisms that shape asylum policy at a more fine-grained level by zooming in on within-country dynamics. Chapter 6 expands my analysis to cross-cutting pressures in Kenya (home to one of the

---

[27] Although see Rosenblum 2004.

largest refugee populations in the world) through content analysis of parliamentary proceedings. Qualitative interpretation and quantitative analysis of statements about refugees show that these differ substantially, depending on whether they are being delivered by members of the foreign policy establishment or parliamentarians who represent domestic constituencies. This evidence further bolsters the argument that asylum policy is indeed shaped by foreign policy and ethnic politics.

The selection of developing country cases for stages two and three is deliberate. Most existing research on immigration and asylum policy has been limited to Western countries, despite the fact that some 85% of refugees reside in developing countries.[28] There is significant variation across the three countries I examine, both in terms of discrimination and delegation and in terms of other conditions that might be expected to affect asylum policies. At the same time, Egypt, Turkey, and Kenya share some of the same refugee groups, which allows for the comparison of policies toward a single refugee group across countries.

Though I comment on more recent events, much of the analysis of these country cases begins with the establishment of the post-WWII international refugee regime and ends before the Arab Spring. A great deal of scholarship is now focused on the Syrian refugee crisis, but this type of retrospective analysis is both important and informative. Looking at previous refugee crises helps us understand the underlying factors and patterns that shape state responses to current and future refugee flows. Moreover, even as the world's attention is drawn to current refugee crises, previous flows have produced populations that remain displaced years or even decades later. That said, my framework also helps us understand Egypt, Turkey, and Kenya's responses to recent and ongoing refugee crises.

The implications of my findings can inform the activities of UN agencies and NGOs by allowing them to target their advocacy and assistance to particular refugee groups, as I describe in the concluding chapter. My theoretical framework can also help concerned states and the international community forecast when exerting pressure will bear fruit and when other tools (such as resettlement) must be used instead. Finally, my findings have implications for a reconceptualization of the relationship between sovereignty and rights. Selective sovereignty shapes the experiences of growing numbers of refugees around the world and, as a result, has important consequences for the international refugee regime.

The next chapter elaborates on my theoretical answer to the discrimination and delegation puzzles and explains the methods and data I use to investigate this theory. It starts by defining the central dependent variable, asylum policy, and introduces a set of indicators that cover admission at the border, freedom to

[28] UNHCR 2020b.

reside outside camps, access to the labor market, and other aspects of the refugee experience. Then I develop the argument that countries' approaches to refugees are shaped by a two-level dynamic involving foreign policy and ethnic politics, such that relations with the sending country and domestic ethnic competition may result in relative inclusiveness, restrictiveness, or delegation.

# 2

# The Role of Foreign Policy
# and Ethnic Politics

Delegation and discrimination are not just intellectual puzzles: they shape the daily work of practitioners and advocates and the lived experiences of millions of asylum-seekers and refugees worldwide. Numerous states have essentially outsourced their asylum policies to the UN. In many countries around the world, the UN Refugee Agency registers asylum-seekers, grants refugee status, administers refugee camps, and provides social services to refugees. At a time when most states are asserting their sovereignty vis-à-vis population flows, it is surprising that many would shift responsibility to an international organization in these ways. Moreover, almost every country favors certain refugees over others. Some refugee groups are welcomed at the border, permitted to live where they choose, provided free medical care and schooling, allowed to open businesses, and even granted citizenship. Others are turned away or detained, warehoused in heavily-guarded camps, denied basic services, barred from earning an income, and sometimes doomed to live in limbo for generations.

This chapter offers a theoretical answer to these puzzles of delegation and discrimination. I begin by defining the central dependent variable, asylum policy. To compare asylum policy across countries and refugee groups, I introduce a set of indicators that cover admission at the border, freedom to reside outside camps, access to the labor market, and other aspects of the refugee experience. Then I develop the theoretical argument that countries' approaches to refugees are shaped by a two-level dynamic involving foreign policy and ethnic politics. I detail the causal pathways whereby relations with the sending country and domestic ethnic competition may result in relative inclusiveness, restrictiveness, or delegation. Policymakers can use refugees to reassure international allies and exert pressure on rivals. At the same time, they have domestic political incentives to favor refugee groups who share their ethnic identity. But when they face conflicting international and domestic pressures, they delegate to the UN. I also discuss possible alternative explanations, such as commitment to humanitarian ideals, the desirability of skilled and/or wealthy refugees, and so on.

This chapter also explains the methods and data I use to investigate this argument and introduces my three-stage, multi-level research design. The first stage, a quantitative analysis of asylum admissions worldwide, allows for an

*Discrimination and Delegation*. Lamis Elmy Abdelaaty, Oxford University Press (2021). © Oxford University Press.
DOI: 10.1093/oso/9780197530061.003.0002

examination of trends across a large sample of countries and years. It demonstrates that admission and delegation are correlated with sending country relations and ethnic affinity and indicates that my argument may be generalizable. The second stage, qualitative case studies of Egypt and Turkey, relies on interviews and archival research to investigate a wider range of asylum policies. These case studies display the causal processes that link asylum policy on the one hand and sending country relations and ethnic affinity on the other. Finally, the third stage extends the analysis with a quantitative and qualitative analysis of parliamentary proceedings in Kenya. Combining these different data collection and methodological techniques, along with careful case selection, allows for a rigorous investigation of my argument and increases confidence in my findings.

## Defining Asylum Policy

Both the delegation and discrimination puzzles relate to states' policy responses to the refugees and asylum-seekers they receive. Solving these puzzles involves explaining the variation in what I call "asylum policy." States may respond to a group with a policy of inclusion, restriction, or delegation.

A necessary first step is defining the terms refugee and asylum-seeker. A refugee is a person who seeks refuge outside their country of origin or nationality due to a well-founded fear of persecution on the basis of race, religion, nationality, social group membership, or political opinion. Alternatively, the refugee may have fled their country due to foreign intervention, interstate war, internal turbulence, or other events seriously disturbing the public order.

An asylum-seeker is an individual who asserts that he or she is a refugee, but whose claim has not yet been definitively evaluated. In other words, an individual may seek asylum and claim to have fled persecution or violence. In most states, that individual's application would then be screened by an RSD process, which examines whether his or her claim is genuine. RSD decides which asylum-seekers will secure refugee status.

Even though these definitions align with international and regional agreements on refugees, I include individuals and groups fleeing persecution and violence whether or not they are granted official refugee status.[1] Using a social scientific, rather than a strictly legal, definition recognizes that the conferral of these categories by governments is a political act. As FitzGerald and Arar point out, the same person might be labeled a refugee, an asylum-seeker, a guest, or an

---

[1] The 1951 Convention relating to the Status of Refugees and its 1967 Protocol only cover persecution that is specifically directed at particular individuals. In contrast, the 1969 OAU Convention Governing the Specific Aspects of Refugee Problems in Africa expands the refugee definition to accommodate situations of mass flight in response to generalized violence.

irregular arrival by different host countries.[2] As shown in chapter 5, the refusal to designate certain groups of people as refugees or asylum-seekers can allow a government to opt in or out of what might otherwise appear to be generally applicable, national-level policies.

Still, these definitions distinguish refugees from internally displaced persons (IDPs) and voluntary migrants. Refugee status requires that an international border be crossed, thereby excluding individuals who flee their homes but remain within the territory of their country. Whereas the movement of refugees and asylum-seekers is conceptualized as flight from persecution or conflict, voluntary migration is assumed to arise from economic motives.

A compelling argument can be made that voluntary and forced migration are not dichotomous, but rather lie on a continuum. In practice, of course, most forced and voluntary migrants have mixed motives for crossing borders. Moreover, elements of coercion and volition are often implicated in both forced and voluntary migration. Refugees may feel compelled to migrate, but others facing similar threats could decide to stay. In addition, refugees are often able to exercise some choice over how, when, and where to go. The 2015 European migration crisis demonstrated that political refugees and economic migrants often use the same routes and modes of travel and that they face similar experiences on their journeys and at their destinations.

I draw a distinction between refugees and voluntary migrants, nonetheless, to mirror current international law and policy. There is a well-established international regime for refugees, based on the 1951 Refugee Convention. The principle of non-refoulement, which has become a principle of customary international law, prohibits returning an individual to a country where their life would be at risk. In contrast, there is no comparable international regime for labor migration and no similar protections for migrants, whom countries are free to deport at will. Along the same lines, most countries' border control policies differentiate between these reasons for moving. In short, my choice to focus on individuals fleeing persecution and conflict is an analytical one, selected in order to match the specific distinctions made by most (if not all) states as well as UNHCR.

I define asylum policy as the set of measures adopted by a national government to regulate the entry, exit, and conditions of residence of foreign asylum-seekers and refugees. This definition includes both laws and regulations as well as their implementation. Indeed, sometimes de jure laws on the books differ from the de facto practices implemented on the ground. Even when national legislation on refugees exists, it may not be fully or accurately implemented. Moreover, seemingly general, national-level laws may vary in their application over time

---

[2] FitzGerald and Arar 2018, 391.

and by refugee group. In addition, as shown in chapter 4, the absence of national legislation need not mean an absence of de facto policy.

My definition of asylum policy also encompasses more than just the decision to grant entry to asylum-seekers. Whether displaced individuals are able to cross borders is critical, but it is not the whole story. Examining the treatment of individuals, whether their asylum applications are accepted or not, is also important for several reasons. First, under the international human rights regime, as well as treaties relating specifically to refugees, displaced individuals are entitled to a set of basic rights in the country that receives them. Second, treatment by host countries determines whether refugees remain there or attempt to move on. Indeed, the sharp increase in sea arrivals to Europe in 2015 is tied to conditions in neighboring countries, where humanitarian aid is stretched thin and refugees are not permitted to earn a living. Third, the treatment of refugees can have long-term consequences. For example, where host countries allow refugees access to social services and employment, refugees may be able to acquire transferable skills or generate remittances that can contribute to state-building and post-conflict reconstruction in their country of origin.

## Policy Indicators

The principle of non-refoulement, that a refugee may not be returned to a country in which they would face a threat to their life or freedom, forms the core of the international refugee regime. The 1951 Refugee Convention also lists minimum standards of treatment relating to non-discrimination, access to courts, access to employment, access to social services, freedom of movement, and so on. It further stipulates that individuals not be penalized or arbitrarily detained for entering a country through irregular means to seek asylum.

These international standards are a logical yardstick for describing a given country's laws and policies. To identify and compare countries' asylum policies, Table 2.1 presents a list of indicators, divided across five broad categories. I derived these from UNHCR's Global Strategic Priorities for 2010–2011, which represent areas where state practice sometimes falls short of international standards.[3]

These indicators together reflect the rights (restrictions) that are granted to (imposed on) refugees. The first set of indicators deal with a country's legal framework governing asylum-seekers and refugees. They comprise accession

---

[3] UNHCR 2011a, 2009. For a similar effort to derive policy decisions from UN recommendations, see Jacobsen 1996.

Table 2.1 Indicators of a state's asylum policy

| | |
|---|---|
| **1. Legal Framework** | |
| International Treaties | Has the country acceded to the 1951 Refugee Convention or its 1967 Protocol? |
| National Legislation | Is there national legislation in force that regulates refugee affairs? |
| **2. Admission and Status** | |
| Entry | Does the government grant entry to asylum-seekers appearing at the border? |
| Screening | Do asylum-seekers have access to status determination procedures? |
| **3. Protection and Security** | |
| Movement | Are refugees restricted to camps or segregated settlements, or can they choose to self-settle? |
| Physical Safety | Are refugees subject to arbitrary detention, and/or do they experience physical harm inflicted by agents of the host country? |
| Refoulement | Does the government expel or return (*refouler*) refugees to their country of origin against their will? |
| **4. Basic Needs** | |
| Services | Do refugees have access to public health services and primary and secondary education? |
| Employment | Are refugees permitted to legally seek wage-earning employment or practice professions? |
| **5. Durable Solutions** | |
| Integration | Do long-time refugees have the option of local integration in the host country? |

to the relevant international treaties, the 1951 Refugee Convention and its 1967 Protocol, as well as the adoption of domestic refugee laws. Ratifying international instruments creates a legal obligation to respect refugee rights. National legislation translates this international commitment to the domestic sphere.

The next two indicators cover admission and status. Individuals flee persecution and conflict by crossing land borders, boarding boats, or traveling via airplane. When displaced individuals appear at entry points, governments must decide whether they will be admitted. Those governments can also opt to put in place a screening process for entrants, one that identifies "genuine" asylum claimants and grants them refugee status.

There are many aspects to refugees' protection and security, but I focus on three major ones: movement, physical safety, and refoulement. Governments determine whether refugees will be forced to remain in camps. They can choose to detain refugees or use violence against them. And they may forcibly return refugees to unsafe home countries.

Other dimensions of asylum policy relate to refugees' ability to meet their basic needs. For example, public healthcare can greatly benefit many refugees if states choose to extend it to them. Similarly, displacement can interrupt children's schooling or prevent them from getting an education in the first place; governments can permit them to attend public schools. Permission to legally enter the labor market enables refugees to earn a living and avoid dependence on charity. Finally, states determine whether refugees have a path to citizenship or long-term status of some sort.

Each of these components of asylum policy varies within any single country, both over time and across refugee groups. It is possible, for instance, that a state ratifies the 1951 Refugee Convention but restricts its coverage to certain groups by refusing to designate others as asylum-seekers or refugees. A state's asylum policy is comprised of the particular configuration of indicators it adopts. In this way, any given country's asylum policy may shift over time. Moreover, a country may have distinct asylum policies for different refugee groups. For each refugee group it receives, a country's asylum policies can lean toward inclusion, restriction, or delegation.

## Inclusive and Restrictive Policies

For each of the asylum policy indicators just described, it is possible to measure inclusiveness and restrictiveness. In many cases, the 1951 Convention itself can be used as a benchmark. For example, the convention contains articles dealing with freedom of movement (Article 26), non-refoulement (Article 33), public education (Article 22), employment (Article 17), and naturalization (Article 34). Other rights, like physical security, are crucial to refugee protection even if they are not listed in the convention. Similarly, enacting domestic legislation and determining refugee status are both essential for the enjoyment of other refugee rights. In general, I describe as inclusive policies that meet the treaty's standards or exceed them. In contrast, policies that fall short of the convention's stipulations are restrictive.

To be considered inclusive vis-à-vis a particular refugee group, a receiving country would apply the 1951 Convention or its 1967 Protocol to that group. It would implement national legislation that applies to that refugee group. Asylee arrivals would be facilitated. Refugee status determination for that group would be conducted in accordance with UNHCR standards. Members of the refugee group would enjoy full freedom of movement and residence. Those refugees would be protected from physical harm and arbitrary detention. Any repatriation to their home country would be strictly voluntary. Members of the refugee group would be able to use public health services and enroll in schools. They would not face legal barriers to entering the formal labor market. Finally, refugees belonging to that group would have a path to citizenship.

At the other end of the spectrum, a state's asylum policy would be considered restrictive vis-à-vis a particular refugee group if it excluded that group from the Refugee Convention's coverage. There would be no national laws that apply to that group, or existing laws would be ignored. Putative asylum-seekers would encounter closed borders. Individuals within that refugee group would not have access to institutionalized status determination procedures. The refugee group would be confined in closed camps. Refugees would experience detentions, torture, or other threats to their physical safety. That refugee group may face mass expulsions or forcible returns. The refugee group may be barred from accessing public hospitals or schools or may be kept out of the formal labor market. No possibility of naturalization would exist.

Of course, inclusive and restrictive policies lie on a spectrum or range, rather than being a simple binary. So intermediate policies are possible. For example, states could apply only parts of the Refugee Convention or use ad hoc directives instead of domestic legislation. Border checks may impede entry or make it difficult. Refugee status determination may fall short of UNHCR regulations. Refugees may be forced to reside in camps but be allowed to travel in and out of them. Small numbers of refugees may face threats to their physical safety or limited expulsions. Accessing social services may be cumbersome, or work permits may be restricted to some occupations. Finally, naturalization may be possible but difficult.

## Delegation of Policies

Delegation is formally defined as a conditional grant of authority from one actor to another, which empowers the latter to act or make decisions on behalf of the former.[4] In the context of refugee affairs, many countries have transferred decision-making on certain asylum policies to the UN Refugee Agency. In particular, UNHCR is involved in training government staff, registering and

---

[4] Hawkins et al. 2006, 7.

screening asylum-seekers, managing camps and assisting urban refugees, establishing policing and justice mechanisms, facilitating voluntary refugee returns, administering health and educational services, providing vocational training and livelihoods programming, and aiding resettlement.[5]

Among UNHCR's most consequential roles is its involvement in RSD. An individual may assert that she is a refugee, but her claim must be evaluated to determine whether she has a well-founded fear of persecution on the basis of race, religion, nationality, social group membership, or political opinion. If she is recognized as a refugee, then she has a right not to be returned to her home country. In other words, RSD has legal consequences because it determines who is eligible for the rights and protections stipulated by the 1951 Convention. RSD is also especially important in countries where bona fide refugees are allowed to access social services, establish businesses, or seek naturalization.

Many governments involve UNHCR staff in their RSD processes, usually codifying this delegation in a cooperation agreement or memorandum of understanding (MoU).[6] In 2018, UNHCR had sole responsibility for RSD in 47 countries or territories, and shared some responsibility for RSD with the national government in 14 others.[7] Delegation of RSD can take one of three forms. The Agency may be involved in one or more stages (registration, interviews, decisions, or appeals) of an otherwise government-run RSD procedure. Alternatively, UNHCR may conduct an independent process that operates in parallel to government-run RSD, as described in chapter 5. The maximum delegation of RSD occurs when UNHCR is in charge of all procedures on a country's territory.

In some cases, refugee status is conferred on a group (or prima facie) basis rather than via the individual-by-individual RSD process just described. During a mass influx, conditions in the asylees' home country may be self-evident and therefore obviate the need to evaluate each individual's claim to refugee status. As with individual RSD, this collective refugee status can be conferred by governments or by UNHCR.[8] Thus, delegation can pertain to group-based refugee status as well as individual RSD.

Countries also delegate refugee camp management to UNHCR. In these contexts, UNHCR organizes the delivery of assistance, arranges the construction and maintenance of facilities, and coordinates security. It also provides a range of services including education, health, nutrition, sanitation, and vocational training. Camps run by UNHCR vary, with some reaching the size of small cities.

[5] Slaughter and Crisp 2008; Kagan 2011.
[6] Smrkolj 2010, 1785.
[7] Annex to UNHCR 2019.
[8] UNHCR 2015.

## The Argument

Refugees are at the intersection of international relations and domestic politics. On the one hand, refugees are inhabitants of one country who cross international borders to seek the protection of another state. Their rights are enshrined in international law, and their plight often attracts international attention. On the other hand, refugees feature in domestic debates about identity and nationalism and sometimes figure prominently in politicians' campaign rhetoric. Refugee flows can put strains on the economy and infrastructure and foment domestic resentment or political instability. Accordingly, a persuasive explanation for refugees' reception should link international and domestic factors.

To explain the variation in asylum policy, I combine foreign policy and ethnic identity in a two-part argument summarized in Table 2.2. For reasons I detail below, policymakers will adopt generous policies when refugees are fleeing a hostile state and share the policymaker's ethnic identity. They will adopt restrictive policies when refugees are fleeing a friendly state and do not share the policymaker's ethnic identity. When there are conflicting pressures from the international and domestic levels, delegation of asylum policy functions is most likely.

This argument resembles a "two-level game."[9] At the international level, the government seeks to align its response to refugees with its diplomatic relations. At the national level, politicians aim to stay in power by leveraging identity politics and catering to domestic groups. As in the two-level game framework, I conceive of a single national political leader in each country. These central decision-makers must pay attention to both levels when choosing between inclusion, restriction, and delegation. International and domestic political audiences are watching their response, and the policymaker is concerned with political survival at each level. So, political leaders adopt the asylum policy that achieves consistency, or at least minimizes discord, between the two levels.

Table 2.2 Theoretical predictions

|  |  | Sending Country Relations | |
|  |  | Hostile | Friendly |
| --- | --- | --- | --- |
| *Affinity with Refugee Group* | Co-Ethnic | Inclusive Asylum Policy | Delegation |
|  | No Ethnic Tie | Delegation | Restrictive Asylum Policy |

---

[9] Putnam 1988; Evans, Jacobson, and Putnam 1993.

Both parts of the argument also rely on the idea of competitive relations. An inclusive policy communicates condemnation of, and enables opposition to, the sending government. So, strategic competition between international rivals motivates inclusive asylum policies. Domestically, competition between ethnic groups will result in inclusive or restrictive asylum policies depending on whether refugees are ethnic kin of the group in power.

While decisions by asylum-seekers and refugees do not play a clear role in this model, they are consequential nonetheless. Decision-theoretic models have viewed refugees as utility maximizers who choose the destination from which they will derive the highest net benefit.[10] As such, the type of treatment refugees expect to receive in a host country (in terms of access to the labor market, guarantees of their physical safety, the possibility of naturalization, and so on) could influence whether they choose that country as their destination. At the same time, both sets of mechanisms have to do with the identity of refugees: nationality at the international level and ethnicity at the domestic level.

In the remainder of this section, I detail the specific causal mechanisms whereby foreign policy and ethnic politics shape asylum policy. Refugees fleeing a rival country offer an opportunity to undermine that country's stability, saddle it with reputation costs, and even engage in guerilla-style, cross-border attacks. Welcoming refugees who are ethnic kin can satisfy domestic constituencies, enlarge the policymaker's support group, and encourage mobilization along ethnic lines. When these international and domestic mechanisms diverge, delegation to UNHCR mitigates the clash.

## The Influence of Foreign Policy

The first part of the argument deals with foreign policy and, more specifically, bilateral relations between the sending and receiving countries. Political relations between states vary widely, but hostility and friendliness can be said to occupy two ends of the spectrum. Hostility involves direct military confrontation at its most extreme but can also be characterized by proxy wars, non-militarized disputes, material support for opposition groups, and other types of competition. Friendly bilateral relations, on the other hand, often feature alliances, trade agreements, and reciprocal high-level visits.

The intuition derives from the observation that the decision to grant formal refugee status to individuals usually implies condemnation of their sending government. The 1969 Organization of African Unity (OAU) Refugee Convention even recognizes this dynamic and tries to counteract it by noting: "The grant of

---

[10]  Riddle and Buckley 1998; Moore and Shellman 2007; Neumayer 2004.

asylum to refugees is a peaceful and humanitarian act and shall not be regarded as an unfriendly act by any Member State."[11] Granting refugee status is an acknowledgement that individuals have a legitimate fear of persecution, thus implicitly reproaching their country of origin for engaging in (or failing to prevent) said persecution. Conversely, when the receiving country supports the sending country, it might mistreat refugees who are political dissidents, militant opponents, or class enemies of the sending government.

There are many historical examples of this dynamic. In January 1990, there was a debate over whether Chinese students should be allowed to remain in the United States after graduation because they feared persecution in China. President George H. W. Bush argued in favor of extending their visas, while many congressional representatives wanted to extend formal asylum status in order to condemn China. In another well-known case, Iranian revolutionaries saw the US decision to permit the Shah of Iran to enter the United States for medical reasons as a form of asylum; this may have been one of the reasons behind the decision to take American hostages.[12]

A policymaker's choice of asylum policy is shaped by three interrelated factors that lead them to treat refugees from rivals generously, while cracking down on refugees from allies. First, a receiving country's asylum policy can undermine or bolster the sending government. Adopting an inclusive asylum policy can encourage citizens of the sending country to flee, while a restrictive policy may dissuade them, with consequences for the sending government's stability. In fact, the East German case demonstrates that a mass exodus can even stimulate regime collapse.[13]

Second, asylum policies can serve to embarrass or commend the sending country. The flight of citizens can be used as evidence that people are "voting with their feet" in an ideological or other conflict. This can serve to discredit an unfriendly sending country in the eyes of the world as well as its own people. The receiving country will not want to impose these reputational (or public relations) costs on friendly countries, however. There are many examples of this dynamic from the Cold War. For example, a 1953 National Security document states that it is US policy to "encourage defection of all USSR nationals," because defection "inflicts a psychological blow to Communism" and "counters Communist propaganda in the Free World."[14] More recently, the Lebanese government refused to recognize those fleeing friendly Syria as refugees, calling them "those fleeing the unrest." According to Syrian activists, some asylum-seekers entering Lebanon through the Beka'a valley were even arrested by the Lebanese army.[15] For its

---

[11] OAU Convention Governing the Specific Aspects of Refugee Problems in Africa.
[12] Weiner 1993, 106–07.
[13] Naimark 1992; Hirschman 1993; Torpey 1992; Mueller 1999; Pfaff 2006.
[14] Qtd. in Zolberg, Suhrke, and Aguayo 1986, 155.
[15] Doyle 2012.

part, the Syrian government prevented individuals from crossing its border into Jordan and laid landmines along escape routes into Lebanon and Turkey.[16]

Third, asylum policies can be used to promote external activities opposing the sending government. Host countries can allow or deny refugees the ability to speak out against their country of origin, send money back home in support of the opposition, or even engage in cross-border guerilla activities.[17] For instance, the failed Bay of Pigs invasion in 1961 was launched using Cuban exiles.

Although most of this discussion is framed in terms of admission policies, the same logic should hold for the treatment of refugees after they have been admitted. At the international level, generous refugee treatment might encourage more individuals to "vote with their feet," providing more opportunities to undermine, embarrass, or support the opposition to a rival regime. Conversely, restrictive refugee treatment would discourage further refugee flows from allies.

## The Influence of Ethnic Identity

The second part of the theory deals with ethnic identity and domestic political competition between ethnic groups. By ethnicity, I mean to refer to the identity cleavages that are salient and politically relevant within a particular country. Depending on the particular society, these may be linguistic, racial, and/or religious.[18] Put differently, ethnicity is a catch-all term that stands in for whichever aspects of identity are significant in any given society. My usage of this term is common among scholars in the comparative politics tradition and follows the example set by path-breaking migration scholars like Weiner.[19]

Consider a stylized example in which there are two or more ethnic groups in the receiving country. One group is in power while the others are excluded from power. Any of these groups may constitute the majority, or they may be balanced numerically. The central decision-maker is assumed to belong to the ethnic group in power. He or she wants to retain political power, but the regime type of the receiving country may be democratic or not.

Here, the policymaker will have three incentives to extend favorable treatment to ethnic kin and unfavorable treatment to ethnic others. First, the policymaker has a better chance of maintaining her hold on power if she accommodates her constituency's desires. Domestic publics generally sympathize with refugees who share with them a common identity, while they might regard ethnic others as

---

16 Jordan-Syria 2012; Syria Laying Landmines along Border 2012.
17 Moorthy and Brathwaite 2016.
18 Following Wimmer, ethnic boundaries are taken to be the result of long-term interaction and negotiation processes in a society. Wimmer 2008.
19 Weiner 1996.

a threat.[20] For example, support for the predominantly Sunni Syrian asylum-seekers in Lebanon has been divided along sectarian lines. Lebanese Sunnis rallied to assist the asylum-seekers, as did Lebanese prime minister Sa'ad al-Hariri's Future Movement. In contrast, the Maronite Christian patriarch declared that Syria's regime was the closest to democracy in the Arab world.[21] Ethnic kinship may not prevent some tensions from eventually arising between citizens and refugees, but these will be less pronounced than antagonism toward refugees who are ethnic others.

Second, the policymaker prefers to increase or at least preserve the relative size of her constituency to ensure her political survival. Generous asylum policies toward ethnic kin can increase the size of the leader's constituency, while restrictive policies toward others can ensure that the constituency's relative size is maintained. In a democracy, this is particularly the case if refugees have the possibility of acquiring voting rights. Even without voting, refugees can form a bloc that could be mobilized, for example, in situations of ethnic conflict. In short, the leader can use asylum policies to ensure that the domestic ethnic balance changes only in favor of her support coalition.

Third, asylum policies can help foster in-group favoritism. Building on instrumentalist accounts of ethnic conflict, leaders may use refugees as part of their efforts to encourage ethnic mobilization.[22] To remain in power, leaders may foster in-group bias (the tendency to favor one's own group) among their constituents.[23] Supporting ethnic kin and cracking down on ethnic others fosters in-group cohesion and favoritism. These tendencies can then help maintain domestic, ethnically based political coalitions.

Admission, as well as post-admission treatment, will be shaped by leaders' need to accommodate their constituencies' desires, as well as the incentive to foster in-group bias. In addition, generous treatment of co-ethnics could encourage more co-ethnics to seek refuge in a particular host country, thereby shifting the domestic ethnic balance in the leader's favor. On the contrary, restrictive treatment of ethnic others could discourage further non-kin flows, thereby keeping the ethnic balance favorable to the leader. In some countries, there is a minority group that is intentionally discriminated against or actively and systematically targeted by the government, like the Roma across most of Europe. Refugee groups that match that minority's ethnic identity will likely face especially restrictive policies.

---

[20] Weiner 1993, 10, 105. Although see Adida 2014.
[21] Doyle 2012.
[22] On instrumentalist theories of ethnic conflict, see Barth 1969; Bates 1983; Waters 1990; Hardin 1995; Fearon and Laitin 1996.
[23] On in-group bias, see Tajfel 1981; Tajfel and Turner 1986.

## The Decision to Delegate

When these domestic and international pressures push in opposite directions, policymakers delegate asylum functions in order to insulate themselves from conflicting pressures. Policymakers are delegating not to get their favored policy but to have someone else take responsibility for politically sensitive decisions. Although delegation can make refugee rights violations more visible, UNHCR is fairly easy to sanction and may self-censor as well. Delegating particular policy functions removes them from the policymaker's toolkit, but he or she retains control of a range of other measures and knows that UNHCR's own limitations preclude it from enacting major changes.[24]

The literature on delegation, based mainly on the principal-agent model, has largely overlooked situations in which a government brings in an international organization to conduct domestic activities. Scholars of international relations have, by and large, conceptualized delegation as a form of interstate cooperation. That is, they have focused on situations in which two or more states agree to grant authority to a third party.[25] While most scholars of delegation in American politics have focused on the single principal case, the agents in that literature tend to be domestic actors rather than international bodies.[26] In contrast to these previous studies, I am considering delegation by a single government (rather than multiple states) to an international organization (rather than a domestic actor). As part of my subsequent discussion of alternative explanations, I show that much of the existing reasoning on delegation does not apply in these situations.

Delegation allows governments to shift the blame to UNHCR. When the UN Refugee Agency grants refugee status to asylum-seekers from friendly states, or to non-kin refugees, states can assert that the decision was not theirs to make. Importantly, UNHCR appears insulated from domestic and international pressures. The Agency is unaccountable to domestic constituents and shielded from lobbying by domestic interest groups. At the same time, UNHCR's independent staff give its activities the appearance of neutrality. My reasoning here resembles scholarly arguments about politicians' use of the International Monetary Fund and other international economic institutions to shirk responsibility for unpopular austerity policies.[27]

On the surface, it might appear as though there are drawbacks to the delegation of asylum policy. Once UNHCR is involved on the ground, it can gather information and be in a position to threaten the host government with bad

---

[24] For general discussion of how nation states established and then used UNHCR to achieve their policy objectives with respect to refugees, see Keely 1996.

[25] Bradley and Kelley 2008, 5–9; Hawkins et al. 2006, 10.

[26] Bendor, Glazer, and Hammond 2001; Gailmard and Patty 2012.

[27] Vaubel 1986; Edwards and Santaella 1993, 425; Remmer 1986, 7, 21; Vreeland 2003, 62.

publicity for rights violations. More importantly, with UNHCR responsible for RSD or camp management, the policymaker loses the ability to use these policy instruments in order to undermine, embarrass, or otherwise oppose a hostile government (or bolster, commend, or support a friendly government). In addition, the policymaker can no longer use refugee recognition in order to accommodate, enlarge/maintain, or manipulate his or her constituency.

However, governments do not generally fear shaming by UNHCR. In fact, it is fairly easy for a policymaker to sanction the Agency if it overreaches. He or she can refuse to honor its refugee status decisions, end its RSD or camp management functions, or simply prevent asylum-seekers from reaching its offices. In addition, UNHCR's desire to continue operating in a receiving country's territory may make it sensitive to that country's preferences. This limits the kinds of criticisms the organization will raise.[28]

The principal-agent approach to delegation identifies "agency slack" (whereby the agent acts independently in ways the principal considers undesirable) as a central problem. However, UNHCR's institutional limitations prevent it from treating refugees too generously. The Agency is perpetually understaffed and underfunded, particularly since it relies almost entirely on voluntary contributions. Indeed, about 44% of its budget went unfunded in 2019.[29] Logistically, this limits the number of applications the organization can process and the number of refugees it can assist. Since UNHCR must also try to protect the individuals it recognizes as refugees, it may have incentives to recognize fewer refugees.[30]

Finally, delegating RSD or camp management to UNHCR still leaves the policymaker in control of the other policy components listed in Table 2.1. The policymaker (or their agents) still controls borders and can engage in arbitrary detention of refugees or deny them access to social and economic rights. Most importantly, the policymaker retains control of naturalization and refoulement decisions. In fact, delegation gives the government a degree of flexibility: it can detain or expel individuals under the pretext that it did not grant them refugee status itself in the first place. Moreover, delegating a policy function does not mean the policymaker relinquishes control for all groups of incoming refugees; he or she can determine which particular groups or nationalities will go through a delegated RSD process, for example.

As the literature on international organizations as autonomous actors reminds us, it is important to consider UNHCR's incentives too.[31] From UNHCR's perspective, a request to take over RSD or camp management is difficult, if not impossible, to decline. Performing these tasks when the government is unable or

---

[28] Loescher 2001, 326.
[29] UNHCR 2020a.
[30] Kagan 2006, 21.
[31] Barnett and Finnemore 2004.

unwilling to undertake them not only lies within the organization's mandate, but also serves the protection functions to which many of the Agency's staff are sincerely committed. At the same time, accepting these responsibilities can be attractive because it maintains UNHCR's position vis-à-vis other humanitarian actors. Moreover, running large status determination or camp operations confers on representatives and other local staff some power and prestige.

Still, UNHCR's official position is that governments ought to be responsible for these operations. When a government decides to take control, the Agency is often more than willing to hand it over. If a government is not willing to take charge, however, insisting too strenuously risks damaging UNHCR's relationship with the authorities. The organization worries about being denied access and about the "protection space" for refugees shrinking. As such, it knows not to threaten governments and to tread carefully when it thinks particular asylum cases will cause political tensions.

To sum up, when domestic and international incentives align, the policymaker has few reasons to delegate to the UN. However, when there are competing domestic and international pressures, the benefits of delegating far outweigh the costs. By delegating, the policymaker avoids paying political costs for controversial decisions, since UNHCR appears neutral to domestic and international audiences. Even so, UNHCR can only have limited influence on other policies and can only assist limited numbers of refugees. Finally, even while delegating RSD or camp management, the policymaker retains control of other policy instruments that can ensure that his or her constituency's size is not altered significantly.

## Observable Implications

In fashioning their asylum policies, discrimination and delegation describe the range of policy options governments can select from vis-à-vis particular refugee groups. For each refugee group, a host government can decide to discriminate or delegate. Discriminating involves policymakers reserving for themselves the ability to respond to refugee groups (favorably or unfavorably), while delegating sees policymakers shift responsibility for refugee groups to the UN. Discrimination and delegation are not sequential decisions, nor does one predict or impede the other. Rather, they present alternative options from which policymakers choose.

In a nutshell, I expect a receiving country to adopt more inclusive asylum policies when it is engaged in hostile political competition with the sending country and more restrictive asylum policies when it is friendly with the sending country. In addition, a receiving country is expected to adopt more generous asylum policies when the refugee group shares the ethnic identity of its government or dominant group and more restrictive asylum policies when there is no ethnic tie. Finally, governments will delegate the formulation or implementation of asylum policies to UNHCR officials when domestic and international incentives point in opposite directions. Delegation should occur in response to co-ethnic refugees who are escaping a friendly sending country or refugees who are ethnic others fleeing a hostile sending country.

Overall, my theoretical framework does not require narrow scope conditions. I expect that where ethnic cleavages are not politically salient, the leader will not face domestic pressures related to the ethnic identity of refugee groups, and the logic of international competition will apply alone. Alternatively, policymakers can focus solely on domestic mechanisms if there is state failure in the sending country which precludes the possibility of strategic relations between the failed state and countries that are receiving its refugees. In either of these situations, conflicting domestic and international pressures will not arise, and therefore delegation should be unlikely.

In any case, for any given country at a single point in time, we should observe differences in policy across refugee groups. Holding time constant, this variation in policy across refugee groups should be explained by relations with the sending country and ethnic affinity. And looking at a single receiving country over time, we should expect major shifts in asylum policy to coincide with breakpoints or discontinuities in either or both relations with the sending country and ethnic affinity. Although we may not expect the ethnic identity of a refugee group to shift over short periods of time, changes in the receiving country's leadership (via regime change or elections) may alter the *relevant* ethnic identity.

To go beyond correlation and establish that the mechanisms that I have outlined are indeed operating, policymakers should cite domestic constituencies and relations with sending countries in order to justify their asylum policies. Observers with access to the decision-making process may also explain policies with reference to ethnic politics and foreign policies. This is most likely to occur in private documents and internal communications and conversations, but may also appear in public statements, memoirs, and published accounts of events.

Within a receiving country, these concerns should also be mirrored in the preferences held by diplomats and legislators. In other words, domestic actors (legislators, political parties, domestic agencies, and interest groups representing a particular ethnic group) should demand inclusive asylum policies for ethnic kin and restrictive policies for ethnic others. Meanwhile, diplomats and the foreign policy bureaucracy should demand generous policies for refugees fleeing a hostile sending country and restrictive policies for refugees from a friendly sending country.

In some situations, therefore, we should observe divergence between the demands of domestic actors on one hand and diplomats and the foreign policy bureaucracy on the other. Further, legislators may cite domestic constituencies, while diplomats reference relations with sending countries, in order to justify their preferred asylum policies. In addition, since members of a single refugee group may be regarded as ethnic kin by some domestic groups and as non-kin by other domestic groups, we may observe divergence among legislators depending on the constituency they represent.

Finally, I argue that UNHCR's status as an international organization and its apparent neutrality make delegation possible and desirable in some contexts. Thus, government officials should claim that UNHCR is in charge and emphasize that it operates in accordance with international standards. Meanwhile, domestic actors should see UNHCR (and not the government) as the actor in control of asylum decision-making. They should also perceive the Agency as neutral.

## Alternative Explanations

This section describes other explanations for patterns of inclusion, restriction, and delegation of asylum-seekers and refugees. I begin by reviewing those factors that, though they may seem to influence asylum policy, cannot explain differences between refugee groups. These explanations (economics, security, regional dynamics, and domestic institutions) either predict a "one size fits all" policy or depend on an underlying logic that echoes my argument. Then I survey some explanations for delegation drawn from principal-agent theory. Some of these characterizations may describe delegation to UNHCR better than others, but none are complete or entirely persuasive. Finally, I list four plausible candidates that emphasize commitment to humanitarian ideals, the desirability of skilled or wealthy refugees, the size of refugee flows, and the arbitrariness of low-level asylum decision-making.

Although there has been little theorizing on host states' asylum policies, economic factors are often advanced to explain state responses to refugees.[32] For example, Jacobsen notes that a host country's economic capacity (among other factors) will shape its ability to absorb refugees.[33] Hosting refugees entails material costs and can therefore be more demanding during economic downturns.

---

[32] Most research on this topic has been descriptive rather than theoretical, as with Basok 1990; Ferris 1985; Milner 2009; Veney 2007. For an exception that applies a single theoretical framework to permanent residence visas, labor visas, non-permanent visas, and asylum, see Freeman 2006.

[33] Jacobsen 1996. Relatedly, Whitaker argues that international funding shortages contributed to a shift in Tanzania's refugee policies. Whitaker 2008.

Refugees increase competition for jobs and social services like housing, education, and health. In developed countries, the welfare state may have to provide for them. And in developing countries, refugees' use of firewood, consumption of water, and grazing of livestock can result in ecological strain.[34] Host countries are often vocal about these concerns, citing them to justify actions like border closures and refugee encampment.

According to this explanation, economic capacity should determine a state's ability to deal with the resource demands imposed by refugee inflows. Countries that have low economic absorption capacity should regard refugee inflows as economically and socially destabilizing. Moreover, they should delegate asylum functions because delegation brings resources and technical assistance to the receiving country, effectively shifting the economic burden to the international organization and the international community. UNHCR can also ease some of the pressure on the host country's resources by resettling recognized refugees to other countries, though the number of annual resettlement opportunities is small.

In short, poorer countries with fewer material resources may adopt more restrictive policies and delegate to the UN because they cannot afford to host refugees or care for them. Of course, a country can still receive international aid without shifting responsibility to the UN. Flows of international aid may result in more inclusive policies, since they give countries the resources needed to host refugees and perhaps even improve the lives of their citizens as well. Bilateral and multilateral negotiations on refugees, like those that culminated in the 2016 EU-Turkey deal, often involve providing host countries with financial assistance.[35] Alternatively, economic capacity could impact a country's ability to implement its preferred asylum policies. Without the resources necessary to keep out refugees, poorer countries may become unwilling hosts to large refugee populations. Meanwhile, wealthier countries may be able to more effectively police their borders. If this reasoning is correct, then all refugee groups in a given receiving country ought to receive similar treatment.

A second set of explanations can be loosely grouped under the heading of security. Weiner, for instance, explores a range of situations in which receiving states may regard migration as threatening.[36] It stands to reason, then, that alarm over internal security or domestic stability may affect asylum policies. However, it is difficult to know what the specific prediction might be. It is difficult to know in advance which groups would be considered most destabilizing and which countries would be most concerned. Perhaps receiving countries who have

[34] Weiner 1993; Loescher 1989.
[35] See also Paoletti 2011.
[36] Weiner 1992.

previously experienced civil violence or terrorist incidents would then want to keep all refugees out (in which case, this explanation would not be able to explain differences between refugee groups). Of course, if only ethnic others are considered threatening, then that lines up with my ethnic affinity argument.

A third set of explanations posits that receiving countries may behave strategically. As Thielemann points out, public goods theory offers insights about free-riding and burden-shifting in the area of refugee protection.[37] Thus, countries may take account of regional trends when designing their asylum policies. If many neighboring states have adopted restrictive approaches, then the one that does not may be concerned about attracting refugees. Since each state would want to avoid the sucker's payoff, the thinking goes, the result would be a regional race to the bottom. With regard to delegation, a country may feel impelled to reassert control over its asylum policies if its neighbors have done so. A country may be concerned for its image, say, if it is the only one in the region that appears dependent on UNHCR. Alternatively, it may fear that refugees will prefer destinations where an international organization is in charge. These arguments about regional dynamics also fail to predict differences in policies across refugee groups.

A fourth set of explanations focuses on political institutions and conditions in the receiving country. If publics are resistant to hosting refugees, then democratization may lead to increased restrictiveness. Indeed, Veney makes a connection between democratization and decreased receptivity to refugees in Kenya and Tanzania in the 1990s.[38] To some degree, this begs the question of what informs public opinion. If public opinion on asylum policy is shaped by economic concerns, then this argument cannot explain differences across refugee groups. Otherwise, if public opinion is shaped by identity concerns, then this explanation may turn into another version of my ethnic affinity argument.

It may also be difficult to reverse policies once they have been put in place, either due to institutional inertia or because of reputational concerns. Of course, this path dependence explanation does not explain why certain policies were adopted in the first place.

There are also explanations, drawn by Hawkins and co-authors from principal-agency theory, that deal specifically with delegation to international organizations.[39] One possibility is that states view UNHCR as a "specialized agent," with the requisite expertise or resources to conduct RSD and manage refugee camps.[40] This account is complicated by the fact that the Agency's

---

[37] Thielemann 2018.

[38] Veney 2007.

[39] Of the potential explanations offered by principal-agent theory for delegation to international organizations, three may appear to apply to delegation to UNHCR: specialization gains, managing collaboration, and ensuring lock-in of policy bias. Hawkins et al. 2006, 13.

[40] Ibid., 13–14.

involvement in these processes is not explicitly provided for in the 1951 Refugee Convention, its 1967 Protocol, or the UNHCR Statute. UNHCR has interpreted its refugee protection mandate to allow it to decide on individual asylum applications, but it officially calls for the development of national asylum systems.[41] At the same time, UNHCR has been critiqued for not complying with the procedural fairness standards it advocates for governments.[42] Moreover, it is not clear why some governments have switched delegation "on" and "off" over the years, at times using their own RSD process or UNHCR's. Several countries even have parallel RSD procedures, whereby some asylum-seekers are processed by the government and others by UNHCR. Indeed, having developed bureaucracies that deal with tourism, immigration, and other people flows, governments should be able to create the mechanisms necessary to process asylum-seekers as well.

Another scenario involves UNHCR functioning as a "collaboration agent" that can prevent the free-rider problem by providing public goods itself.[43] Still, if UNHCR is providing a public good by taking on RSD, then it should be puzzling that some countries delegate and others do not. In other words, delegation itself would become subject to the free-rider problem. Countries that delegate RSD to UNHCR are likely to see some positive number of asylum applications accepted. Each country should therefore face incentives to reject all asylum applications and free-ride on other countries who have delegated RSD.

Finally, UNHCR could be acting as a "policy-biased agent" that helps domestic coalitions lock in their desired policy preferences through delegation.[44] Under this reasoning, a political party with a preference for some minimum level of asylum admissions may delegate RSD in order to prevent future governments from blocking admissions. A government may also delegate in response to lobbying from powerful domestic interest groups who favor the lock-in of asylum admissions (such as employers in migrant-dependent industries or ethnic relations of those asylum-seekers). In order for this argument to work, however, mandates must be difficult to undo. This is decidedly not the case for delegation to UNHCR. Governments have revoked the Agency's RSD authority altogether on numerous occasions, indirectly made it difficult for asylum-seekers to file applications (for example, by stationing police officers outside the Agency's offices), and overturned specific asylum recognition decisions (by, for instance, deporting refugees recognized by UNHCR). At the same time, UNHCR may not necessarily be more likely to grant asylum. For many refugee groups, acceptance rates at UNHCR offices are higher than those of some governments and lower

---

[41]  See, for example, UNHCR 1977.
[42]  One such critique can be found in Alexander 1999.
[43]  Hawkins et al. 2006, 16.
[44]  Ibid., 19–20; Moravcsik 2000.

than others.[45] In short, the propositions provided by principal-agent theory do not convincingly explain the decision to delegate to UNHCR.

Other alternative explanations are more promising. For instance, responses to refugees may be shaped by empathy and public opinion influenced by compassion. In other words, states may fashion their policies to reflect "principled beliefs" that align with international human rights norms as described by Goldstein and Keohane.[46] States may conform with norms like non-refoulement (which forbids returning a refugee to a country where they might face persecution) out of genuine altruism and empathy or because they seek international legitimacy and national esteem.[47] This account can also be linked to solidarist and cosmopolitan conceptions of international society, which stress Kant's principle of universal hospitality.[48]

If humanitarianism influences asylum policies, then countries ought to be more generous to refugee groups who are fleeing more pervasive persecution or danger (e.g., widespread human rights violations or large-scale deadly violence). If their own resources are insufficient, countries should delegate asylum policies to UNHCR in order to ensure international humanitarian standards are met. It is also possible for receiving countries to experience compassion fatigue, such that an initially warm welcome sours as the refugee population's plight continues. Of course, if a receiving country is more attuned to the suffering of ethnic kin, that would lend support to my argument about ethnic identity.

Alternatively, as Borjas's writing on immigration suggests, individual characteristics of refugees may shape the selection of some over others.[49] For instance, aging societies may be more welcoming of an injection of younger refugees. Moreover, labor skills may make some refugee groups more desirable than others. And wealthy refugees may be less likely to strain social services. This explanation would expect asylum policies to favor certain individuals rather than entire refugee groups.

The magnitude of the refugee flow, in absolute or per capita terms, may also influence asylum policies. For example, Milner's framework for explaining asylum politics in Africa incorporates the scale of refugee movements alongside other factors.[50] If it anticipates a large or lasting refugee crisis, a country may adopt restrictive policies in order to deter future refugees and prevent a "floodgates" situation. It may also crack down on bigger refugee groups in order to disincentivize their remaining in the country. It is unclear, however, whether delegation would

---

[45] See Kagan 2006, 20, fn. 75.

[46] Goldstein and Keohane 1993. See also Risse, Ropp, and Sikkink 1999; Rosenblum and Salehyan 2004.

[47] Finnemore and Sikkink 1998.

[48] Hurrell 2011; Benhabib 2004.

[49] Borjas 1989, 2014.

[50] Milner 2009.

be more or less likely for larger refugee groups. On the one hand, governments may want to retain control of large refugee groups because policies toward them will be more consequential. On the other, larger flows of asylum-seekers could outstrip the government's administrative capacity and lead to delegation for that reason.

The final possibility is evoked by the title of an important book, *Refugee Roulette*. Ramji-Nogales, Schoenholtz, and Schrag demonstrate that, even for applicants from a single country, there are divergences among asylum officers' and among judges' grant rates.[51] Perhaps asylum policies are somewhat arbitrary, determined by the idiosyncratic characteristics and decisions of low-level government employees. When a receiving country's refugee population is small, there may be few reasons for central decision-makers to concern themselves with formulating a consistent asylum policy. If this is the case, then there should be no discernible patterns in the treatment of various refugee groups.

## Research Design and Data

This section identifies the research methods used to investigate my argument and test it alongside these various alternative explanations. In particular, I follow a three-stage and multi-level design that is summarized in Figure 2.1. Rather than simply present a collection of multiple methods, I purposely mix quantitative and qualitative analyses. In addition, each successive stage corroborates and

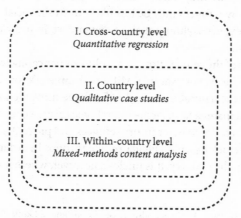

I. Cross-country level
*Quantitative regression*

II. Country level
*Qualitative case studies*

III. Within-country level
*Mixed-methods content analysis*

**Figure 2.1** Three-stage and multi-level research design

[51] Ramji-Nogales, Schoenholtz, and Schrag 2009.

expands on the prior stage. The findings from these different analyses point in the same direction, making my argument more compelling.

In the first stage, quantitative analysis explores general patterns in countries' decisions to grant refugee status and delegate status determination procedures. Using statistical regression, I am able to demonstrate a relationship between asylum policy, foreign policy, and ethnic politics, while controlling for other variables. This stage establishes that my findings hold across countries. In the second stage, qualitative case studies examine asylum policymaking in two countries, Egypt and Turkey. Each case study involves an examination of a wide range of policies toward several major refugee groups over time. This stage examines the more fine-grained mechanisms that underlie the previous stage's correlational relationship. The third stage goes a step further by exploring within-country dynamics related to inclusion, restriction, and delegation through content analysis of parliamentary proceedings in Kenya. I analyze these debates both qualitatively and quantitatively. This stage allows me to delve into the statements of individual actors within a specific country context.

## Country Selection

I focus on Egypt, Turkey, and Kenya for several reasons. Egypt, which has signed on to the 1951 Refugee Convention and hosts a relatively small number of refugees per capita, is broadly representative of most refugee recipients. Turkey has experienced several mass influxes, maintains a "geographical limitation" that only recognizes Europeans as refugees, and boasts the largest refugee resettlement program in the world, all factors that make it an outlier. And Kenya is often considered an important case because it hosts one of the world's largest refugee populations, it is home to one of the largest refugee camps, and it is the site of a grave, protracted refugee situation.

Even though my quantitative analysis relies on global data, the selection of developing countries for further examination is deliberate. Most existing research on immigration and asylum policy has been limited to Western countries.[52] However, some 85% of refugees reside in developing countries. Turkey had the world's largest refugee population in 2019, and Lebanon ranked first in number of refugees hosted per capita.[53] Some developing countries have experienced successive refugee movements from multiple crises, and some have been hosting long-standing refugee populations for years or even decades.

[52] For example, Hamlin 2014; Loescher and Scanlan 1986; Miller, Camp Keith, and Holmes 2015. Recent studies have demonstrated the value of examining migration and citizenship in developing country contexts. Klotz 2013; Sadiq 2009.

[53] UNHCR 2020b.

There is also significant variation across these three countries. For instance, Egypt, Turkey, and Kenya vary on their adoption of domestic legislation, their use of refugee camps, and their relations with UNHCR. Egypt lacks any domestic legislation pertaining to refugees, Turkey passed its Asylum Regulation in 1994, and Kenya adopted a Refugee Act in 2006. While Kenya has adopted a strict refugee encampment policy, Turkey relocates refugees to designated "satellite cities," and Egypt permits them to live where they choose. Finally, whereas Kenya completely turned over refugee status determination and camp management to UNHCR, both Egypt and Turkey kept some refugee groups outside the Agency's purview.

The three countries also vary on domestic conditions that might be expected to affect asylum policies, like regime type, intrastate violence, and economic conditions. Egypt is autocratic throughout the period under study, compared to Turkey and Kenya which underwent democratization processes in the 1980s and 1990s, respectively. Turkey and Kenya have experienced large-scale ethnic violence, while Egypt has not. The World Bank and the UN have classified Turkey (an OECD member) as an upper-middle-income economy, Egypt as a lower-middle-income economy, and Kenya as a low-income economy. Further, while refugees have long been a major public opinion issue in Kenya, probably due to the country's large refugee population, this was not the case in Turkey and Egypt prior to 2011. With these considerable differences across the three countries, findings that are consistent with my argument in all three would indicate that the results are likely generalizable—at least to developing countries—and not driven by idiosyncratic case-specific attributes.

At the same time, the three countries share some of the same refugee groups, as shown in Table 2.3. Iraqi refugees have gone to both Egypt and Turkey. Sudanese, Somali, Ethiopian, and Eritrean refugees live in Egypt and Kenya. This allows for the comparison of policies toward a single refugee group across countries. In effect, the refugee group is being held "constant" in these cross-country comparisons.

Table 2.3 Shared refugee groups in Egypt, Turkey, and Kenya

| | | | Refugee Group | | |
|---|---|---|---|---|---|
| | | Sudanese | Iraqi | Somali | Ethiopian & Eritrean |
| Host Country | Egypt | x | x | x | x |
| | Turkey | | x | | |
| | Kenya | x | | x | x |

For each of these countries, I analyze inclusion and restriction of different refugee groups as well as patterns of delegation. Within each country, asylum policy varies over time and across refugee groups. Thus, each country contains multiple cases of inclusion, restriction, and delegation. Moreover, each country experienced various configurations of sending country relations and ethnic affinity. The task, then, is to gauge the extent to which each country's refugee group-specific asylum policies are captured by my theoretical framework.

My analysis for Egypt and Turkey begins in 1951, the date of the Refugee Convention. The postwar establishment of the international refugee regime is a reasonable starting point, since it sets out the standards governing refugee rights. For Kenya, the analysis begins with the country's independence in 1963. The analysis ends in 2010 for all three countries, that is just before the upheavals and changes triggered by the Arab Spring, the Syrian civil war, and constitutional reform in Kenya.

## Data Collection

For the quantitative analysis, I compiled a dataset that combines information from the UNHCR Statistical Online Population Database, the Affinity of Nations Index, Penn World Table, the Political Terror Scale, the Major Episodes of Political Violence dataset, the Correlates of War Inter-State War Dataset, the Political Instability Task Force State Failure Problem Set, and the CEPII Distances dataset. In addition, I coded a proxy for refugee group affinity, using the Ethnic Power Relations and Minorities at Risk datasets in combination with secondary sources.

Qualitative data collection involved fieldwork in Cairo, Egypt; Ankara and Istanbul, Turkey; and Nairobi, Kenya. Between 2010 and 2012, I conducted a series of semi-structured interviews with policymakers, researchers, and representatives of relevant international organizations and non-governmental organizations (NGOs). A useful starting point was the list of organizations and government agencies that UNHCR designates as implementing and operational partners in each country. Interviews with policymakers and researchers attempted to discern official policy and the reasons behind its adoption. In addition, representatives of international organizations and NGOs often experience state policy firsthand in the course of their work, and studying their experiences through interviews is useful. Interviews involved questions on the individual's background and his/her organization's work; the conditions of refugees with which the individual/organization works; the country's official stance on refugees, legislation, and implementation; and the respondent's assessment of the sources of asylum policy.

In addition, I examined documents at the UNHCR Archives in Geneva, Switzerland. The documents in these archives detail the Agency's activities in countries around the world between 1951 and 1994. Specifically, I focused on Series 1 to 3 of Fonds 11. I examined folders related to UNHCR's External Relations, Specific Refugee Situations, Eligibility, Accreditation, and Administration and Finance in each of Egypt, Turkey, and Kenya. Overall, I consulted 62 folders and collected over 6,000 document images in English, French, and Arabic.

I also gathered primary and secondary sources from the Grey Files Special Collection at the Center for Migration and Refugee Studies at the American University in Cairo, the grey literature collection at the Refugee Studies Centre at the University of Oxford, and the combined libraries of the British Institute in Eastern Africa and the French Institute for Research in Africa. These materials included legislation, government press releases, human rights reports, and statistical surveys.

Finally, I examined the proceedings of the Kenyan parliament to create an archive of content related to foreign asylum-seekers and refugees. I used the online archive of the Kenya National Assembly Official Record (Hansard) to locate every instance between 1963 and 2010 in which the keywords "refugee" or "asylum" were used. I also searched for the Swahili verb root -kimbi- (to run or escape) to capture instances where references were being made to refugees (m-/wa-kimbizi), asylum (kimbilio), and asylum-seeking (-kimbilia).

The following chapter presents the first stage of my empirical research. It investigates discrimination and delegation by analyzing refugee status determination across countries, across refugee groups, and across time. Even when controlling for a range of other factors, countries' acceptance rates, as well as the likelihood that they will delegate decision-making on asylum applications, appear to be influenced by foreign policy and ethnic politics.

# 3

# Cross-National Trends in Refugee Status

Millions of asylum-seekers await a single decision that may save, or end, their lives. That decision: whether they will be granted refugee status along with its promise of protection. The majority will have worked to persuade government authorities in their country of asylum that they have a well-founded fear of persecution. What considerations may lead the government to reject their applications while accepting those of other refugees?

Elsewhere, asylum-seekers will have registered at a UNHCR office and sat for an interview with a UNHCR employee. When they receive written notification of a positive or negative decision, it will be on UNHCR letterhead. In these countries, why is it that an international organization is adjudicating asylum and not the government's own bureaucracy?

In the previous chapter, I developed a theoretical framework in which policymakers in refugee-receiving countries weigh international and domestic concerns. At the international level, policymakers consider relations with the refugee-sending country. At the domestic level, policymakers consider political competition among ethnic groups. When these international and domestic incentives conflict, shifting responsibility to the UN allows policymakers to placate both refugee-sending countries and domestic constituencies.

In this chapter, I test this theoretical argument using statistical analysis of global data on refugee status. The findings indicate that, all else equal, foreign policy and ethnic identity shape whether countries admit, reject, or shift the responsibility for refugees. Moreover, the results are robust to restricting the sample of observations, using alternative measurements, introducing additional control variables, and making different modeling choices. The results indicate that my argument applies broadly across countries, across refugee groups, and across time, setting the stage for the country-specific analyses that appear in subsequent chapters.

The remainder of this chapter proceeds as follows. The first section provides a brief overview of refugee status determination (RSD). The second section describes the measurement of delegation, admission and rejection, bilateral relations and ethnic affinity, and control variables. The third section presents an analysis of delegation and discrimination and discusses robustness checks. The final section concludes by summarizing this chapter's findings and drawing the link to the analysis in chapter 4.

*Discrimination and Delegation.* Lamis Elmy Abdelaaty, Oxford University Press (2021). © Oxford University Press.
DOI: 10.1093/oso/9780197530061.003.0003

## Why Study Refugee Status Determination?

RSD is the legal or administrative process that examines whether an applicant for asylum is indeed a genuine refugee. This procedure matters a great deal for asylum-seekers: for many, their lives are literally at stake. Having escaped persecution or large-scale violence, only a decision granting them refugee status will protect these individuals from deportation. Refugee status is also often the gateway to a range of rights, including access to employment and social services.

Crucially, RSD screens individual asylum-seekers' claims. It is therefore distinct from group-based (or, as it is also known, prima facie) refugee status. In some cases, members of a large-scale influx are collectively accorded prima facie refugee status based on readily apparent conditions in their home country. This group-based designation has been used for Afghan refugees, for example. In situations like these, an examination of each individual's claim to refugee status does not take place. Although prima facie refugees are in the majority worldwide, individual status determination still accounts for millions. In 2019, 60% of new refugees were recognized through individual status determination procedures.[1]

Investigating individual RSD, rather than prima facie refugee status, ensures that we do not mistake weak government capacity or, say, proximity to conflict zones for an inclusive asylum policy. Governments vary in their capacity to control border crossings, and many receiving countries have porous and imperfectly policed borders. For instance, Lebanon decided to introduce entry restrictions in early 2015 but could not seal unofficial crossings along large sections of its mountainous border with Syria. Unlike prima facie refugee status (and, perhaps, the total number of asylum applications lodged), individual asylum decisions should not depend on the government's ability to patrol the border or ease of access for refugees. At the same time, most countries do have some mechanism for determining individuals' eligibility for refugee status. According to data from the UNHCR Statistical Online Population Database, at least 155 countries had an RSD procedure of some sort in operation between 1996 and 2005.[2]

Admission processes and rates are also more suitable for a comprehensive cross-national analysis than laws or regulations. As subsequent chapters will demonstrate, various refugee-receiving countries lack domestic legislation on refugees altogether (e.g., in chapter 4, I show that Egypt's asylum policy consists of ad hoc decision-making and administrative decrees rather than national

---

[1] UNHCR 2020b.
[2] UNHCR n.d.

refugee legislation). Even for those countries that have adopted specific asylum legislation, implementation gaps may exist (chapter 5 describes Turkey's inconsistent application of its 1934 Law on Settlement, which ostensibly recognizes individuals of Turkish descent as "national refugees").

Finally, granting entry to asylum-seekers is often the most visible and highly publicized aspect of countries' asylum policies. But RSD is not generally a high-stakes event involving top-ranking government officials. Instead, the procedure involves numerous day-to-day decisions by individual bureaucrats, officers, and/or judges. The asylum bureaucracy in the United States comprises over 300 asylum officers and about 250 immigration judges, for example.[3] Previous research has documented large discrepancies in asylum approval rates among these individual adjudicators.[4] Investigating whether concerns related to foreign policy and ethnic politics percolate down to influence such micro-level decisions constitutes a "hard test" of my argument.

## Measuring Variation Worldwide

This chapter's analysis examines when countries delegate decision-making on asylum applications and why governments accept or reject individually screened applicants. My argument expects a given government to vary its treatment of refugees over time, depending on the origin and identity of those refugees. Testing this argument globally requires an analysis of each receiving country's responses, the reception of refugees from different sending countries, and changes over time.

I gathered data about every country in the world that decided on asylum applications during a ten-year period (1996–2005) and organized this dataset by "directed dyad-year." A dyad-year is simply a pair of countries in a given year, like Bangladesh and India in 1997. It is "directed" when the pair of countries is sequenced or ordered, in this case by asylum-seekers' country of origin then their country of (potential) refuge. So, "Bangladesh-India 1997" is the directed-dyad year that captures Bangladeshi nationals who applied for asylum in India in 1997. In contrast, "India-Bangladesh 1997" is the directed-dyad year that captures Indian applicants for asylum in Bangladesh in that year. For every directed dyad-year, I assembled statistics regarding delegation, admission and rejection, bilateral relations, ethnic affinity, and a host of additional variables. This section describes how each of these variables was measured.

---

[3] Miller, Camp Keith, and Holmes 2015, 10; US Department of Justice 2017.
[4] Ramji-Nogales, Schoenholtz, and Schrag 2009.

## Delegation

It has long been UNHCR's position that RSD is the legal responsibility of governments.[5] Identifying individuals who meet the refugee definition is necessary for states, whether or not they are signatories to the 1951 Refugee Convention, to protect individuals against refoulement. Legal obligations aside, we might expect governments to want to have a say in who remains on their territory and accesses their services. Still, as described in chapter 1, a number of countries have empowered UNHCR to act on their behalf with regard to RSD. One of the questions this book seeks to answer is when and why countries delegate in this way.

In order to measure the degree of UNHCR involvement in RSD, I use an ordinal, or rank-ordered, variable. This variable indicates whether *Refugee Status Determination* in each receiving country was conducted solely by the government (1), jointly with UNHCR (2), or solely by UNHCR (3) in that year. This information was extracted from the UNHCR Statistical Online Population Database.[6] I take greater UNHCR involvement in RSD to represent more delegation, since it indicates the conferral of more authority to UNHCR.

Figure 3.1 shows the distribution of responsibility for RSD over time. The total number of delegating countries remained roughly the same, with a modest increase in joint delegation (from 2 countries in 1997 to 13 in 2005) and a small decline in full delegation (from 44 countries in 1997 to 32 in 2005). However, the sample grew over time to include more non-delegating countries (78 countries in 2005 compared to only 17 in 1997). This dramatic increase is probably due to improvements in UNHCR's data collection for countries where it is not involved in RSD.

Not only resource-deprived countries delegate decision-making on asylum applications. During the period under study, UNHCR conducted status determination in several countries that belong to the OECD, like South Korea. Despite being classified as high-income economies by the World Bank, countries like Cyprus and Saudi Arabia have also delegated to UNHCR. Meanwhile, the governments that conducted status determination themselves were a diverse group. They included 68 countries who were not World Bank high-income economies, OECD members, or EU members, and 26 of them were located in sub-Saharan Africa.

---

[5] UNHCR 2014.
[6] UNHCR n.d. Joint status determination typically means that UNHCR is responsible for one or more components (such as registration, interviews, decisions, or appeals) in an otherwise national procedure.

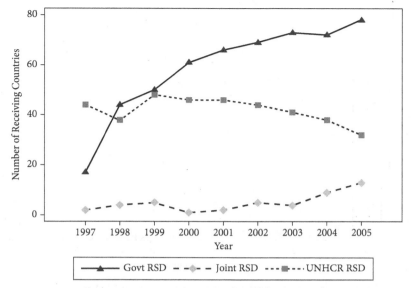

**Figure 3.1**  Delegation of refugee status determination (RSD) over time
Note: This graph includes 952 receiving country-year observations.

## Admission and Rejection

Even though they may hail from the same country, asylum-seekers will face vastly
different odds of being admitted depending on their destination. To capture this
variation in admission and rejection, I rely on the receiving country's "recognition rate" for asylum-seekers from each sending country. The recognition rate is
usually interpreted to reflect the proportion of asylum applications approved in
any one year.[7] The variable *Asylum Recognition Rate* reflects the recognition rate
when the receiving country's government was solely responsible for RSD. Once
again, I rely on the UNHCR Statistical Online Population Database for this data.[8]
I take a higher recognition rate to represent a more inclusive policy on the part of
the receiving country.

[7]  More precisely, UNHCR calculates the recognition rate as the number of decisions recognizing
asylum claims in any one year, relative to the number of claims decided upon.
[8]  UNHCR n.d. The UNHCR Statistical Online Population Database reports two types of recognition rates: refugee recognition rates and total recognition rates. The latter covers individuals who
have been accorded complementary protection status, rather than recognition as a 1951 Convention
refugee. Complementary protection status is generally used for individuals who, though not eligible
for convention refugee status, may still have sound reasons for not wishing to return to their home
country. The two statuses usually entail different rights and entitlements for the asylum-seeker, with
complementary protection often considered a subsidiary or temporary form of protection. The analysis in this chapter covers only refugee recognition rates.

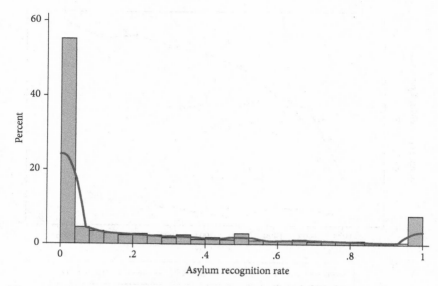

**Figure 3.2** Histogram and kernel density for asylum recognition rate
Note: This graph includes 18,859 directed dyad-year observations. The Epanechnikov function was used to produce the kernel density estimate.

Figure 3.2 shows the distribution of recognition rates in my dataset. Based on the data, most countries tend toward rejecting asylum applications; many directed dyad-years had a 0% recognition rate. As a result, the median recognition rate is a bleak 0.8%, or acceptance of only 8 out of every 1,000 asylum-seekers.

## Bilateral Relations and Ethnic Affinity

My argument is that a refugee-receiving country's responses are shaped by two key factors: bilateral relations with the refugee-sending country and ethnic affinity with the refugee group. There is no single, straightforward way to measure relations between sending and receiving countries. For *Sending Country Relations*, I use data from the Affinity of Nations Index, which is based on states' votes in the UN General Assembly. In particular, I use the measure "s2un4608i," which is based on two category votes (i.e., excluding abstentions) and includes interpolation for missing values.[9] This variable ranges from −1 (for least similar interests) to 1 (for most similar interests). Using this proxy assumes that UN voting is closely correlated with underlying foreign policy interests and political

[9] Gartzke 2010.

ties between countries. This is a fairly reasonable assumption, even if UN votes are symbolic. Even though UN General Assembly votes are not costly, states tend to vote according to their foreign policy positions.

Unsurprisingly, most pairs of countries appear to be on good terms most of the time. The average value of this variable in my dataset is a cordial 0.66. Only a small number of dyad-years between 1997 and 2005 appear on the most hostile end of this variable (at −1).

With regards to ethnic affinity, an ideal measure would capture the ethnic composition of refugee flows between countries. However, UNHCR does not collect information on the ethnicity of refugees, and secondary sources are insufficient to code this variable for all directed dyads over time. Even a recently released dataset on the Ethnicity of Refugees identifies only the three largest refugee groups residing in each country, while also limiting itself to refugee movements between neighboring countries.[10]

Instead, I use a proxy that captures whether, for each directed dyad-year, an ethnic group is in power in the receiving country but excluded from power in the sending country. I coded this *Refugee Group Affinity* variable using the Ethnic Power Relations (EPR) and Minorities at Risk (MAR) datasets, in combination with secondary sources.[11] It takes the value 0 (no ethnic tie) or 1 (co-ethnic). For example, the Azerbaijan-Armenia directed dyad receives a score of 1 because ethnic Armenians are in power in the receiving country (Armenia) but excluded from power in the sending country (Azerbaijan). In my sample, about 97% of directed dyad-years had no ethnic tie and only 3% received co-ethnic refugees. Using this proxy assumes that most refugees are members of a community that is excluded from power in their country of origin.[12]

I also calculated weighted averages of these two variables, to account for a receiving country's relations with all sending countries (*Sending Country Relations$_{avg}$*) and its affinity with all refugee groups (*Refugee Group Affinity$_{avg}$*) in a given year. In other words, I calculated an average Affinity of Nations Index weighted by the number of applications made from each sending country. Similarly, I weighted the Refugee Group Affinity proxy by the number of applications from each sending country, then calculated the average. These manipulations presume that, when faced with refugee flows from many countries, a

---

[10]  Rüegger and Bohnet 2018.

[11]  The EPR dataset identifies access to power for politically relevant ethnic groups in each country, but it identifies transnational ethnic linkages only across contiguous countries. Cederman, Min, and Wimmer 2009; Vogt et al. 2015. The MAR dataset uses consistent codes for communal groups living in multiple countries, but efforts to expand its scope beyond at-risk groups are still at an early stage. Minorities at Risk Project 2009; Birnir et al. 2015.

[12]  If the exclusion of ethnic groups from power systematically shaped bilateral relations, that would affect my results due to multicollinearity. However, the correlation between sending country relations and ethnic affinity is low in my sample ($\rho = 0.084$).

policymaker may choose to delegate or not depending on the proportion of friendly-origin vs. rival-origin refugees and depending on the proportion of ethnic kin vs. other refugees. Finally, since I postulate that relations with sending country and ethnic affinity have an interactive (rather than additive) effect on delegation, I interact these two variables as well.

## Other Variables

A number of control variables are included in the regression to account for other factors that could shape asylum decision-making. Shifting responsibility to or away from UNHCR may be a response to the previous year's admission rates, so I include the lagged asylum recognition rate (*Asylum Recognition Rate$_{t-1}$*). I also control for whether the receiving country is a member of UNCHR's Executive Committee (*ExCom Member*). Countries that sit on this committee may find delegation more acceptable since they have some control over UNHCR's policies. A control variable coding whether the receiving country has acceded to the 1951 Convention or its 1967 Protocol (*Refugee Treaty*) is included in the delegation equation as well. Since these treaties set out criteria for refugee status, countries that have ratified them may be more likely to establish a status determination procedure.

We might also expect that countries will be more likely to delegate as the burden of processing applications becomes heavier. Delegation frees up the receiving country's resources and ensures that applications will be processed according to international standards. To capture this dynamic, several variables are included in the regression. The natural log of the lagged refugee stock in the destination country (*ln Refugee Stock$_{t-1}$*) was computed using UNCHR's Statistical Online Population database, as was the lagged number of individual asylum applications received per capita (*Applications per capita$_{t-1}$*) and the number of countries from which asylum applications were received in the previous year (*Number of Origin Countries$_{t-1}$*). I also include the receiving country's *ln GDP per capita*, the natural log of real GDP per capita in 2005 constant prices, as obtained from the Penn World Table (PWT).[13] Finally, I include a lagged delegation variable (*Refugee Status Determination$_{t-1}$*) because governments with an already operational status determination procedure in place may be likely to continue using it.

Economic capacity may also shape receptivity to refugees, so the receiving country's *ln GDP per capita* is included in the regression for admission and rejection. In addition, conditions in the sending country, or the potential causes of

---

[13] Heston, Summers, and Aten 2009.

refugee flows, may affect the asylum policy of the receiving country. Specifically, refugees fleeing more difficult circumstances or pervasive danger may be more warmly received. The *Origin's ln GDP per capita* was taken from the PWT.[14] In addition, the *Origin's Political Terror* reflects government human rights violations.[15] Information on *Origin's Domestic Violence/War* was collected from the Major Episodes of Political Violence dataset.[16] To indicate whether the sending country was involved in an interstate war in any given year (*Origin's Interstate War*), I use the Correlates of War (COW) Inter-State War Dataset v4.0.[17] In addition, the scaled annual number of deaths from genocide/politicide (*Origin's Genocide/Politicide*) was taken from the Political Instability Task Force (PITF) State Failure Problem Set.[18] Finally, I control for distance between sending and receiving countries by taking the natural log of kilometers between their capitals (*ln Distance*) from the CEPII Distances dataset.[19]

To be sure, there may be other factors that I have left out. To ensure that these omitted variables do not bias the results, my analysis also includes fixed-effects. Destination fixed-effects hold constant those receiving country characteristics that I did not, or cannot, measure or observe.[20] Similarly, year dummies control for those unobserved attributes that may impact all directed dyads in each particular year. The following section discusses the findings.

## Analyzing Asylum Decision-Making

A receiving state cannot accept or reject asylum applications without conducting RSD. Put differently, a government cannot use RSD to discriminate between asylum-seekers if it has outsourced that process to another independent actor. Thus, my statistical model must account for two decisions: the choice of whether or not to delegate and the choice of how much to discriminate.

A "double-hurdle" model is most appropriate here because it estimates two decisions, often termed participation and quantity, which can correspond to delegation and discrimination.[21] The delegation (or participation) decision is when

---

[14] Ibid.

[15] In years in which both Amnesty International and the US State Department derived-ratings were present, their simple average was taken. Where one of the two ratings was missing, the other was used instead. Gibney, Cornett, and Wood 2010.

[16] Marshall 1999.

[17] Sarkees and Wayman 2010.

[18] Marshall, Gurr, and Harff 2010.

[19] CEPII n.d.

[20] Unconditional logit fixed-effects estimates can be biased and inconsistent due to the incidental parameters problem. Lancaster 2000; Neyman and Scott 1948. To deal with this issue, I include time-averages of the independent variables for each destination country rather than using destination dummies. Papke and Wooldridge 2008.

[21] Cragg 1971.

a receiving country decides whether to conduct RSD itself. The discrimination (or quantity) decision is when it decides how many asylum-seekers to admit through that process.[22] Crucially, and in keeping with my theoretical model, the double-hurdle model treats delegation and discrimination as occurring simultaneously (not sequentially).

To analyze the delegation decision, I examine all directed dyad-years (21,897 in total between 1997 and 2005) in which the receiving country had any RSD procedure in place that decided on some positive number of applications. A receiving country in which no asylum decisions were made drops out of the analysis because we cannot observe its status determination in action. Since the variable *Refugee Status Determination* is ordinal, I use an ordinal logit regression to estimate the delegation of RSD.

In my analysis of the discrimination decision, I investigate all directed dyad-years (18,859 between 1997 and 2005) in which the receiving country's government was solely responsible for that RSD. Focusing on governmental acceptance rates tests my argument about the effect of foreign policy and ethnic politics on countries' decisions to pursue inclusive or restrictive policies. I use a fractional logit regression to estimate asylum recognition rates because *Asylum Recognition Rate* is a proportion.[23]

The findings in full are reported in Table 3.1 and are discussed in detail below.[24] Overall, the models appear to fit the data well. The baseline model correctly predicts *Refugee Status Determination* in 96.3% of the observations and correctly classifies *Asylum Recognition Rate* in 64.5% of the observations.[25]

## Why Do States Outsource Refugee Status Determination?

The argument laid out in chapter 2 suggests that countries delegate asylum policymaking to the UN when domestic and international incentives collide. If I am correct, then delegation should be most likely when countries receive co-ethnic refugees from a friendly country and when they receive ethnic others from a hostile country.

---

[22] A zero recognition rate means that a country has chosen to reject all the asylum applications it received. A zero is observed data, not missing or censored data, so this does not represent a sample selection problem. Wooldridge 2010, 692.

[23] Papke and Wooldridge 1996.

[24] Cross-sectional dependence and serial correlation are not likely to be a problem, because the data covers a large number of directed dyads over a small number of years (N>T). Still, models with cluster-robust standard errors are reported to control for autocorrelation and heteroskedasticity.

[25] These figures were generated with the STATA user-written command "epcp" after transforming the fractional logit discrimination regression into a weighted logistic model.

**Table 3.1** Double-hurdle regression for refugee status determination and asylum recognition rate

| Variables | Delegation Step: Ordinal Logit for Refugee Status Determination | Discrimination Step: Fractional Logit for Asylum Recognition Rate | | | |
| --- | --- | --- | --- | --- | --- |
| | | *(1)* Baseline Model | *(2)* Year FEs | *(3)* Destination FEs | *(4)* Year & Destination FEs |
| Sending Country Relations | — | −1.151*** (0.087) | −1.151*** (0.088) | −0.415*** (0.152) | −0.320** (0.154) |
| Refugee Group Affinity | — | 0.381** (0.181) | 0.379** (0.180) | 0.595*** (0.207) | 0.609*** (0.208) |
| Sending Country Relations$_{avg}$ | −6.212*** (1.322) | — | — | — | — |
| Refugee Group Affinity$_{avg}$ | −1.358*** (0.213) | — | — | — | — |
| Relations$_{avg}$ × Affinity$_{avg}$ | 8.172*** (1.397) | — | — | — | — |
| Asylum Recognition Rate$_{t-1}$ | −0.092 (0.112) | — | — | — | — |
| ExCom Member | 0.182** (0.091) | — | — | — | — |
| Refugee Treaty | −1.423*** (0.108) | — | — | — | — |
| ln Refugee Stock$_{t-1}$ | −0.055*** (0.014) | — | — | — | — |
| Number of Origin Countries$_{t-1}$ | −0.035*** (0.002) | — | — | — | — |
| Applications per capita$_{t-1}$ | 0.604*** (0.142) | — | — | — | — |
| ln GDP per capita | −0.151*** (0.044) | −0.022 (0.036) | −0.012 (0.037) | −0.375 (0.265) | −2.419*** (0.440) |
| Refugee Status Determination$_{t-1}$ | 3.352*** (0.081) | — | — | — | — |

*Continued*

Table 3.1 *Continued*

| Variables | Delegation Step: Ordinal Logit for Refugee Status Determination | Discrimination Step: Fractional Logit for Asylum Recognition Rate | | | |
|---|---|---|---|---|---|
| | | (1) Baseline Model | (2) Year FEs | (3) Destination FEs | (4) Year & Destination FEs |
| Origin's ln GDP per capita | — | −0.142*** (0.031) | −0.141*** (0.031) | −0.276*** (0.033) | −0.283*** (0.034) |
| Origin's Political Terror | — | 0.461*** (0.035) | 0.464*** (0.035) | 0.887*** (0.037) | 0.898*** (0.038) |
| Origin's Domestic Violence/War | — | −0.204*** (0.071) | −0.214*** (0.072) | −0.379*** (0.076) | −0.373*** (0.076) |
| Origin's Interstate War | — | −0.100 (0.130) | −0.075 (0.133) | −0.068 (0.150) | 0.004 (0.154) |
| Origin's Genocide/ Politicide | — | 0.042 (0.052) | 0.041 (0.052) | 0.009 (0.047) | 0.012 (0.048) |
| ln Distance | — | −0.088** (0.039) | −0.088** (0.039) | −0.502*** (0.048) | −0.500*** (0.048) |
| Constant | — | 1.471*** (0.518) | 1.938*** (0.536) | −5.471 (4.206) | −5.127 (4.273) |
| Cut 1 | 2.076*** (0.481) | — | — | — | — |
| Cut 2 | 3.598*** (0.513) | — | — | — | — |
| N | | 27588 | 27588 | 27588 | 27588 |
| Log-Likelihood | | −14925.110 | −14915.924 | −12340.838 | −12309.463 |
| Akaike Information Criterion | | 29896.22 | 29895.85 | 24903.68 | 24858.93 |
| Bayesian Information Criterion | | 30085.4 | 30159.05 | 25816.67 | 25845.94 |

Note: Models 2 and 4 include year dummies, but coefficients are not reported. Robust standard errors, clustered on 5,658 directed dyads, are in parentheses. *$p<.10$, **$p<.05$, ***$p<.01$.

**Table 3.2** Average marginal effect of explanatory variables on the probability of delegation

| Variable | Estimated at | | AME |
|---|---|---|---|
| Sending Country Relations$_{avg}$ | Refugee Group Affinity$_{avg}$ = | 1 (Co-Ethnic) | 0.094*** (0.017) |
| | | 0 (No Ethnic Tie) | −0.027*** (0.004) |
| Refugee Group Affinity$_{avg}$ | Sending Country Relations$_{avg}$ = | −1 (Hostile) | −0.333*** (0.089) |
| | | 1 (Friendly) | 0.034*** (0.003) |

Note: Cells display average marginal effects for Pr(Refugee Status Determination=3) from Model 1. Robust standard errors are in parentheses. *$p<.10$, **$p<.05$, ***$p<.01$.

The coefficients for my two central independent variables—relations with the sending country and ethnic affinity with the refugee group—and their interaction are all statistically significant. In order to better interpret the substantive effects of these variables, Table 3.2 lists average marginal effects for the probability that RSD is conducted solely by UNHCR. Simply stated, this table estimates the impact of a one unit increase in each of *Sending Country Relations$_{avg}$* and *Refugee Group Affinity$_{avg}$* on the probability of full delegation to UNHCR. Recall that the variable *Sending Country Relations$_{avg}$* equals one when average relations are friendliest and negative one when they are most hostile; *Refugee Group Affinity$_{avg}$* equals one when all refugees are co-ethnics and zero when there are no ethnic ties.

The effect of refugee group affinity on delegation depends on the value of sending country relations, and vice versa. Delegation becomes more likely for co-ethnic refugees as relations with their country of origin improve: a one unit increase in *Sending Country Relations$_{avg}$* raises the probability of delegation by 9.4 percentage points on average when refugees are co-ethnics. However, a similar improvement in bilateral relations makes delegation less likely for refugees who do not share an ethnic tie, decreasing the probability of delegation by 2.7 percentage points on average. When bilateral relations are hostile, delegation is 33 percentage points less likely on average for co-ethnic refugees compared to those with no ethnic tie. But when bilateral relations are friendly, a one unit increase in *Refugee Group Affinity$_{avg}$* has a positive effect on the probability of delegation, raising it by 3.4 percentage points on average. These average marginal effects are all statistically significant at the 99% level.

The predicted probabilities displayed in Table 3.3 further clarify the estimated relationship between refugee ethnicity, bilateral relations, and delegation. Full

**Table 3.3** Average predicted probability of delegation, by value of explanatory variables

|  |  | *Sending Country Relations*$_{avg}$ | |
|---|---|---|---|
|  |  | −1 (Hostile) | 1 (Friendly) |
| *Refugee Group Affinity*$_{avg}$ | 1 (Co-Ethnic) | 0.000 (0.000) | 0.187*** (0.003) |
|  | 0 (No Ethnic Tie) | 0.204*** (0.009) | 0.153*** (0.001) |

Note: Cells display average predicted Pr(Refugee Status Determination=3) from Model 1. Robust standard errors are in parentheses. *p<.10, **p<.05, ***p<.01.

delegation is most likely when a country receives co-ethnic refugees from friendly sending countries (20.4% probability) and when it receives refugees from hostile countries with no ethnic tie (18.7% probability). Conversely, RSD conducted solely by UNHCR occurs with only a 15.3% probability with non-kin refugees fleeing friendly countries. For co-ethnics fleeing hostile countries, the lack of statistical significance suggests that the predicted probability may be equal to zero.[26]

These results lend support to my argument. Granting complete status determination authority to UNHCR is most likely when bilateral relations and refugee group affinity pose conflicting pressures. The probability of delegation is highest for co-ethnic refugees from hostile countries and for non-kin from friendly countries. Improvements in bilateral relations make delegation more likely for co-ethnics and less likely for non-kin. Meanwhile, a shift toward co-ethnicity raises the probability of delegation for refugees from friendly countries and decreases it for those fleeing hostile countries.

Though not central to my argument, the coefficients on the control variables are worth noting. Only lagged asylum recognition rate has a coefficient that is not statistically significant. The coefficient for *ExCom Member* is positive and statistically significant at the 95% level. Joining UNHCR's Executive Committee increases the probability of delegation by 0.3 percentage points on average. Perhaps countries are more likely to delegate because sitting on this committee allows them to shape UNHCR's activities. Meanwhile, the coefficient for *Refugee*

---

[26] For friendly sending countries, pair-wise comparisons confirm that there is a statistically significant difference (at the 99% level) in the predicted probability of delegation for co-ethnic refugees compared to those with no ethnic tie. For refugees with no ethnic tie too, there is a statistically significant difference in the predicted probability of delegation for hostile compared to friendly sending countries.

*Treaty* is negative and statistically significant, such that ratifying the treaty decreases the probability of delegation by 2.4 percentage points on average. I can only speculate about the reasons for this finding: signatories may be more likely to conduct their own RSD than non-signatories because any compliance with the treaty hinges on identifying those individuals to whom it applies. Meanwhile, non-signatories have fewer reasons to be concerned about compliance with a treaty they have not signed.

The variables controlling for lagged refugee stock and number of origin countries do not behave as expected. The coefficient on *ln Refugee Stock$_{t-1}$* is negative, indicating that an increase in that variable lowers the probability of delegation. The coefficient on *Number of Origin Countries$_{t-1}$* also has a negative sign. Thus, it does not appear that countries delegate as status determination becomes more resource-intensive due to sizeable refugee stocks or a more diverse pool of applicants. Receiving countries that host larger refugee populations may fear that delegation to an international organization will swell these numbers further, perhaps because UNHCR's presence may act as a pull factor. Governments may want to keep status determination in their own hands as their asylum applicants become more heterogeneous, so that they can better discriminate among these applicants.

The estimates for the remaining control variables seem more straightforward. *Applications per capita$_{t-1}$* has a positive effect on the probability that UNHCR will be placed in charge of RSD. Meanwhile, an increase in *ln GDP per capita* lowers the probability of delegation. In other words, delegation becomes more likely as the number of asylum applications rises and less likely as the receiving country's economic conditions improve. These effects indicate that countries' delegation decisions may be influenced by resource constraints. Finally, the positive coefficient on *Refugee Status Determination$_{t-1}$* suggests that countries that delegate are likely to continue to do so.

## Why Do States Accept or Reject Asylum Applications?

Once again, I hypothesize that countries adopt more inclusive policies toward co-ethnic refugees and those fleeing hostile countries. Conversely, I expect more restrictive policies toward refugees from friendly sending countries and those with whom there is no ethnic tie. Thus, my argument suggests that higher recognition rates should be associated with lower values of *Sending Country Relations* and higher values of *Refugee Group Affinity*.

As expected, the coefficient on *Sending Country Relations* is negative and statistically significant, while *Refugee Group Affinity* is positive and statistically significant. For easier interpretation, Figure 3.3 plots average marginal effects from

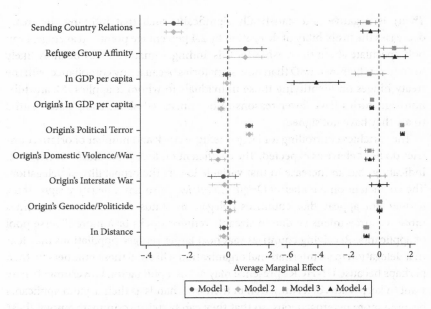

**Figure 3.3** Average marginal effects from fractional logit regressions of asylum recognition rates

Note: Error bars represent 99% confidence intervals. Capped spikes represent 95% confidence intervals. Year dummies are included in Models 2 and 4, but marginal effects are not plotted. Models 3 and 4 include destination fixed-effects.

the fractional logit regression estimating asylum recognition rates. A one-point improvement in *Sending Country Relations* decreases the asylum recognition rate by 26.2% on average. Meanwhile, a shift from no ethnic tie to co-ethnicity raises the asylum recognition rate by 8.7% on average.

Figure 3.4 plots the average predicted asylum recognition rate for different values of the two key independent variables *Sending Country Relations* and *Refugee Group Affinity*. According to the argument I laid out in chapter 2, co-ethnics from a hostile country will be treated most generously, while refugees who lack an ethnic tie and come from a friendly country will face the most restrictive treatment. Model 1 predicts that the former group will have a 90% asylum recognition rate on average, while the latter will only receive a 42% recognition rate. The difference between these two predicted margins is about 48% and is statistically significant at the 99% level.

With regards to the control variables, the receiving country's *ln GDP per capita* is only statistically significant in Model 4, which includes both year and destination fixed-effects. The coefficient for this variable has a negative sign, such that wealthier countries are less likely to grant entry to refugees. This result indicates

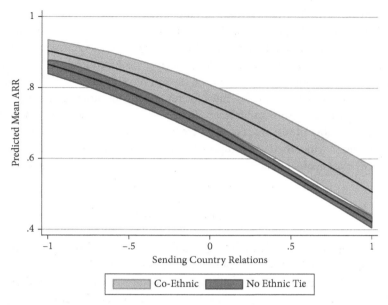

**Figure 3.4** Average predicted asylum recognition rate (ARR)

Note: Model 1 was used to predict average asylum recognition rates. Shaded areas represent 90% delta method confidence intervals.

that receptivity to refugees is not primarily shaped by states' ability to meet the material costs of hosting these populations.

The findings relating to conditions in the country of origin are mixed. The coefficients for *Origin's Interstate War* and *Origin's Genocide/Politicide* are not statistically significant. The coefficients for *Origin's ln GDP per capita* and *Origin's Political Terror* signal that asylum-seekers fleeing difficult or dangerous conditions are more likely to be accepted. A one-point improvement in *Origin's ln GDP per capita* decreases the asylum recognition rate by about 3.2% on average. An increase in the *Origin's Political Terror* also has a marginal effect of around 10.5%. These two results indicate that as economic and human rights conditions in a sending country worsen, receiving countries will grant a larger proportion of its asylum-seekers refugee status.

At the same time, however, the coefficient on *Origin's Domestic Violence/War* is negative. In other words, refugees fleeing civil conflict are less welcome on average. It is difficult to speculate on the reasons underlying this novel finding. It is plausible, though, that refugees fleeing civil war are less able to persuade authorities that they are eligible for refugee status under the 1951 Refugee Convention. Since that treaty ties refugee status to individual-level persecution, people fleeing generalized violence may not qualify. At the same time, receiving countries may view asylum-seekers from civil wars as a possible mechanism for the spread of conflict. Receiving states may wish to avoid those refugees, since they are perceived to transmit destabilizing ideas, resources, and recruits across borders.[27]

Finally, *In Distance* between sending and receiving countries has a negative and statistically significant effect on the asylum recognition rate. Governments have higher asylum recognition rates for refugees from more proximate origin countries. This relationship between distance and acceptance rates may stem from any number of reasons. For instance, members of the asylum bureaucracy may be more sympathetic to refugees from neighboring countries with whom they are better acquainted.

## Checking the Findings' Robustness

To ensure that these results are robust, I examined a battery of additional regressions that are briefly described here. The first set of checks for robustness are related to the sample of observations in my dataset. In many of the directed dyad-years examined in the previous discussion, only a small number of asylum applications were submitted in the first place. It might be concerning if these very small status determination operations were responsible for my results. So I estimated a double-hurdle model for the subsample of observations in which 100 or more decisions were made during the year, dropping 20,392 observations. I also estimated a model for the subsample of observations in which 100 or fewer decisions were made, dropping 7,153 observations. Restricting the analysis in these ways did not alter my results for bilateral relations and refugee group affinity significantly.

My argument regarding bilateral relations presumes that the sending country has a functioning government, that is, one with which it is possible for receiving countries to have a friendly or hostile diplomatic relationship. And my argument about refugee group affinity assumes that ethnicity is salient in the receiving country, such that policymakers there care about the ethnic identity of incoming refugee groups. Accordingly, I estimated the model while restricting the sample to exclude directed dyad-years where ethnicity was not salient in the receiving country (according to the EPR dataset) and where the sending country experienced state failure (described as geographically substantial or complete collapse of state authority by the PITF State Failure dataset).[28] The coefficients for bilateral relations and refugee group affinity were roughly the same for this subsample.

---

[27] Salehyan and Gleditsch 2006.
[28] Rüegger and Bohnet 2018; Cederman, Min, and Wimmer 2009.

A second set of robustness checks revolved around alternative ways of measuring the variables included in the model. This step ensures that my findings are not an artifact of a particular operationalization decision. For sending country relations, I substituted the measure "s3un4608i" from the Affinity of Nations Index. I also estimated my models using ideal point estimates based on UN votes, rather than Affinity scores.[29] As an alternative way to measure refugee group affinity, I used the Ethnicity of Refugees dataset in combination with the EPR dataset to indicate whether a refugee group shared the same ethnicity as the group in power in the receiving country.[30] My findings remained robust to these changes.

With regards to control variables, replacing *ln Distance* with contiguity from the COW Direct Contiguity dataset did not substantially alter my results.[31] The outcome was similar when scaled deaths from genocide/politicide was replaced with incidence of genocide/politicide from the PITF State Failure dataset. I also ran regressions with summed civil and ethnic violence and war magnitude scores from the Major Episodes of Political Violence dataset as well as intra-state war from the COW Intra-State War Dataset v4.0.[32] For interstate war, I used the intensity level and cumulative intensity of war from the UCDP/PRIO Armed Conflict Dataset v.4-2011.[33] In all cases, my results with respect to sending country relations and refugee group affinity remained largely the same.

In a third set of checks for robustness, I added additional control variables to the regression to investigate whether my findings were shaped by omitted variable bias. A democratic receiving country may be less likely to delegate, particularly if its citizens are wary of transferring responsibility to an unaccountable international organization. Moreover, admission and rejection may be shaped by the level of democracy in the sending country, with those fleeing repressive regimes more likely to be welcomed. However, my findings are robust to adding regime type variables for the sending and receiving countries, whether these measures reflected the Polity IV Project's Revised Combined Polity score or the sum of Freedom House's political rights and civil liberties indices.[34] Left-right ideology in the receiving country might also impact the propensity to delegate and the desire to admit refugees. Controlling for left-right ideology in the sending and receiving countries, using the Manifesto Project Dataset, did not substantially change the results either.[35]

---

[29] Volkens et al. 2016.
[30] Separate variables were created to indicate whether that refugee group was numerically dominant or represented a majority of the refugee population.
[31] Stinnett et al. 2002.
[32] Sarkees and Wayman 2010; Sarkees 2000.
[33] Gleditsch et al. 2002.
[34] Marshall and Jaggers 2002; Freedom House 2011.
[35] Volkens et al. 2016.

Lastly, I examined alternative model specifications by adding variable interactions as well as using other functional forms in a final set of robustness checks. The effect of the previous year's asylum recognition rate on the decision to delegate may depend on who was conducting status determination at that time, so I interacted *Asylum Recognition Rate*$_{t-1}$ with *RSD*$_{t-1}$. Since the number of applications received may have a different effect on delegation for wealthy countries compared to poorer countries, I also created an interaction for *ln GDP per capita* with *Applications per capita*$_{t-1}$. Finally, I ran a multinomial logit regression for delegation, as well as separate ordinary least squares regressions for each hurdle. Once again, the results for sending country relations and refugee group affinity remained unchanged in terms of statistical significance and direction of effect.

## Conclusion

UNHCR is involved in RSD worldwide. As described in chapter 1, the Agency played some role in 77 countries in 2011 and undertook status determination single-handedly in 54. This delegation of decision-making on asylum applications is consequential for refugees, especially in light of various shortcomings in UNHCR's implementation of status determination.[36] The prevalence of an international organization determining who may remain on a state's territory also has implications for our understanding of sovereignty.

At the same time, there is substantial variation in the proportion of asylum applications approved by governments. A single country's admission rates can vary widely between different refugee groups, from rejecting every single applicant to accepting them all. These decisions are matters of life or death for the asylum-seekers who may be released from detention, spared deportation, given assistance, and so on.

This book argues that delegation and discrimination decisions are shaped by foreign policy and ethnic politics. In this chapter, I used a global dataset and statistical analysis to answer two questions: When are countries likely to delegate decision-making on asylum applications to the UN Refugee Agency? And when they retain these decision-making functions themselves, why do countries accept or reject applications?

The results lend support to my argument, and they are extremely robust. Though other factors matter as well, this chapter demonstrates that receiving

---

[36] UNHCR's status determination procedures have been criticized for withholding evidence from applicants, disallowing them the right to legal representation, denying them access to an independent appeals process, and refusing to reveal to unsuccessful applicants the reasons for their rejection. Kagan 2016.

countries are more likely to welcome refugees who are co-ethnics as well as those fleeing hostile sending countries. And they are more likely to transfer responsibility to UNHCR when international and domestic incentives push in opposite directions (i.e., when co-ethnic refugees flee friendly countries, or when refugees with no ethnic tie originate from rival states).

Previous research has shown that there is substantial variation in approval rates for refugees from any single country of origin, even among EU countries who have sought to harmonize their asylum policies.[37] This chapter suggests that these divergences may stem, at least in part, from cross-national patterns in sending country relations and affinity with refugee groups.

Of course, this analysis focused only on individual refugee admission and status during a specific time period, 1996–2005. Still, this chapter's findings indicate that my argument may apply broadly across countries, across refugee groups, and across time even when controlling for other factors. The next chapter builds and expands on these findings by presenting detailed causal evidence from a qualitative case study of Egypt.

[37] Neumayer 2005.

# 4

# Politics Overtakes Policy in Egypt

Egypt is a "typical" refugee recipient in several respects. It is a developing country, like most other states in which the majority of the world's refugees reside. It has signed on to both the 1951 Refugee Convention and its 1967 Protocol, as have 141 other countries. Finally, it hosts a relatively small number of refugees, numbering about 95,000 in 2010. This figure represents 16 refugees to each dollar in GDP per capita (the worldwide average is 21) and one refugee for each 1,000 inhabitants in the country (the global average is three).[1]

The Egyptian case is also particularly interesting in its own right. Egypt was on the drafting committee for the 1951 Refugee Convention.[2] The country long hosted one of the world's five largest urban refugee populations and was chair of UNHCR's Executive Committee in 2010–2011.[3] When Egyptian border guards shot some 33 Africans trying to cross into Israel in 2009, the USCRI included the country on its list of the worst places for refugees.[4]

The conventional wisdom about Egypt's asylum policy is that there is, in fact, no policy. One expert I interviewed wondered: "Does Egypt have, or care to have, a refugee policy?" He doubted there was an underlying pattern to the government's responses to refugees, suggesting that the "government may not think about refugees very much . . . it couldn't care less."[5] Another researcher described the country's asylum policy as "inconsistent" and "ad hoc."[6] Indeed, Egypt does not have domestic refugee legislation or a single, clearly-articulated, official asylum policy.

This chapter demonstrates that, contrary to the conventional wisdom, there are clear patterns in Egypt's responses to refugees. Fluctuations in the government's actions over time, and their variation by refugee group, reveal the

---

[1] UNHCR 2011b.

[2] Convention Relating to the Status of Refugees (entered into force April 22, 1954); Protocol Relating to the Status of Refugees (entered into force Oct. 4, 1967); OAU Convention Governing the Specific Aspects of Refugee Problems in Africa (entered into force June 20, 1974).

[3] Sperl 2001, 1.

[4] USCRI 2009.

[5] Martin Jones (Vice Chairman, Egyptian Foundation for Refugee Rights). Personal interview by author. American University in Cairo, Cairo, Egypt, June 22, 2010.

[6] Ray Jureidini (Director, Center for Migration and Refugee Studies). Personal interview by author. American University in Cairo, Cairo, Egypt, June 15, 2010.

*Discrimination and Delegation.* Lamis Elmy Abdelaaty, Oxford University Press (2021). © Oxford University Press.
DOI: 10.1093/oso/9780197530061.003.0004

influence of foreign policy and ethnic politics. These political factors shape that country's responses to refugees, even in the absence of an official asylum policy. In the words of one researcher, when it comes to refugees in Egypt, "politics has overtaken policy."[7]

Chapter 3 showed that asylum admissions and delegation are correlated with sending country relations and ethnic affinity. This chapter's in-depth study of Egypt expands that analysis to a broader range of asylum policies and traces the changes in these over time. I examine Egypt's policy responses toward its largest refugee groups since the establishment of the post-WWII international refugee regime and until just before the Arab Spring. Alongside other sources, I draw on interviews at the Egyptian Ministry of Foreign Affairs, UNHCR, the International Organization for Migration, the Center for Migration and Refugee Studies at the American University in Cairo, and a number of refugee-related NGOs. I also present evidence from archival sources containing correspondence between UNHCR's branch office in Cairo and the Agency's headquarters in Geneva.

The remainder of this chapter is organized into five sections. The first examines differences in the treatment of refugee groups by Egyptian authorities, while the second focuses on the government's relationship with UNHCR. The third section assesses the extent to which these patterns in Egypt's asylum policies align with my theoretical expectations, and the fourth section explores alternative explanations. The final section concludes.

## Discrimination

Egyptian asylum policy is often described as having been traditionally generous but becoming more restrictive in recent years.[8] As the remainder of this section shows, however, the development of the Egyptian government's asylum policies over time is more complex. In this section, I provide some contextual information before delving into government responses vis-à-vis six refugee groups: Palestinians, Sudanese, Iraqis, Somalis, Eritreans, and Ethiopians. This analysis demonstrates that Egypt's policies are not ad hoc, nor have they uniformly trended from generosity to restrictiveness. Rather, Egypt's treatment of different refugee groups in practice seems to match sending country relations and ethnic affinity.

---

[7] Hania Sholkamy (Assistant Professor, Social Research Center). Personal interview by author. American University in Cairo, New Cairo, Egypt, June 20, 2010.
[8] UNHCR 2009.

## Context

Egypt ratified the 1951 Refugee Convention in 1981, along with its 1967 Protocol and the 1969 OAU Refugee Convention.[9] As mentioned earlier, Egypt has no national refugee legislation or domestic procedures for asylum in effect. The government's official position has been that, since ratified international instruments are directly enforceable in national courts, additional domestic legislation is unnecessary.[10] Rather than being codified in domestic implementing legislation, policies on health, education, and employment for refugees have often been promulgated in the form of ministerial decrees.[11]

Article 53 of the Egyptian Constitution states that: "Egypt is obliged to grant the right of political asylum to any foreigner who has been persecuted for his defense of the interests of people, or of human rights, peace, or justice. The extradition of political refugees shall be prohibited." But in practice, this special category of "political refugee" (which is granted asylum by the Office of the President) seems to have been reserved for high-profile cases like Shah Mohammad Reza Pahlavi of Iran, President Jaafar Nimeiry of Sudan, or Queen Fatima el-Sharif of Libya.[12]

For the average refugee, the most relevant government bodies are the Department of Refugee Affairs within the Ministry of Foreign Affairs, and the Ministry of Interior. The former mainly issues letters to obtain residence permits and works to secure the release of detained asylum-seekers and refugees. The latter is responsible for issuing residence permits for asylum-seekers and refugees. These permits are for temporary residence pending resettlement or repatriation; naturalization of refugees is not permitted. UNHCR lobbies both bodies when asylum-seekers and refugees are detained, but the Department of Refugee Affairs is the main target of advocacy work by UNHCR, NGOs, and refugee communities.[13]

In the absence of any major repatriation, resettlement, or secondary movement trends, the majority of refugees arriving in Egypt have tended to stay in the

---

[9] Convention Relating to the Status of Refugees; Protocol Relating to the Status of Refugees; OAU Convention Governing the Specific Aspects of Refugee Problems in Africa. The Egyptian government entered reservations to five articles in the 1951 Refugee Convention, relating to personal status (art. 12(1)), rationing (art. 20), public education (art. 22(1)), public relief (art. 23), and labor legislation and social security (art. 24). Egypt has also signed the 1994 Arab Convention on Regulating Status of Refugees in the Arab Countries, but this treaty has not come into force.

[10] Article 151 of the Egyptian Constitution states that international treaties ratified by Egypt and published in the Official Gazette have the force of law and in all cases supersede domestic law. Zaiotti 2006, 336, fn. 11.

[11] UNHCR 2004.

[12] Badawy and Khalil 2005, 24–25; Zohry and Harrell-Bond 2003, 50.

[13] Grabska 2006, 19; Al-Sharmani 2008, 10; Hilal and Samy 2008b, 47, 8; Badawy and Khalil 2005, 25.

country. There are no refugee camps in Egypt, and the majority of refugees reside in the capital, Cairo, and the second largest city, Alexandria.

According to UNHCR estimates, 70,000 Palestinians lived in Egypt in 2010, making up three-quarters of the refugee population there.[14] Sudanese refugees were the second largest group (11% of the refugee population), with over 10,000 refugees and nearly 12,500 asylum cases pending. The country hosted refugees from 36 other countries, including Iraq (7%) and Somalia (6%), with growing numbers of Eritreans and Ethiopians.

The discussion that follows deals with each of these refugee groups in turn. In line with this book's argument as laid out in chapter 2, differences between refugee groups correlate with relations with the sending country and ethnic affinity. Moreover, major shifts in asylum policy coincide with breakpoints or discontinuities in relations with the sending country.

## Palestinians

The first significant flow of Palestinian refugees occurred with the declaration of the state of Israel and the Arab-Israeli war that ensued.[15] Relations between Egypt and Israel were decidedly hostile over the next three decades and were marked by major wars in 1948, 1956, 1967, and 1973.[16] Egyptian-Israeli relations were transformed, however, with the signing of the Camp David Accords in 1978. At the same time, Palestinian refugees shared an ethnic affinity with Egyptians: the majority ethnicity for Palestinians and the dominant ethnic identity for Egypt were both "Arab Muslim."[17]

Thus, I expect to observe an initially inclusive asylum policy toward Palestinian refugees, shifting in a more restrictive direction in the late 1970s. Indeed, the discussion that follows shows that Palestinian rights, which had expanded in the 1950s and 1960s, were abruptly and dramatically curtailed in 1978/1979.

---

[14] Of course, the size of refugee populations is difficult to know with certainty. Some asylum-seekers never register with UNHCR, while others have been rejected by the Agency but remain in the country.

[15] Although Palestinian refugees have been described as a "special" or "unique" case in some of the refugee studies literature, I use the same analytical approach for Palestinians and all other refugee groups described in this chapter. For a discussion of unique aspects of the Palestinian refugee case, see Dumper 2006. For an argument against Palestinian "exceptionalism" in scholarship on asylum policy, see Kagan 2009.

[16] I characterize relations with a sending country as friendly or hostile depending on whether there were disputes, material support for opposition groups, alliances, trade agreements, or high-level visits in a given year.

[17] To identify the ethnic identity of refugee groups throughout, the MAR and EPR datasets were used in combination with secondary sources. Minorities at Risk Project 2009; Cederman, Min, and Wimmer 2009. In cases where refugees from a single country of origin represented a number of different ethnic identities, I discuss the identity of the majority of refugees.

Egyptian authorities were initially caught off guard by the 1948 influx of Palestinians, probably ranging from 11,000 to 13,000, but they assumed the displacement crisis would be short-lived. The country's King Farouk quickly established the Higher Committee of Palestinian Immigrant Affairs and allocated LE300,000 (over one million in 2010 US dollars) in government funds for its relief efforts. He also created three camps—Abbasiyya, Qantara Sharq, and Azarita—though Palestinians were permitted to leave these camps and obtain a residence permit to remain in Egypt if they had financial means and an Egyptian guarantor. After the 1949 armistice agreement placed the Gaza Strip under Egyptian administration, thousands were sent to Maghazi camp in Gaza. Others left to join relatives abroad, with the government paying their fares in some cases. By 1950, only a few thousand Palestinians remained in Egypt.[18]

At this time, the border between Egypt and Gaza was closely monitored and controlled, although the government flirted with international projects to settle some refugees in the Sinai Peninsula. Within Egypt proper, the Higher Committee was transformed into an aid agency, providing government assistance to those Palestinians who had a residency card recording refugee status. Palestinians were not permitted to work, though this was related to the perception that they would soon be able to return home. In accordance with an Arab League decree, Egypt also declined to grant citizenship to Palestinian refugees. The situation of Palestinians in Egypt remained largely unchanged immediately following the overthrow of the Egyptian monarchy in 1952.[19]

Eventually, President Gamal Abdel-Nasser approved a budget to create work opportunities in Gaza and gradually eased restrictions on employment and ownership for Palestinian refugees residing in Egypt. In 1962, Law 66 gave Palestinians the same employment options as Egyptian nationals, inaugurating what is often called the "golden era" for Palestinians in Egypt. Education, health, and other services were made available to Palestinians as well. These policies and the wave of refugees created by the 1967 war resulted in a significant influx of Palestinians into Egypt. According to government estimates, by 1969 there were 33,000 Palestinians in Egypt.[20]

A major turning point for the Palestinian population in Egypt came in the late 1970s under President Anwar Sadat. Egypt's relations with the Palestine Liberation Organization (PLO) had seriously begun to sour with Sadat's 1977 trip to Jerusalem to address the Israeli Knesset. Following the assassination of Egyptian culture minister Yusif al-Sibai by the Abu Nidal faction in 1978, there was a flurry of arrests, surveillance, and detentions of Palestinians. Sadat

---

[18] El-Abed 2009, 17–19; Brand 1991, 43–45.
[19] El-Abed 2009, 36–37, 39–40; Brand 1991, 51–52, 54.
[20] El-Abed 2009, 20, 28, 40–45.

proceeded to dismantle Nasser's legislation that favored the Palestinians, tightening restrictions on employment and education. Law 48 of 1978 made the employment of foreigners in the public sector subject to reciprocity with other countries, effectively barring stateless Palestinians. The same year, the Ministry of Education decreed that Palestinian children be transferred from public to private schools, excepting children of employees of the PLO, the Administration Office of the Governor of Gaza, public sector employees, and retirees. Soon Palestinians were required to pay university fees in foreign currency and were not permitted to enroll at certain faculties such as medicine, engineering, and political science.[21]

Palestinians next flowed into Egypt under President Hosni Mubarak. After Israel's invasion of Lebanon in 1982, some members of the PLO apparatus relocated to Egypt. A larger influx occurred during the 1990–1991 Gulf War. Some Palestinians fleeing the Iraqi invasion or expelled from Kuwait after the war held valid Egyptian residence permits and were permitted to enter the country. However, tens of thousands of others who held Egyptian travel documents were turned back. Palestinians (including registered students and long-time residents) were detained at the airport and deported, especially to Sudan. In 1995, Libyan leader Muammar Qadhafi expelled more than 1,000 Palestinian holders of Egyptian travel documents to the Egyptian-Libyan border. Although the Egyptian government granted transit visas to some, most were denied entry or passage and remained stranded at the Salloum border camp until Qadhafi agreed to let them back into Libya two years later.[22]

Mubarak largely continued or extended Sadat's restrictive policies, with minor improvements. In 1992, a ministerial decision required that foreigners, including Palestinians, not exceed 10% of the student body at public universities. At the same time, children of employees of the PLO and public sector employees, as well as children who had been born in Egypt and completed all their basic education there, found their university fees reduced by 90%. In 1982, Law 25 introduced a quota for foreigners in the private sector. Still, in 2003, Decree 136 exempted Palestinians (and Sudanese) from paying the full fee to receive a work permit.[23]

In July 2004, a new law was passed granting Egyptian women the same rights as Egyptian men with regard to conferring nationality on their children. Given that an estimated third of all Egyptian women married to non-nationals were married to Palestinians at the time, this law was considered a major development. However, the law applied automatically only to persons born after its activation.

[21]  Ibid., 46, 48–49, 91, 105–08.
[22]  Ibid., 29, 51, 86; USCRI 1997; USCRI 1998.
[23]  El-Abed 2009, 92, 108–09, 13–14; Grabska 2006, 20.

For individuals born to an Egyptian mother before the law was enacted, there was a one-year grace period to apply to the interior ministry for citizenship. In practice, Palestinian applicants appeared to have been turned away especially when the child of the mixed marriage was over 16.[24]

This reluctance to naturalize children of mixed Egyptian-Palestinian marriages fell under a broader Egyptian refusal to grant citizenship to Palestinian refugees. Residence permits for Palestinians had to be renewed every three or five years, depending on their arrival date. Residency was contingent upon providing a reason for remaining in Egypt, such as education, licensed work, or marriage to an Egyptian, and a fee was charged.[25]

Egypt closed the Rafah border crossing in 2007 after the Hamas takeover of Gaza and until after the Israeli flotilla raid in 2010. During this time, Palestinians that left Egypt with valid travel documents were not allowed to reenter without a visa, which Egyptian consulates abroad summarily denied. Following a break in the Gaza-Egypt border wall in 2008, Egyptian authorities attempted to force over 1,000 Palestinians in the Sinai back into Gaza.

To summarize, Egypt initially perceived the 1948 refugee crisis as temporary and responded with encampment and the distribution of government-funded relief and assistance. Palestinian rights were gradually expanded in the 1950s and 1960s, despite a concurrent increase in the number of Palestinian refugees residing in Egypt. However, the situation of Palestinians in Egypt deteriorated abruptly and dramatically in 1978/1979 as relations between Egypt and Israel improved. This restrictive trend continued until 2010, though suppression of Palestinians was limited by Egyptians' "affinity or solidarity" with these refugees.[26] At the same time, it may be that the presence of Palestinian refugees in Egypt was an obstacle to the adoption of integration policies toward refugees from other countries, "who should not be seen to benefit from more favorable terms than the Palestinians" who were ethnic kin after all.[27]

## Sudanese

Sudanese asylum-seekers and refugees flowed into Egypt in several waves corresponding with the first civil war (1955–1972), the second civil war (1983–2005), and the Darfur conflict (2003–present). Mainly Southerners and Darfur Black Muslims, they did not share an ethnic tie with Egyptians. Moreover, Egyptian-Sudanese relations fluctuated wildly. The two governments initially experienced

---

[24] El-Abed 2009, 52–54.
[25] Ibid., 80.
[26] Ibid.
[27] Sperl 2001, 11–12; Al-Sharmani 2008.

a dispute over the Halaib border region in 1956 and 1957 following Sudanese independence. Relations quickly improved, however, and remained friendly until Sudanese president, and close Egyptian ally, Jaafar Nimeiry was overthrown in 1985. Egyptian hostility toward successive Sudanese presidents was manifested in the support it provided to opposition parties and rebel movements. It was only in the late 1990s that bilateral relations were normalized.[28]

Accordingly, I expect Sudanese refugees to experience several shifts between more and less restrictive asylum policies. Specifically, the pattern of bilateral relations and ethnic affinity ought to lead to more restrictive treatment during 1958–1984 and 1999–2010. As a brief preview: information about Sudanese refugees in Egypt is unfortunately sparse prior to the 1990s, but there is evidence of increased restrictions in the early 2000s. Though they were treated relatively favorably prior to this shift, Sudanese refugees were not welcomed to the same degree as Palestinian refugees.

Until 1995, Sudanese migrants, asylum-seekers, and refugees in Egypt formally enjoyed a status close to nationals due to bilateral agreements between Egypt and Sudan. For instance, the 1976 Nile Valley Treaty provided for reciprocal treatment, including unrestricted entry for Sudanese as well as unfettered access to employment, education, healthcare, and ownership of property. As a matter of law, it was not necessary for refugees to seek asylum in order to obtain these benefits. In 1992, Decree No. 24 by the Minister of Education allowed Sudanese children to enroll in Egyptian public schools, though with extensive and often difficult to meet documentation requirements.[29]

Following the 1995 assassination attempt on Mubarak's life in Ethiopia, allegedly supported by the Sudanese government, the Nile Valley Agreement was revoked and the border with Sudan closed. Visa and residence permit requirements were imposed on all Sudanese attempting to enter the country, while those resident in Egypt were subject to increased security checks. Suddenly, all Sudanese (including asylum-seekers and refugees) were not allowed to work without a permit. Despite the restrictions on the entry of regular Sudanese migrants, it is worth noting that Sudanese refugees were welcomed during a dispute between Mubarak and Sudanese president Omar al-Bashir in the late 1990s.[30]

In other words, the mid-1990s were a turning point only in that the government began distinguishing between Sudanese refugees and other migrants. Prior to 1995, Sudanese nationals in general had a privileged position. While this group undoubtedly included bona fide refugees, the latter were not identified or

[28] Hilal and Samy 2008b; Zohry and Harrell-Bond 2003; Metz 1992; Brecher and Wilkenfeld 1997.
[29] Badawy and Khalil 2005, 26; Sperl 2001, 20.
[30] Hilal and Samy 2008b, 35; Sperl 2001, 20.

recognized as such by the Egyptian government. In other words, Egypt did not have an "asylum policy" for Sudanese before 1995. Asylum-seekers and refugees were able to blend into the larger Sudanese flow and enjoy the same access to employment, education, healthcare, and ownership of property. When the government began differentiating between refugees and other migrants, it restricted the latter while welcoming the former. Even as other migrants faced stricter border control, refugees continued to be welcomed into the country.

The situation for refugees arriving in the early 2000s took a different turn. Soon after the outbreak of the conflict in Darfur, Darfurian refugees reported being chased in the streets of Cairo by Sudanese security and asked to provide information about Darfurian activists in Egypt.[31] In fact, "Egypt coordinates with Sudan" with respect to Sudanese refugees.[32]

In 2004, the signing of the "Four Freedoms Agreement" seemed promising on its face. The treaty provided for reciprocal rights for Egyptian and Sudanese nationals regarding work, freedom of movement, residence, and property ownership. Under the agreement, all Sudanese migrants (including asylum-seekers and refugees) would not be required to obtain entry visas, residence permits, or work permits. However, this agreement was not implemented in practice.[33]

A few years later, attempts by significant numbers of migrants, asylum-seekers, and refugees (mostly Eritreans and Sudanese) to enter Israel illegally through Egypt's Sinai desert raised concerns on the part of both governments. In late June 2007, Egyptian president Mubarak met with Israeli prime minister Ehud Olmert in Sharm el-Sheikh. Following the meeting, Olmert said he had reached an "understanding" with Mubarak on "ways to deal with infiltration into Israel via the Egyptian border." Days later, Egypt's new shoot-to-stop policy was inaugurated and claimed its first victim. The Egyptian government publicly justified its policies by claiming that organized Sinai-based criminal smuggling networks posed a threat to national security.[34] The UN High Commissioner for Human Rights said she knew of "no other country where so many unarmed migrants and asylum-seekers appear to have been deliberately killed this way by government forces."[35] Meanwhile, the Sudanese Consul in Cairo cast doubt on the numbers and identity of those attempting to cross the border into Israel. He alleged Israel was inflating the numbers to cast itself as an attractive "safe haven" for Arabs and Africans, adding that non-Sudanese "infiltrators" were claiming to be Darfurian to get refugee status.[36]

[31]   Hilal and Samy 2008b, 35.
[32]   Martin Jones (Egyptian Foundation for Refugee Rights). Personal interview by author. June 22, 2010.
[33]   Hilal and Samy 2008b, 35; Grabska 2008, 79.
[34]   Human Rights Watch 2008, 31–32; Amnesty International 2008; Anteby-Yemini 2008.
[35]   Maigua 2010.
[36]   Hamdallah 2010. For the Eritrean embassy's response, see Othman 2010.

Sudanese asylum-seekers and refugees attempting to cross the border into Israel were detained and transported to Cairo, interrogated, beaten and tortured, and then returned to Sudan. In 2007, following the deportation of 48 Sudanese refugees by Israel to Egypt, Egypt then returned at least 20 of them to Sudan. These deportations were especially serious given that the Sudanese government banned its citizens from traveling to Israel and reportedly punished offenders with torture, life imprisonment, or the death penalty. In April 2008, authorities returned 49 Sudanese including 11 recognized refugees and asylum-seekers accused of participating in gang violence, before their hearing.[37] It is worth noting that these developments coincided with Egypt's support for President Bashir in the face of his indictment by the International Criminal Court.

Along with other sub-Saharan asylum-seekers and refugees, Sudanese have faced racism and discrimination by Egyptian police as well as by locals. They report being verbally harassed and sometimes attacked by street thugs. Most Sudanese are concentrated in five neighborhoods in and around Cairo: Ain Shams, Arba wa Nus, Maadi, Nasr City, and 6th of October City. Occasionally, Egyptian police launched raids to round up anyone who looked "black," including registered asylum-seekers and recognized refugees. These detainees often experienced beatings and were held until UNHCR intervened for their release.[38]

In short, bilateral treaties had long stipulated that all Sudanese nationals be accorded rights roughly on par with Egyptian citizens. When the Egyptian government imposed restrictions in the mid-1990s, many of these applied to Sudanese migrants rather than refugees. The turning point for Sudanese asylum-seekers and refugees came in the late 1990s with a notable upswing in detentions and deportations.

## Iraqis

The outflow of Iraqis that began with the 2003 US invasion rose sharply with the upsurge in violence marked by the 2006 al-Askari Mosque bombing. The US was effectively occupying Iraq throughout this period, and Egypt was a US client and strategic ally. As Arab Sunnis, the majority of Iraqi refugees in Egypt share an affinity with Egyptians.[39]

My argument predicts that Iraqis, fleeing a friendly sending country and sharing an ethnic affinity with Egyptians, ought to receive treatment less generous

---

[37] Human Rights Watch 2008; US Department of State 2009.
[38] Azzam 2006, 15–16; Zohry and Harrell-Bond 2003, 55; Human Rights Watch 2003.
[39] Fargues et al. 2008.

than golden era Palestinians and less restrictive than post-1990s Sudanese refugees. Indeed, the analysis that follows shows that Iraqis were denied access to social services but nonetheless did not experience widespread detentions and deportations.

Most Iraqis were initially able to enter Egypt with one-month tourist, student, or investment visas obtained from travel agencies in Iraq. They were expected to register with the Ministry of Interior within ten days of their arrival. Refugees could then register with UNHCR and receive prima facie asylum-seeker status.[40]

In late 2006, that is within months, a more restrictive visa policy was introduced. Egypt began requiring that Iraqis report to an Egyptian consulate for a visa interview, effectively obliging them to go first to Syria or Jordan before arriving in Egypt. Visas already issued also became more difficult to renew. In 2008, Iraqis arriving by air from Jordan and Syria were deported back to these countries. The following year, at least four Iraqis arriving at Cairo International Airport were denied admission.[41]

Some government officials invoked security concerns, including fear of Shia proselytizing, to justify these decisions. It is striking that Egyptian authorities would defend their less-than-welcoming policy responses, and attempt to shape the reaction of their domestic public, by falsely claiming that Iraqi refugees in Egypt were ethnic others (i.e., Shia rather than Sunni). Others claimed that Egypt was discouraging the flight of Sunnis from Iraq in order to prevent the latter from becoming a Shia state.[42]

Unlike Sudanese and Palestinian refugees, Iraqi children were not allowed to attend Egyptian public schools to receive primary and secondary education. Even though the Minister of Education had issued a decree in 2000 allowing all refugee children access to free public primary education, this decree imposed difficult documentation requirements, such as a birth certificate, an original school certificate from the country of origin, and a letter from the embassy of the country of origin. In practice, implementation of this decree was hindered because officials within the Ministry of Education as well as at the governorate and school level were either unaware or had inconsistent interpretations of it.[43]

With respect to employment, Iraqis joined other refugees in being treated as would any other foreigner in the country. Law No. 137 of 1981 required foreigners (including refugees) to obtain a work permit from the Ministry of Manpower. Obtaining a work permit was in many cases difficult, if not impossible. Foreigners

[40] Rosen 2007; Yoshikawa 2007; Fargues et al. 2008, 27; Sadek 2010, 49.

[41] Fargues et al. 2008, 16; Hilal and Samy 2008b, 43; Rosen 2007; USCRI 2009; Roman 2009, 4; Badawy 2009, 3.

[42] Refugees International 2007.

[43] Zohry and Harrell-Bond 2003, 51; Badawy 2009, 6; Refugees International 2007; Grabska 2008, 78.

were not permitted to compete with the local workforce and therefore had to have special expertise and qualifications in addition to being barred from certain professions, such as tourism, exports, and customs-related jobs. The employer was also required to pay a work permit fee amounting to LE1,000 (US$174).[44]

The vast majority of Iraqis in Egypt were from Baghdad, many residing in 6th of October City. Unlike other refugee groups in Egypt, Iraqis were not permitted to form their own associations or community-based organizations.[45] There was no law stating this prohibition, but Iraqis consistently failed to secure registration for their associations on security grounds.[46] Members of the community were reportedly under "intense security surveillance."[47]

Iraqi refugees do not appear to have been deported or detained by the Egyptian authorities. Unlike refugees from sub-Saharan Africa, "racism" was not an issue with Iraqis, so the government was "more lenient" with them.[48] However, without access to public services or the formal labor market, Iraqis in Egypt faced the continuous depletion of the economic resources with which they traveled to Egypt.[49]

To recap, the Egyptian government acted quickly to restrict Iraqis arrivals within months. Denied access to public education and the labor market, the refugees were also prohibited from forming community-based organizations. At the same time, they did not experience significant threats to their physical safety on par with Sudanese refugees in Egypt.


## Other Refugee Groups

There is less information available about the treatment of Somalis, Ethiopians, and Eritreans in Egypt, but it is indicative nonetheless. Here, I describe Egypt's responses to each of these refugee groups in turn.

The onset of the Somali Civil War in 1991 resulted in a large movement of Somalis to Egypt. Somali refugees in Egypt are mainly Darood, Hawiye, Issak, Dir, and Rahenweyn. Thus, like Sudanese refugees, Somalis are ethnic others in Egypt. However, because Somalia was a failed state throughout the period

---

[44] Grabska 2006, 21.

[45] In addition, the establishment of the Iraqi Information Office by St. Andrew's Refugee Services had been difficult due to government opposition to Iraqis congregating. Fiona Cameron (Assistant Director, St. Andrew's Refugee Services Children's Education Programme). Personal interview by author. St. Andrew's Church, Cairo, Egypt, August 25, 2010.

[46] Fargues et al. 2008, 27, 37; Sadek 2010, 51; Trapped between Egypt and Iraq 2008.

[47] Badawy 2009, 6.

[48] Sara Sadek (Outreach Coordinator, Center for Migration and Refugee Studies). Personal interview by author. American University in Cairo, Cairo, Egypt, June 9, 2010.

[49] Hilal and Samy 2008b, 45; Fargues et al. 2008, 73.

under consideration, it is difficult to speak meaningfully of Egyptian relations with a Somali government.[50] I expect Somali refugees to be treated less restrictively than late-1990s Sudanese refugees, since Somalis lack the added effect of friendly bilateral relations. The evidence presented here shows this to be the case, with Somali refugees experiencing fewer threats to their physical safety than Sudanese refugees.

When a small number of Somali refugees arrived in 1988, UNHCR's internal communications noted that the Egyptian government had expressed an "official commitment to non-refoulement" but was loath to "create a 'refugee problem.'" The government, long a Somali military ally, was willing "to give hospitality (residence visas) without using the word refugee." The Somali government concurred that refugee status was "not justified."[51]

Around the same time, we also see internal disagreements between Egyptian government bodies. In November 1988, five Somalis were refouled by the Ministry of Defense (and three Iraqis by State Security). The Ministry of Foreign Affairs decried the lack of coordination with it.[52] That these different parts of the government held different views on the return of Somalis indicates that they may have been weighing different concerns.

Starting in 1991, some Somali refugees and asylum-seekers fleeing the civil war traveled directly to Egypt via Kenya or the Gulf region, while others were secondary movers who spent some years in other host societies (e.g., Libya, Saudi Arabia, Kenya, or Yemen) before moving on to Egypt. In order to enter Egypt by air, land, or sea, all Somalis were required to display a visa and passport. Although most refugees traveled with Somali passports purchased in an unofficial Mogadishu office, Egyptian authorities nonetheless recognized these documents. This was especially remarkable given that most countries reject Somali passports as valid travel documents.[53] Somali refugees were concentrated in two districts of Cairo, Ard El-Liwa and Nasr City.

Although Somali asylum-seekers enjoyed prima facie recognition until 1999, in subsequent years their recognition rates fell, prompting demonstrations against UNHCR until it revised its policy in 2003. Around the same time, Egypt stopped granting entry visas to Somali applicants. Still, Somali refugees appeared to enjoy more supportive treatment from the authorities, with few cases of

[50]  Al-Sharmani 2003; Moret, Baglioni, and Efionayi-Mäder 2006; Zohry and Harrell-Bond 2003.

[51]  UNHCR Branch Office in Cairo, 25 October 1988, "Somali (Issaks) Influx in A.R.E.," *UNHCR Archives*, Fonds 11, Series 3, 100 ARE SOM Refugee Situations—Special Groups of Refugees—Refugees from Somalia in Egypt, Folio 1.

[52]  Mustapha Djemali [Head of Desk III, Regional Bureau for South West Asia, North Africa and the Middle East] to Liaison Officer in Washington, 24 November 1988, "Refoulement Incidents Involving 3 Iraqis and 5 Somalis from Egypt," *UNHCR Archives*, Fonds 11, Series 3, 10 ARE External Relations—Relations with Governments—Egypt [Volume A], Folio 17.

[53]  Al-Sharmani 2003, 7; Moret, Baglioni, and Efionayi-Mäder 2006, 33.

security harassment or deportation.[54] Thus, Somali refugees were treated slightly better than Sudanese refugees.

With regard to Ethiopian refugees, they flowed into Egypt in 1977–1989 to escape the repressive "Red Terror" campaign and again in 1991–1992 when the Mengistu Haile Mariam regime fell. The border conflict between Ethiopia and Eritrea (1998–2000) also led refugees from both countries to flee to Egypt. When UNHCR in Sudan invoked the cessation clause revoking refugee status in 2000, Eritrean refugees who lived there and feared forced return also traveled to Egypt.[55]

Relations between Egypt and Eritrea had been warm ever since the latter secured its independence. In fact, Egyptian backing for Eritrean separatists was one source of hostility between Egypt and Ethiopia in the late 1970s. Disputes over Nile diversion projects and Egypt's support for Somalia's irredentist ambitions damaged relations between Egypt and Ethiopia further. Even though the two countries managed to smooth matters over in the 1980s, relations soured once again when Egypt sided with Eritrea in the Eritrean-Ethiopian border war of 1998–2000. Almost immediately after the war, however, Egypt and Ethiopia were able to salvage their bilateral relationship through a series of high-level official visits.[56] Both Eritrean and Ethiopian refugees in Egypt can be characterized as Black Muslim and Christian, and therefore, lack an ethnic tie with Egyptians. Meanwhile, sending country relations are different for each sending country: friendly with Eritrea and fluctuating with Ethiopia. My argument, therefore, expects restrictiveness for Eritrean refugees throughout and for Ethiopian refugees only when Ethiopian-Egyptian relations are friendly (i.e., 1987–1997 and 2001–2010).

There is very limited information on the treatment of these (smaller) refugee groups. That said, an incident that took place in April 1989, when relations between Egypt and Ethiopia were cordial, is revealing. Following a soccer match in Cairo, six members of the Ethiopian national team attempted to seek asylum at the US embassy and were referred to UNHCR. The "defection" received significant Egyptian and international press coverage, and Egyptian authorities were "embarrassed." In the Ethiopian capital Addis Ababa, the Ethiopian Minister for Foreign Affairs got in touch with the Egyptian ambassador. Several days later, the Egyptian Ministry of Foreign Affairs conveyed to UNHCR that four of the asylum-seekers had "expressed regrets for their gesture and their wish to return to Ethiopia." However, when UNHCR interviewed the two remaining soccer players, "it emerged that . . . none of the six footballers wished to return to their country . . . they would prefer to die in Egypt . . . " But a

---

[54]   Grabska 2008, 84; Al-Sharmani 2008, 4; Al-Sharmani 2003, 10; Sperl 2001, 22.
[55]   Cooper 1992, 13–14; Zohry and Harrell-Bond 2003, 57–58.
[56]   Cooper 1992; Erlikh 2002; Zohry and Harrell-Bond 2003.

decision had been taken at "the highest level" of the Egyptian government that none of the six asylum-seekers would be granted refugee status. The Egyptian president had reportedly received a telephone call from the Ethiopian president. UNHCR's representative in Cairo concluded that, if his office was to find the Ethiopians eligible for refugee status, the Agency would have to resettle them "quickly and discreetly."[57]

By the late 2000s, Egypt's relationship was warm with both Ethiopia and Eritrea. In 2008 and 2009, the government detained a number of Eritrean and Ethiopian asylum-seekers and refugees for illegal entry, denying UNHCR access to them. Nearly 1,200 Eritreans were detained in 2008 then collectively deported after breaching Egypt's southern border.[58] For its part, the Eritrean government was supportive of Egypt's border shootings policy, saying "we cannot say that Eritreans are being treated badly by the Egyptian authorities, because international law prohibits smuggling."[59] In short, for Eritreans and Ethiopians, the limited information available seems to point to restrictive treatment, as my argument expects for ethnic others from friendly sending countries.

Overall, the analysis in this section demonstrates systematic trends and noticeable shifts in the treatment of refugee groups in Egypt. Far from being ad hoc or uniform, these patterns indicate discrimination between refugee groups. For example, Palestinian refugees experienced the most inclusive asylum policy until the late 1990s, while Sudanese refugees saw the most restrictive treatment beginning in the late 1990s. Iraqi refugees did not have access to the generosity that Palestinians experienced, but they were also largely spared the widespread detentions and deportations that Sudanese refugees saw. Even the little information available regarding Somalis, Eritreans, and Ethiopians seems to support my argument regarding the influence of foreign policy and ethnic politics on Egypt's responses to refugees.

## Delegation

Delegation to UNHCR is a prominent feature of Egypt's asylum policy. However, and in line with my theoretical expectations, the analysis of discrimination presented earlier showed that the Egyptian government still controlled most aspects of the refugee experience, including border admissions, detentions, deportations, and access to social and economic rights. Delegation of RSD still left the

---

[57] Vincent Cochetal [Conseiller Juridique Adjoint, UNHCR Headquarters in Geneva], 28 April 1989, "Note pour le Dossier," *UNHCR Archives*, Fonds 11, Series 3, 100 ARE ETH Refugee Situations—Special Groups of Refugees—Ethiopian Refugees in Egypt.
[58] USCRI 2009; Human Rights Watch 2008, 28–29, 67–68; Amnesty International 2008.
[59] Othman 2010.

government in control of most elements of asylum policy, thus mitigating any potential downsides of this shift in responsibility.

Delegation, I argued in chapter 2, occurs because governments are attempting to shift the blame for policies that may antagonize domestic or international audiences. Claiming that a neutral third party, like UNHCR, is responsible for these policies eases pressure. Meanwhile, UNCHR's limitations ensure that delegation will not backfire. In this section, I provide contextual information before examining several instances in which Egyptian authorities successfully pointed to UNHCR in order to deflect pressure. Finally, I document specific cases in which UNHCR self-censored and deferred to Egypt's preferences.

## Context

In what Kagan has termed a "responsibility shift," UNHCR performs a number of "quasi-government functions" in Egypt.[60] The Agency established its office in the country following the signing of a 1954 MoU with the Egyptian government.[61] For all asylum-seekers and refugees excepting Palestinians, RSD is conducted by UNHCR. In addition, UNHCR is at the center of a network that offers refugees services ranging from medical assistance and legal aid to educational programs and job placement. A number of implementing partners (including faith-based institutions and community-based organizations) coordinate their activities with UNHCR.[62] It is worth noting that Egypt only joined UNHCR's ExCom in 2004, becoming its chair for 2010–2011.

In contrast to UNHCR, the UN Relief and Works Agency for Palestinian Refugees in the Near East (UNRWA) does not operate in Egypt.[63] There are a few Palestinian refugees registered with UNHCR, but the vast majority experience a

---

[60] Kagan 2011.

[61] "Accord entre le haut commissaire des nations unies pour les réfugiés et le gouvernement Egyptien," 2 February 1954, *UNHCR Archives*, Fonds 11, Series 1, Box 76, 2/3/20 UAR Administration and Finance—Staff Privileges and Immunities—UAR, Folio 1. For an analysis of the MoU's provisions, see Badawy 2010.

[62] Grabska 2006, 28–32; Samy 2009.

[63] After UNRWA was formed in 1950, it operated in the Gaza Strip but not in Egypt proper. It is unclear why this was the case, though it may be due to the fact that the vast majority of Palestinians had indeed been concentrated in camps in the Gaza Strip. UNRWA 1955. It is worth noting that the Egyptian government had not requested assistance from the UN Relief for Palestine Refugees, so that when UNRWA took over from its predecessor in 1950, Egypt was not within the organization's predefined area of relief work. According to official accounts from the UN, insufficient resources prevented UNRWA from subsequently extending its services to Palestinians in Egypt. Bartholomeusz 2009. However, El-Abed asserts that the Egyptian government deliberately eschewed UNRWA assistance in 1950, in order to discourage Palestinians from remaining in Egypt proper. El-Abed 2009, 36. Today, UNRWA runs a small office in Cairo which is mainly responsible for liaising with the Arab League.

"protection gap." In fact, UNHCR only began including estimates of Palestinians in its refugee and asylum-seeker statistics in 2002. Palestinians who applied for residence permits were processed separately by the Ministry of Interior rather than UNHCR.

In short, the main division in the delegation of Egypt's asylum policy is between Palestinians and all other refugees. UNRWA does not operate in the country and Palestinians are excluded from UNHCR's mandate. Meanwhile, asylum-seekers from Sudan, Iraq, Somalia, and other countries are processed and assisted by UNHCR. My theoretical argument would expect the government to attempt to shift the burden to UN agencies for Palestinian refugees starting in the late 1970s, for Sudanese refugees starting in the mid-1980s, and for Iraqi refugees throughout their presence in the country. The pattern of delegation in Egypt comes close to, but does not fully fit, my theoretical expectations.

Still, as the evidence presented in this section demonstrates, many of the mechanisms I laid out in chapter 2 seem to influence the relationship between the Egyptian government and UNHCR. Specifically, the Egyptian government has emphasized UNHCR's neutrality and independence in order to deflect blame. At the same time, UNHCR has engaged in self-censorship and deferred to the government.

## Deflection of Blame

In chapter 2, I argued that delegation to UNHCR allows governments to shift blame for policies that could antagonize domestic or international audiences. The Agency's independence gives it the appearance of neutrality, enabling governments to assert that decisions were not theirs to make. The evidence presented here shows the Egyptian government highlighting UNHCR's neutrality and indicates that it decided to delegate so as not to offend its friendly Sudanese counterpart. In addition, Egypt's attempts to deflect blame were successful with Somali officials.

The Egyptian government has declared, at ExCom and elsewhere, its intention to take responsibility for the process of conferring refugee status, or RSD. In 1984, Presidential Decree No. 188 stipulated the creation of a permanent committee within the Ministry of Foreign Affairs to conduct RSD. The committee would include representatives from the Ministries of Foreign Affairs, Justice, and the Interior as well as the Office of the President. Still, despite numerous discussions with UNHCR over this issue, this turnover of responsibility was delayed.[64]

---

[64] Egypt 1984; Grabska 2006, 25.

This reluctance to take control of RSD is puzzling in light of the relatively small number of refugees in Egypt. Indeed, in an interview, a foreign ministry official indicated that setting up a national asylum system for "40,000 [non-Palestinian refugees] is not a resource problem" but that RSD conducted by UNHCR "ensure[s] objectivity and integrity."[65] Some observers have attributed the Egyptian government's reluctance to conduct RSD itself to the large number of Sudanese in the country. By recognizing Sudanese refugees, the Egyptian government would be indirectly criticizing the Sudanese government and admitting that government's role in atrocities in Sudan.[66]

The Egyptian government has found UNHCR's appearance of neutrality to be politically expedient on multiple occasions. An exchange of letters between UNHCR's branch office in Cairo and the Agency's headquarters in Geneva provides evidence of this dynamic. In a confidential memo from September 1988, UNHCR's representative in Egypt reported that he had met with the Egyptian minister of state for foreign affairs, Boutros Boutros-Ghali. Boutros-Ghali conveyed that the Somali president had "expressed [his] disappointment" to the Egyptian ambassador in Mogadishu that four Somali military students had been granted political asylum in Egypt. Boutros-Ghali instructed a subordinate to send a response indicating that since those four had "presented themselves to the UNHCR Office and were found to be of concern, the Government thus cannot oblige the students to go back to their country against their own will, and left this matter to UNHCR to solve their affairs."[67] In this instance, the Egyptian government was able to point to UNHCR's involvement to deny its own responsibility.

Indeed, Somali officials were persuaded that UNHCR was acting independently. In 1989, First Secretary of the Somali embassy in Cairo Mohamed Ali Serar headed to UNHCR's office. He had been instructed to communicate his embassy's "disappointment for the protection given by the [branch office] to Somalis" in Egypt. Serar emphasized, in particular, Somali diplomats who refused to return to Somalia following the end of their foreign assignment, the former manager of Somali Airlines in Cairo who had allegedly embezzled funds, and Somali students who claimed to belong to the Issak clan. He

---

[65] Official, Ministry of Foreign Affairs. Personal interview by author. Ministry of Foreign Affairs, Cairo, Egypt, September 4, 2010.

[66] Grabska 2008, 76.

[67] Abdul Mawlah El-Solh [UNHCR Representative to the Arab Republic of Egypt] to Mustapha Djemali [Head of Desk, Regional Bureau for South West Asia, North Africa and the Middle East, UNHCR Headquarters in Geneva], 11 September 1988, "Memorandum: Meeting with H.E. the Egyptian Ministry of State for Foreign Affairs," *UNHCR Archives*, Fonds 11, Series 3, 10 ARE External Relations—Relations with Governments—Egypt [Volume A], Folio 16.

"seemed not satisfied with [UNHCR's] answers" and said he would "raise the question of the Somali refugees and UNHCR's practices with the Egyptian authorities."[68]

Later that year, Serar again complained to UNHCR. He began by clarifying that "the Somali government saw no reasons for Somalis to be refugees." Still, "if a Somali citizen considers himself as such and UNHCR wishes to assist him," then this was "a matter between the individual and UNHCR." The problem, Serar asserted, was that Somalis who were not students had joined the Somali students' association, politicized that organization, and instigated violence. He asked UNHCR to persuade "its refugees" to leave the students' association.[69] It is striking that the Somali diplomat was voicing his concerns to UNHCR, rather than the government that had allowed these individuals to enter Egypt and to reside there. It would appear that UNHCR seemed to him to be a neutral organization, acting independently of the Egyptian government.

These episodes demonstrate that Egypt tried to deflect blame by pointing to UNHCR's neutrality. Egyptian officials claimed that delegation ensured the integrity of the RSD process, but were likely motivated by the desire not to antagonize the Sudanese government. In addition, Somali officials were seemingly convinced when the Egyptian government denied responsibility for admitting refugees. These sending countries failed to recognize that the Agency was itself highly constrained, as the following discussion shows.

## Deference and Self-Censorship

I suggested in chapter 2 that delegation is not as costly to governments as we might think. Since UNHCR hopes to continue operating on a country's territory, it is likely to curb its criticisms of that country's conduct and to be especially sensitive to that country's preferences. In addition, the Agency's generosity is bounded by its limited funds. The vignettes presented in this section corroborate my argument regarding these constraints.

There is evidence that UNHCR regularly engaged in self-censorship. For example, UNHCR avoided publicly calling for local integration of refugees, which the Egyptian government had categorically refused. UNHCR often refrained

---

[68] Abdul Mawlah El-Solh, 30 January 1989, "Note for the File: Protest by Somali First Secretary in Egypt," *UNHCR Archives*, Fonds 11, Series 3, 100 ARE SOM Refugee Situations—Special Groups of Refugees—Refugees from Somalia in Egypt, Folio 2.

[69] UNHCR Branch Office in the Arab Republic of Egypt to UNHCR Headquarters in Geneva, 7 August 1989, "Meeting with Mr. Mohamed Ali Serar, 1st Secretary at the Somali Embassy in Cairo," *UNHCR Archives*, Fonds 11, Series 3, 100 ARE SOM Refugee Situations—Special Groups of Refugees—Refugees from Somalia in Egypt, Folio 2.

from condemning deportations because it "calculates that there is no way to reverse deportation decisions."[70]

One early episode has UNHCR agonizing about the possible damage to its relationship with Egyptian authorities should someone seek sanctuary at a UN building in Egypt. In 1968, negotiations were underway to establish an administrative center for the UN in Cairo. Reviewing the draft agreement, UNHCR staff were most concerned about a clause stipulating that the UN would not permit the building to be used as a sanctuary for individuals seeking to avoid arrest or extradition. The director of the Legal Division noted that "the UN might be obliged to deliver to the UAR [United Arab Republic] authorities, e.g., a Jew who sought asylum in the UNHCR Office of the Centre in order to avoid arrest. This would put the HC [High Commissioner] in a very peculiar position." Moreover, adding a stipulation providing for the right to seek political asylum "would hardly be acceptable to the UAR authorities and, having raised the point and lost it, the UN would be in a weaker position than before."[71] While it would be preferable that the original provision be removed, "we are not in a position to judge what would be the reaction of the UAR authorities to such a proposal." Ultimately, the Legal Division recommended that the document be left as is, and UNHCR would "face the problem when it presents itself."[72] Clearly, UNHCR's desire to maintain a working relationship with the Egyptian government shaped its behavior in this instance.

The Egyptian government also exercised pressure on UNHCR to ensure that it would not be too generous. In September 1986, UNHCR's representative in Egypt met with Minister of State for Foreign Affairs Boutros-Ghali. In that meeting, Boutros-Ghali stressed that the UNHCR should "step up its efforts" to resettle refugees without having them remain in Egypt for too long. Egyptian authorities had "strongly . . . requested" that UNHCR "put pressure" on refugee students who had completed their studies and/or not been accepted for resettlement, and who had arrived in Egypt from another country of asylum. If those refugees did not leave, then this "might create reluctance [by] authorities to facilitate [the] entry [of] new refugees to Egypt."[73] Since the Egyptian government

---

[70] Ahmed Badawy (Chairman, Egyptian Foundation for Refugee Rights). Personal interview by author. EFRR Office, Cairo, Egypt, August 3, 2010.

[71] A. Rørholt [Director, Legal Division] to M.J. Heidler [Executive Officer], 19 August 1968, "Agreement relating to the Administrative Centre of the United Nations in Cairo," *UNHCR Archives*, Fonds 11, Series 1, Box 76, 2/3/20 UAR Administration and Finance—Staff Privileges and Immunities—UAR, Folio 16.

[72] A. Rørholt to C.D. Stavropoulos [Under Secretary, Legal Counsel New York], 26 August 1968, "Agreement relating to the Administrative Centre of the United Nations in Cairo," *UNHCR Archives*, Fonds 11, Series 1, Box 76, 2/3/20 UAR Administration and Finance—Staff Privileges and Immunities—UAR, Folio 17.

[73] Abdul Mawlah El-Solh, 16 October 1986, Cable, *UNHCR Archives*, Fonds 11, Series 3, 10 ARE External Relations—Relations with Governments—Egypt [Volume A], Folio 1.

controlled the country's borders, and because UNHCR wielded limited influence, it had little choice but to tread carefully. If UNHCR did not resolve the issue of overstaying students and unresettled refugees, then it risked the government denying new refugees access to the country.

UNHCR proved receptive to the directives it received from the Egyptian government. In a letter to an Egyptian foreign ministry official in 1988, the UNHCR branch office noted that resettlement would not be offered to students and medical cases, "to prevent an excessive attraction of new refugees coming to Egypt with the only objective of emigrating to certain countries."[74] Similarly, a cable to headquarters affirmed the branch office's policy not to provide financial assistance or resettlement to Somalis "in order not to create [a] pull factor."[75] In this instance, UNHCR appears remarkably sensitive to something that ought to be the government's concern: whether more refugees would head to Egypt as a result of the availability of aid and resettlement opportunities. While the government may have been able to influence UNHCR, the reverse seemed unlikely. For one expert, an indication that UNHCR did "not have much effect on policy" was that its statements are not widely reported in the Egyptian press.[76]

There was another telling incident in October 1994, in which UNHCR and Egyptian authorities effectively banded together against demonstrating refugees. According to regional office officials, one hundred southern Sudanese participated in a peaceful protest at UNHCR's waiting area, at not receiving prima facie recognition, economic hardships, and delays in processing applications. The demonstrators refused to vacate the premises. So, UNHCR contacted the Ministry of Foreign Affairs the following day and the director of the refugee affairs department intervened, but negotiations failed, as did the strategy of denying access to food and other supplies. At 1:30 a.m. the next day, the Ministry of Foreign Affairs requested the intervention of security forces. UNHCR appeared pleased with this development, saying that "[d]emonstrators were removed quickly and efficiently, three were slightly injured but treated and released immediately, and ultimately everyone went home safely."[77] This episode

[74] UNHCR Branch Office in the Arab Republic of Egypt to Mahmoud A. Abdel-Hadi [Director, Immigration & Refugees Department, Ministry of Foreign Affairs], 6 March 1988, *UNHCR Archives*, Fonds 11, Series 3, 10 ARE External Relations—Relations with Governments—Egypt [Volume A], Folio 12.

[75] UNHCR Branch Office in the Arab Republic of Egypt, 25 October 1988, "Somali (Issaks) Influx in ARE," *UNHCR Archives*, Fonds 11, Series 3, 100 ARE SOM Refugee Situations—Special Groups of Refugees—Refugees from Somalia in Egypt, Folio 1.

[76] Martin Jones (Egyptian Foundation for Refugee Rights). Personal interview by author. June 22, 2010.

[77] Mustapha Djemali [UNHCR Regional Representative in Egypt] to M. Boukry [Head of Desk III, Regional Bureau for South West Asia, North Africa and the Middle East], 23 October 1994, "Sit-in by Sudanese Nationals," *UNHCR Archives*, Fonds 11, Series 3, 100 ARE SUD Refugee Situations—Special Groups of Refugees—Sudanese Refugees in Egypt, Folio 5.

would prove to be a precursor for another sit-in a decade later: In September 2005, about 2,000 Sudanese asylum-seekers and refugees engaged in a sit-in at Mustapha Mahmoud Square near the offices of UNHCR to protest its suspension of RSD procedures, as well as their conditions. In December, thousands of security personnel forcibly removed the protestors to various holding centers in and around Cairo, killing about 30 refugees and asylum-seekers, including women and children, during the removal.[78] Subsequently, UNHCR offices were moved outside Cairo to 6th of October City.

Moreover, UNHCR's "funds dictate how many [refugees] they can recognize."[79] With regard to Sudanese in Egypt, a set of handwritten comments from a UNHCR senior legal adviser in April 1993 are particularly illuminating. He notes UNHCR's position, emphasizing the "relatively trouble-free legal status" of this group under the Nile Valley Treaty. "To start to consider them as refugees now might ignite a flood of legal and other problems" which the Agency may not have "the intent or capacity" to handle. He reminds his colleagues that some estimates put the number of Sudanese in Egypt at 4 million. Accordingly, "UNHCR should consider seriously the consequences of any decision to become involved whether from a legal or material point of view."[80] The Agency, then, was keenly aware of its own limitations.

The analysis in this section demonstrates that Egypt successfully deflected blame by emphasizing UNHCR's neutrality. At the same time, UNHCR proved to be sensitive to the government's preferences and therefore less than neutral in practice.

## Summary of Findings

Where the previous sections analyzed discrimination and delegation in Egypt's asylum policies, this section focuses on the implications for my argument. After summarizing my findings, I assess the extent to which they match my theoretical predictions. Overall, the findings show patterns consistent with my argument.

[78] Azzam 2006; US Department of State 2006; Al-Sharmani 2008, 19. In 2004, UNHCR had suspended RSD procedures for Sudanese following the signing of several peace agreements to end the second Sudanese civil war. In that year, a Sudanese refugee demonstration was initiated in front of the UNHCR office by an Egyptian NGO. Rioting ensued and a confrontation between refugees and the Egyptian police ended with the detention of 22 protesters who were eventually released. Hilal and Samy 2008a, 7.

[79] Lina Attalah (Managing Editor, Al-Masry Al-Youm English Edition). Personal interview by author. Al-Masry Al-Youm Office, Cairo, Egypt, June 30, 2010.

[80] Roberto Quintero-Marino [Senior Protection Officer, UNHCR Branch Office in Kenya] to Karen Abu-Zayd [Head, Kenya Unit, UNHCR Headquarters in Geneva], 19 July 1993, "Sudanese in Egypt," *UNHCR Archives*, Fonds 11, Series 3, 100 ARE SUD Refugee Situations—Special Groups of Refugees—Sudanese Refugees in Egypt, Folio 4.

Despite the conventional wisdom regarding asylum policies in Egypt, they appear far from ad hoc.

In the face of the first significant wave of Palestinians in 1948, Egypt provided government assistance but no access to the labor market. A gradual expansion in Palestinian rights culminated in a 1962 law and the golden era for Palestinians in Egypt, who had almost unrestricted access to education, employment, and health services. Moreover, Palestinians fleeing the 1967 war were able to cross the border into Egypt. No other refugee group in Egypt experienced as inclusive an asylum policy as did the Palestinians during this time. Once Egypt's relations with Israel changed, however, most of these privileges were taken away. In the late 1970s, the favorable legislation was reversed and Palestinians found themselves excluded from public schools and work in the public sector. Palestinians were turned back or stranded at the border in subsequent years. This trend continued through the late 2000s, when Egypt closed the Rafah border crossing. Thus, there was a shift in asylum policy toward Palestinians in 1977.

Until 1995, bilateral treaties between Egypt and Sudan meant that the Sudanese at large (whether refugees or other migrants) could enter the country freely, access social services, and participate in the formal labor market. The Egyptian government did not set out to provide generous treatment to Sudanese refugees in particular, and refugees did not need to identify themselves as such since they could take advantage of the substantial privileges accorded to any Sudanese national in Egypt. In the mid-1990s, restrictions were imposed on the entry of other migrants, but refugees were still admitted. In other words, the mid-1990s were a turning point only in that the government began distinguishing between refugees and other migrants. Even as migrants faced stricter border control, refugees continued to be welcomed into the country. Still, they did not enjoy the kind of access to the labor market that Palestinians had during their golden era.

In terms of asylum policies directed at Sudanese refugees qua refugees, a shift occurred in 1998/1999. At that point, the government began cracking down on Sudanese refugees, who continued to face detentions and deportations in subsequent years. These threats to physical safety faced by the Sudanese surpassed those faced by Palestinian refugees. As mentioned earlier, Darfurian refugees reported being chased in the streets by Sudanese security, most probably with tacit Egyptian government approval.

Despite the fact that they were relatively wealthy and highly-skilled, Iraqi refugees did not receive the sort of welcome that Palestinians had in the pre-Camp David period. Iraqi refugees entering Egypt in 2006 were initially able to take advantage of relaxed visa policies, but these were tightened within months. They were prohibited from forming community-based organizations and did not have access to the formal labor market or to public education. However, Iraqis appeared to be relatively better off than Sudanese refugees in that they did not face significant refoulement or physical safety issues.

Somali refugees were generally granted admission to Egypt, despite the fact that most countries did not recognize Somali passports. In contrast with other sub-Saharan refugees, the detention and deportation of Somalis was fairly rare. Both Somalis and Sudanese are ethnic "others" in Egypt, so perhaps the more negative Sudanese experience points to the added effect—for Sudanese refugees—of friendly relations between Egypt and Sudan starting in the late 1990s. There is less information on the treatment of Eritreans and Ethiopians. These refugee populations are relatively small (fewer than 1,700 were registered with UNHCR in 2010) and, as a result, have received less attention from researchers.[81] However, we do know that in recent years they have suffered extensively from detentions and deportations.

While some policy indicators reflect no change at all for any refugee group, others suggest periods of significant improvement or deterioration. For example, Egypt did not change its policies regarding refugees' freedom of movement or naturalization. Still, the year 1978 marked the beginning of strict border control, detentions and deportations, and the barring of access to public services and employment for Palestinians. For Sudanese refugees, the late 1990s saw a significant downward shift in conditions, with mass arrests and expulsions.

In short, there are clear differences in treatment across refugee groups and over time. This theme was emphasized by several interviewees as well. For example, NGO personnel noted that Sudanese refugees had traditionally been treated well, but more recent refugees from Darfur had a different experience.[82] In short, a "monolithic description" of refugee experiences would be inaccurate; we "need to look at nationality . . . Palestinian, Iraqi, or African."[83] Refugees themselves understood that their national origin may shape their treatment: one NGO interviewee reported that there had been cases of Ethiopian refugees claiming they were Eritrean and vice versa.[84]

There are also findings related to the Egyptian government's relationship with UNHCR. First, UNHCR has proven to be a useful device to deflect blame. For example, as mentioned earlier, observers note that the Egyptian government continued to delegate RSD to UNHCR because it did not want to antagonize the Sudanese government. Second, the organization may sometimes defer to

[81] UNHCR n.d.

[82] Gasser Abdel-Razek (Country Director, Africa and Middle East Refugee Assistance-Egypt). Personal interview by author. AMERA-Egypt Office, Cairo, Egypt, June 7, 2010.

[83] Lina Attalah (*Al-Masry Al-Youm* English Edition). Personal interview by author. June 30, 2010.

[84] Ahmed Badawy (Egyptian Foundation for Refugee Rights). Personal interview by author. August 3, 2010.

the authorities' preferences and engage in self-censorship in order to maintain the government's cooperation. Finally, there is little evidence that UNHCR has a significant impact on policy. The Egyptian government engaged in the detention and deportation of asylum-seekers and refugees and continued to exclude Palestinians from UNHCR protection. In effect, the government was ensuring that UNHCR's scope of activity remained narrow. The Agency's awareness of its own limitations reinforces this dynamic.

Table 4.1 summarizes the patterns in Egypt's asylum policy, with those groups and time periods that match my theoretical predictions marked in bold. My theoretical argument performs fairly well, though not perfectly. Across the different time periods, inclusiveness and restrictiveness largely match with theoretical predictions. However, the Egyptian government did not shift responsibility for Palestinian refugees as expected.

Besides tracking changes or continuities in the treatment of each refugee group (i.e., within-group comparison), comparisons of relative treatment can be made between them as well (i.e., across-group comparison). It is clear that the Palestinian golden era saw by far the most inclusive asylum policy in Egypt's history. In contrast, the treatment of Sudanese refugees in the most recent period (1999–2010) is the most restrictive, characterized by extensive detention and deportation.

It is also worth noting that there is no evidence that sending country relations were endogenous to refugee policies. That is, there is no evidence that the refugee flows themselves or the treatment of refugees by Egypt was responsible for the patterns of hostility or friendship between sending and receiving country. In every case, sending country relations appeared not to be shaped by refugee policies and patterns.

On the whole, the analysis of Egypt's asylum policies supports my argument about the influence of foreign policy and ethnic politics on discrimination and delegation. The next section explores a number of possible alternative explanations—including economic concerns, strategic calculations,

Table 4.1  Predicted asylum policies in Egypt

| | | Sending Country Relations | |
| --- | --- | --- | --- |
| | | Hostile | Friendly |
| *Affinity with Refugee Group* | Co-Ethnic | Inclusive (Pal 1948–1977) | Delegation (Pal 1978–2010) (Irq 2006–2010) |
| | No Ethnic Tie | Delegation (Sud 1995–1998) | Restrictive (Sud 1999–2010) |

humanitarian impulses, and domestic considerations—to assess the role that other factors may have played in shaping asylum policy in Egypt.

## Alternative Explanations

While a number of alternative explanations can be drawn from the literature on refugees, none of these can explain the patterns in Egypt's asylum policy described in this chapter. First, the conventional wisdom about Egypt's asylum policies referenced at the beginning of this chapter casts the country's behavior as arbitrary. The descriptions in this chapter demonstrate, however, that there are discernable patterns in the country's responses to refugee groups. At the same time, there is evidence of involvement by high-level political officials.

A second set of explanations points to the role of economics. Between 1948 and 2010, Egypt's real GDP per capita grew from about US$800 in 1950 to over US$4,800 in 2010. Increases in GDP per capita were fairly steady, although average growth rose after the open door economic policy was declared in 1974.[85] However, the availability of material resources did not seem to shape Egypt's willingness to host refugees. We do not observe a shift (sudden or gradual) to more generous policies, or a shift away from delegation, in the mid-1970s. The country has also not attempted to attract international assistance in return for shouldering the refugee burden.[86]

Moreover, there is no evidence that an inability to police borders, due to lack of economic capacity, shaped asylum policies in Egypt. Economic concerns also did not appear to shape the selection of particular refugees over others. As mentioned earlier, the country's asylum policies did not seem to especially favor the wealthiest and most highly skilled refugees (Iraqis).

Third, concerns about national security are not a persuasive explanation for the patterns in Egypt's asylum policies either, because no refugee groups would appear to be inherently more dangerous than others. Sudanese refugees were repressed long before they engaged in the 2005 sit-in. Fear of Shia proselytizing, with respect to Iraqi refugees, seemed to be a manufactured concern since the vast majority of Iraqis in Egypt were Sunni. Finally, Egypt did not adopt uniformly restrictive policies toward all refugee groups when it experienced a wave of terrorist attacks in the 1990s.

A fourth set of explanations points to strategic behavior by receiving countries. However, Egypt did not experience sudden shifts in policy alongside the

---

[85] GDP per capita is reported at 2005 constant prices. Heston, Summers, and Aten 2012; World Bank 2019.

[86] Barbara Harrell-Bond (Founder, Center for Migration and Refugee Studies). Personal interview by author. American University in Cairo, Cairo, Egypt, June 16, 2010.

arrival of large numbers of refugees. Palestinian refugees, in particular, received the most inclusive treatment despite being the country's largest refugee group. I was also unable to locate any evidence that Egypt was evaluating the behavior of other receiving countries in the region before making discrimination or delegation decisions.

Fifth, since Egypt remained a one-party state, for all practical purposes, throughout most of the period under study, democratization was not a likely factor influencing asylum policies. Still, other institutional factors may have mattered. Though Egypt seemed perfectly capable of shifting policies for Palestinians and Sudanese refugees, path dependence may explain Egypt's delegation pattern.

Finally, responses to refugees may be shaped by empathy. Yet, in the Egyptian case, there is no evidence that policies were shaped by humanitarian concerns or were influenced by the cause of refugee flows or the conditions of refugees. Iraqi, Sudanese, and Somali refugees were treated differently despite the fact that all of these groups were escaping civil strife. It is also worth noting that not all groups received an initial welcome that gradually wore off, as the compassion fatigue argument would lead us to expect. Overall, these alternative explanations do not provide a satisfactory account of the patterns and shifts in Egypt's asylum policy.

## Conclusion

The analysis above challenges the "no policy" conventional wisdom described at the beginning of this chapter. It is true that Egypt has not made explicit its asylum policy through national legislation, official documentation, or public statements. However, several practices clearly stem from senior-level decision-making and persist over time or are repeated over several different instances. For example, chartering airplanes to deport refugees is probably not possible without a decision from the top.

Why did different refugee groups have divergent experiences with the government in Egypt? This chapter compared asylum policies in Egypt across refugee groups and over time. The description of the group-specific asylum policies presented in this chapter lends some support to my argument that inclusiveness, restrictiveness, and delegation are explained by ethnic affinity and sending country relations.

Charting Egypt's asylum policies shows that there is significant variation across refugee groups and over time. The theoretical framework put forward in chapter 2 is largely able to predict generosity and restrictiveness, indicating that group-specific asylum policies might be shaped by each refugee group's ethnic identity and Egypt's relations with their sending country. At the same time, hypotheses commonly invoked in the literature on refugee flows (stressing, for example, the host country's economic absorption capacity and humanitarianism) appear insufficient to explain the variation in Egypt's asylum policies.

Though I do not present a full analysis here, Egypt's more recent responses to Syrian refugees appear to be consistent with my theoretical framework as well. As the Syrian civil war intensified, Egyptian president Mohamed Morsi declared his support for the Syrian opposition to the Bashar al-Assad regime. Syrian refugees were permitted to enter Egypt without a visa and were granted access to education and healthcare. Observers noted that Syrians, ethnic kin arriving from a hostile country, were welcomed and treated well compared to Sudanese and Ethiopian refugees. Following Morsi's overthrow, however, Egypt quickly revived diplomatic ties with Syria. Conditions for Syrian refugees in Egypt shifted almost overnight. Syrians were required to obtain a visa and security clearance before arriving in Egypt and detentions and deportations for these refugees surged.[87]

Egypt is a fairly typical refugee recipient in terms of its level of economic development, its relevant treaty ratifications, and the relative size of its refugee population. By comparison, Turkey is an outlier—it has experienced multiple large refugee influxes and is one of a handful of countries that only grants refugee status to Europeans. Chapter 5 presents an analysis of discrimination and delegation in that country. Despite major differences between Egypt and Turkey, interstate relations and domestic politics appear to shape asylum policies in Turkey as well.

---

[87] Kressler 2017; Krajeski 2013.

# 5

# Selective Protection in Turkey

Like Egypt, Turkey was one of the 26 countries that collectively drafted the 1951 Refugee Convention. Today, out of 148 state parties to the convention or its protocol, it is one of a handful of countries that maintain a "geographical limitation." Along with just three other countries (Congo, Madagascar, and Monaco), Turkey restricts refugee status only to individuals who have fled due to "events occurring in Europe."

Besides being an outlier that only recognizes Europeans as refugees, Turkey has also experienced several mass refugee influxes. Iraqi Kurds in the tens and then hundreds of thousands fled to Turkey in 1988 and 1991. In 1989, Turkey received hundreds of thousands of ethnic Turks from Bulgaria. The Bosnian and Kosovar Wars also led to large waves of refugees. And with the ongoing Syrian crisis, Turkey currently hosts the largest refugee population in the world. It also boasts one of the biggest refugee resettlement programs.

Due to the geographical limitation, most accounts of Turkish asylum policies emphasize the "selective protection" provided to European compared to non-European refugees. In contrast, my analysis in this chapter reveals that Turkish policies are more nuanced. A simple dichotomy between European and non-European refugees is too blunt and can be misleading. Even seemingly general policies that exist on the books are applied selectively, a pattern that betrays the influence of foreign policy and ethnic politics on Turkey's asylum policies.

In this chapter, I analyze Turkey's asylum policies as well as UNHCR's role in the country from the establishment of the Agency until just before the Syrian crisis. To do so, I consulted archival sources containing correspondence between UNHCR's branch office in Turkey and the Agency's headquarters in Geneva. In addition, I draw on interviews at the Turkish Ministry of Foreign Affairs and Ministry of Interior, UNHCR, the Migration Research Center at Koç University, and a number of domestic and international NGOs.

By analyzing the case of Turkey as a refugee-receiving country, this chapter enables a side-by-side comparison with the more typical Egyptian case laid out in chapter 4. Even though there are many differences between the two countries, the patterns in asylum policy in both Egypt and Turkey are consistent with my argument regarding when countries are likely to include, exclude, and delegate on refugees. The side-by-side comparison shows that foreign policy and ethnic politics shape responses to refugees in similar ways in dissimilar

*Discrimination and Delegation.* Lamis Elmy Abdelaaty, Oxford University Press (2021). © Oxford University Press.
DOI: 10.1093/oso/9780197530061.003.0005

countries, and that my argument is therefore likely to be applicable to other contexts as well.

This chapter proceeds as follows. The first section details Turkey's responses to the different refugee groups it has received. The second section examines the government's interactions with UNHCR. The third section evaluates the extent to which my findings about Turkey's asylum policies match my theoretical expectations, while the fourth section considers alternative explanations. The fifth and final section concludes.

## Discrimination

Much of the existing scholarship on Turkey's asylum policies presumes a straightforward dichotomy between European and non-European refugees. To the contrary, the remainder of this section demonstrates that Turkey's treatment of different refugee groups over time is more nuanced. After providing useful contextualizing information, I describe Turkey's responses to five refugee groups: Bulgarians, Iraqis, Iranians, Bosnians and Kosovars, and refugees from Soviet and post-Soviet states. This analysis shows that Turkey does not simply discriminate between European and non-European refugees. Instead, Turkey's policies are most consistent with sending country relations and ethnic affinity.

### Context

During the drafting conference for the 1951 Refugee Convention, Turkey was probably one of the countries that pushed for the inclusion of geographical and temporal limitations.[1] Accordingly, under Article 1B, states may restrict their obligations only to individuals who fled events in Europe prior to 1951. When it signed the 1967 Protocol, Turkey lifted the temporal limitation but maintained the geographical limitation. Later, in the mid-1980s, a foreign ministry official underscored that the limitation was "a long-term policy and that there are no intentions of lifting it."[2]

Meanwhile, at the domestic level, Turkey long lacked legislation relating to refugees and asylum-seekers. Instead, provisions from laws like the 1934 Law

---

[1] Kirişci suggests that Turkish officials may have been reacting to the Palestinian and Indian/Pakistani refugee crises that took place in the 1940s. Kirişci 2001, 71, 74.

[2] Fransisco Galindo-Velez [Deputy Representative, UNHCR Branch Office in Turkey], 21 October 1986, "Note for the File: Meeting with Mrs. Fügen Ok, Ministry of Foreign Affairs," *UNHCR Archives*, Fonds 11, Series 3, 10 TUR External Relations—Relations with Governments—Turkey [Volume A], Folio 7.

on Settlement, the 1950 Passport Law, the 1950 Law on the Residence and Movement of Aliens, and the 1964 Citizenship Law were applied.[3]

As a matter of law, the country espoused a distinct usage of the terms refugee (mülteci), asylum-seeker (sığınmacı), and immigrant (göçmen). Depending on their country of origin and ethno-religious identity, individuals could be considered convention refugees, non-convention refugees (called asylum-seekers), or national refugees (called immigrants).[4]

The government only extended de jure refugee status to Europeans. This designation was most commonly applied to individuals from Eastern Europe and the Soviet Union during the Cold War. Even though Turkey granted this status to those fleeing communism, it was understood that they would be resettled elsewhere.[5] Meanwhile, non-Europeans could be recognized as asylum-seekers and permitted to reside in Turkey temporarily, pending resettlement. The majority of these individuals came from the Middle East, particularly Iran and Iraq.[6]

Finally, under the 1934 Law on Settlement (No. 2510), only individuals of "Turkish descent and culture" could immigrate to Turkey, settle permanently, and obtain the country's citizenship. A Council of Ministers determined which individuals or communities qualified under this law. Although individuals of Turkish origin are referred to as immigrants (göçmen) under the 1934 Law on Settlement, several scholars have also used the term "national refugee" to refer to them. Indeed, the majority of those benefiting from this law were either expelled from their home countries or felt compelled to escape. It has been applied to Turkish-speakers from the Balkans, Caucasus, and Central Asia, but its provisions have also been extended to communities not usually considered to be ethnic Turks (including Albanians, Bosnians, Circassians, Georgians, Pomaks, and Tatars).[7]

The Settlement Law designated two types of immigrants: independent immigrants (serbest göçmen) and settled immigrants (iskanlı göçmen). The former did not need support from the government, and once their application was complete, they could enter Turkey and settle wherever they wished. The latter were sponsored and assisted by the state and could be provided with land, cattle, and equipment, though they were usually required to settle in a specific area. Although the practice of state-sponsored immigration was terminated in 1970, exceptions were made for three groups: Turkic-speaking Afghan refugees from Pakistan in 1982; Meskhetian (or Ahıska) Turks from Uzbekistan in 1992/1993; and Bulgarian Turks in 1989.[8]

---

[3] Latif 2002, 23; Kirişci 2001, 71, 76.
[4] Latif 2002, 21–22.
[5] Kirişci 2001, 75.
[6] Latif 2002, 21–22.
[7] Kirişci 2001, 73–74; 1996b, 387–88.
[8] Kirişci 1996b, 388.

With regard to settlement patterns, Turkey at times established temporary camps to deal with sudden and large-scale refugee influxes, such as the inflow of Iraqi Kurds in 1988. Under regulations passed in 1994, other asylum-seekers were required to reside in a "satellite city" designated by the Turkish government.[9] Of course, some refugees also opted to live "illegally" in large urban centers like Istanbul.

In the following, I examine policies toward five refugee groups in turn: Bulgarians, Iraqis, Iranians, Bosnians and Kosovars, and refugees from Soviet and post-Soviet states. Hundreds of thousands of Bulgarian Turks crossed the border in 1989 to flee Bulgaria's assimilation campaign, with many repatriating following regime change in Bulgaria the following year and the remainder becoming naturalized. With Iraqi refugees, there were major influxes of ethnic Kurds fleeing Saddam Hussein's al-Anfal campaign in northern Iraq in 1988 and fleeing his suppression of the Kurdish rebellion in 1991. The majority of these Iraqi refugees were repatriated with the creation of a "safe haven" in northern Iraq in 1991, while others were resettled. In contrast, there was an almost steady stream of Iranians into Turkey beginning with the 1979 Iranian revolution. Bosnian and Kosovar refugees arrived (and returned) in large waves with the Bosnian War in 1992 and the Kosovo War in 1998. Finally, refugees fled Eastern Europe and the Soviet Union beginning in 1970 and until the end of the Cold War, though few of them remained in Turkey permanently. After the end of the Cold War, refugees fleeing the Second Chechen War entered Turkey in 1999.

In line with this book's central argument, Turkey's responses to these different refugee groups correspond to bilateral relations and ethnic affinity. Moreover, major shifts in asylum policy over time coincide with changes in sending country relations. Indeed, the analysis that follows reveals that the European/non-European distinction is too simplistic. Rather, differences in treatment between refugee groups seem to be linked to ethnic affinity and sending country relations.

## Bulgarians

By far the largest group to benefit from state-sponsored immigration were the 310,000 Bulgarians who escaped Todor Zhivkov's assimilation campaign in the summer of 1989. Turkey's relations with Bulgaria were decidedly hostile during this time. Not only were the two countries on opposite sides during the Cold War, but Bulgaria had directed significant discrimination and assimilation programs at its ethnic Turkish minority. Most of the refugees who fled to Turkey

---

[9] Calabrese 1998, 11, fn. 56.

were Bulgarian Turks and Pomaks who shared an ethnic affinity with the country's predominantly Turkish citizens.[10]

Accordingly, I expect Bulgarian refugees to experience an inclusive asylum policy. Indeed, as shown here, Turkey opened its borders to this group, providing them with government assistance and the opportunity to apply for Turkish citizenship.

In late May 1989, Turkey complained to the High Commissioner that Bulgaria was expelling ethnic Turks, but stressed that "Turkey will grant asylum to all those who want to come."[11] The government initially attempted to negotiate an orderly migration with the Bulgarian government, but when these attempts failed, it quickly opened its borders and suspended the immigrant visa requirement in June. New legal provisions allowed Bulgarian Turks to be rapidly recognized as immigrants, rather than refugees. As a result, they could take advantage of a far wider range of privileges than those available to convention refugees, including government-funded housing and employment projects, as well as the ability to apply for Turkish citizenship. The refugees were permitted to convert their Bulgarian currency into Turkish liras and to import their cars without paying customs duties. While about 170,000 refugees repatriated after the regime change in Bulgaria in 1990, the others remained in Turkey.[12] Even UNHCR noted that Turkey's assistance of these refugees had been "very generous," despite the country having made "no request for support" from the international community.[13]

This had not been the first mass expulsion of Bulgarian Turks. In August 1950, the Bulgarian government informed Turkish authorities that "about 250,000 Bulgarian citizens of Turkish ethnic origin . . . have expressed their desire to emigrate voluntarily to Turkey" and ought to "be admitted . . . within three months."[14] The status of ethnic Turks in Bulgaria was governed by the

---

[10] Petkova 2002.

[11] Ercüment Yavuzalp [Permanent Representative of Turkey to the UN Office in Geneva] to Jean-Pierre Hocké [UN High Commissioner for Refugees], 31 May 1989, *UNHCR Archives*, Fonds 11, Series 3, 100 TUR BUL Refugee Situations—Special Groups of Refugees—Bulgaria Refugees in Turkey [Volume A], Folio 2.

[12] Kirişci 1991a, 515; Kaşlı and Parla 2009, 210; Amnesty International 1994, 3; Kirişci 1996b, 390, 93; 2000, 13.

[13] 5 March 1991, "Briefing Note for the HC's Meeting with the Turkish Permanent Representative," *UNHCR Archives*, Fonds 11, Series 3, 10 TUR External Relations—Relations with Governments—Turkey [Volume B], Folio 31.

[14] Bulgarian Ministry of Foreign Affairs to Turkish Ambassador in Sofia, 10 August 1950, "Note—Verbale No 304-50-1," *UNHCR Archives*, Fonds 11, Series 1, Box 354, 22/2 Refugees from Bulgaria in Turkey 22-2-I, Folio 5C. This portion of the correspondence reads: "environ 250,000 citoyen bulgares d'origine ethnique turque . . . ont jusqu'ici exprimé le désir d'émigrer volontairement en Turquie. Il serait indispensable . . . que les émigrants en question soient admis sans retard en Turquie et cela de manière que l'émigration prenne fin dans un délai de trois mois à courir de la date de remise de la présente note."

1925 Turkish-Bulgarian Treaty of Friendship and the 1925 Turkish-Bulgarian Convention of Establishment, which provided for voluntary emigration. However, a Turkish government publication explained, this was actually "a mass deportation of non-assimilables, whose property has been seized" and "a number of Bulgarian agents were introduced into Turkey in the guise of immigrants."[15] Still, Turkey's delegation explained at the UN: "[a]s with other refugees of Turkish origin, the Turkish government followed a policy of assimilating those refugees from Bulgaria, and of eventually giving them Turkish nationality."[16]

These refugees were "accorded all the rights which Turkish citizens enjoy" even before their naturalization was formally completed.[17] They benefited from "land and houses provided . . . free by the Government." Indeed, a UNHCR report concluded that "their status is, in certain respects, even more favorable than that of ordinary Turkish nationals." The report went on to observe: "There is a striking discrepancy between the favorable legal position of refugees of Turkish ethnic origin and the economic aid given to them, and the precarious legal status of non-Turkish refugees and their pitiful economic condition which results therefrom."[18] One member of parliament, Cezmi Türk (Refah Parti-Seyhan), said he preferred to call Bulgarians "brothers," rather than refugees.[19]

In explaining this warm reception, scholars have often emphasized domestic political considerations exclusively. Refugees accepted under the Law on Settlement can quickly become voting citizens. From the perspective of the government, therefore, treating them generously could be seen as a political investment.[20]

Indeed, ethnic Turks from other countries have been similarly received. For example, in the early 1980s, 5,200 Afghans were resettled from UNHCR camps in northern Pakistan to Turkey. A specific law (Law 2641) was passed to admit and settle this group in March 1982. Three months later, the refugees were placed

---

[15] Cumhuriyet Matbaasi, 1951, "Question of Turkish Refugees from Bulgaria," *UNHCR Archives*, Fonds 11, Series 1, Box 354, 22/2 Refugees from Bulgaria in Turkey 22-2-I, Folio 5A.

[16] Heinz Schindler to UN High Commissioner for Refugees, 4 December 1951, "High Commissioner's Advisory Committee on Refugees, First Session, Provisional Summary Record of the Fourth Meeting," *UNHCR Archives*, Fonds 11, Series 1, Box 354, 22/2 Refugees from Bulgaria in Turkey 22-2-I, Folio 1A.

[17] Turkish Ministry of Foreign Affairs, 3 June 1952, "Note sur les réfugiés en Turquie et les problèmes qu'ils posent," *UNHCR Archives*, Fonds 11, Series 1, Box 354, 22/2 Refugees from Bulgaria in Turkey 22-2-I, Folio 5B. The note says: "On accorde aux émigrants, dès leur arrivée en Turquie . . . tous les droits dont jouissent les citoyens turcs sans attendre l'accomplissement des formalités quant à l'acquisition de la nationalité turque."

[18] Knud Larsen [UNHCR Representative in Greece] and Paul Weis [Legal Adviser] to UN High Commissioner for Refugees, 20 May 1952, "Report on Mission to Turkey," *UNHCR Archives*, Fonds 11, Series 1, Box 354, 22/2 Refugees from Bulgaria in Turkey 22-2-II, Folio 7.

[19] Turkey 1953, 20: Cilt 48, Birleşim 580.

[20] Kirişci 1991a, 516; 1996b, 388.

on flights to Turkey. They were settled in villages in the Eastern Anatolia Region of Turkey and were provided with financial and material assistance, including housing.[21]

However, not all ethnic Turks were welcome in Turkey. It is instructive to compare the reception given to Bulgarian Turks with that of Gagauz Turks. In contrast to the initial welcome extended to Bulgarian Turks, Gagauz Turks (who are Orthodox Christians) were rebuffed by Turkish officials when they made a number of attempts to flee to Turkey from Moldova in 1990. If an increase in voting citizens were the only consideration, Gagauz Turks ought to have been warmly embraced by Turkish authorities. However, as Kirişci points out, Turkish immigration and refugee policies have only favored those of Turkish origin so long as they were also of Sunni-Hanafi background.[22]

Importantly, Turkey's responses to Bulgarian Turks shifted as the country's relationship with Bulgaria changed, even though the shared ethnic kinship remained the same. With the end of the Zhivkov government and the collapse of communism, it became difficult for Bulgarian Turks to immigrate to Turkey. In 1991 and again in 1994, Bulgarian Turks were deported on the grounds that they were no longer persecuted. Despite the presence of well-organized pressure groups representing Bulgarian Turks in Turkey, and their representatives in the Turkish parliament, the government simply stopped issuing immigrant visas to Bulgarian Turks. As of September 1992, applicants were accepted only if they were "independent" immigrants hoping to reunify with family members who entered Turkey in 1989. It is worth noting that there was a substantial improvement in relations between Bulgaria and Turkey with the end of the Cold War.[23]

In short, Turkey welcomed hundreds of thousands of ethnic Turks from Bulgaria in 1989, granting them citizenship in many cases. This warm reception echoed the country's response to a previous mass expulsion of Bulgarian Turks in 1950. Although ethnic Turks from other countries were treated similarly, a comparison with the Orthodox Christian Gagauz Turks from Moldova who were rejected demonstrates that religious identity likely played a role as well. Foreign policy considerations were likely influential too, since Bulgarian Turks were no longer welcome once Turkey's relations with Bulgaria improved with the end of the Cold War.

---

[21] Kirişci 1991a, 522; 1996b, 399.
[22] Kirişci 1991a, 521–22; 1996b, 390, 99; 2000, 14.
[23] Kirişci 1991a, 516; 1991b, 554; 1996b, 389.

# Iraqis

Turkey experienced three major influxes from Iraq. In 1988, tens of thousands of Kurds fled Saddam Hussein's al-Anfal campaign in northern Iraq after the end of the Iran-Iraq war. Following Iraq's invasion of Kuwait in 1990, there was a flow of foreign workers and their families into Turkey. After the end of the Gulf War in 1991, with Iraqi forces crushing the Kurdish uprising in northern Iraq, hundreds of thousands sought refuge in Turkey. While the majority of refugees in 1988 and 1991 were Kurds who lacked an ethnic tie with Turks, other asylum-seekers from Iraq have included religious and ethnic communities like Turkmens, Shia Arabs, and Christians. In addition, former military personnel, draft evaders, and deserters also sought asylum in Turkey. The majority of these Iraqi refugees were repatriated in 1991 with the creation of a "safe haven" in northern Iraq, while others were resettled. Although refugees from Iraq continued to seek refuge in Turkey, their numbers were far smaller. The relationship between Turkey and Iraq had been cordial and featured extensive trade. However, the 1990–1991 Gulf War worsened relations, as Turkey participated in the war and enforced sanctions on Iraq.[24]

Given this pattern of ethnic identity and foreign policy, my argument would predict that Iraqi refugees experience a restrictive asylum policy before 1990. The evidence below demonstrates that Turkey encamped and sought to repatriate the Iraqi Kurds who arrived in 1988. There did not appear to be a shift in asylum policy to coincide with the change in Iraqi-Turkish relations in 1990, however. Of course, Turkey's central government has long discriminated against the country's sizable ethnic Kurdish minority. It is likely that the Turkish government's wariness of its domestic ethnic Kurd outgroup further harshened its response to Iraqi Kurdish refugees.

Iraqi Kurds who fled to Turkey in 1988 were admitted but restricted to harsh camps pending their return or resettlement. When Saddam launched an assault in northern Iraq in August 1988, some 50,000 Kurds who feared a repeat of the Halabja massacre began streaming across the border into Turkey. The Turkish minister of defense was initially opposed to admitting them, a position possibly linked to the fact that armed activities by the separatist Kurdistan Workers' Party (PKK) were on the rise at the time. Nonetheless, the prime minister quickly announced that Turkey would open its borders and "temporary accommodation centers" (TACs) were established in Diyarbakır-Yenikent, Mardin-Kızıltepe, and Muş-Yenikent.[25]

---

[24] Latif 2002, 9, 18–19; Tschirgi 2003; Hale 2000.
[25] Latif 2002, 9–10; Kaynak 1992, 24, 53.

Although they were received with much publicity and at great expense, Turkish officials preferred to refer to these asylum-seekers as "temporary guests" or "peshmergas" (Kurdish fighters). They were restricted to three closely monitored camps, with the expectation that their presence in Turkey would only be temporary. Attempts to provide them with international assistance were largely rejected by the Turkish authorities.[26] UNHCR had "every day repeated our offer of assistance in whatever way [the] government might find appropriate."[27] The Agency was permitted to conduct an "unofficial preliminary assessment visit" to refugee sites but was told to "keep [a] low profile."[28] This resistance to international assistance persisted despite UNHCR assurances that it would "in no way affect nor create a precedent for use against Turkey's position vis-à-vis the geographical limitation."[29] According to an internal UNHCR briefing note, the government "declared they [Iraqi Kurds] were not of UNHCR's competence" due to "political and international sensitivities surrounding the Kurdish question."[30]

Conditions in the Iraqi Kurdish refugee camps were grim. A member of the German parliament, Angelika Beer, visited the camps in 1989 and described the living conditions as "completely unbearable." The Diyarbakır camp was "filled beyond capacity" and sanitary conditions there were "dire." Living conditions at Mardin camp were "completely catastrophic" with "few water sources," refugees "exposed to extreme climate conditions," and "completely inadequate" medical care. Beer continued, "[t]o describe the sanitary conditions as scandalous or acutely health-jeopardizing would be an understatement." Both camps housed refugees "in prison-like conditions . . . surrounded by barbed wire and patrolled by armed soldiers of the Turkish army." As a result, the Iraqi Kurds lived "in constant fear and uncertainty of being sent back to Iraq."[31]

---

[26] Latif 2002, 10–11; Kirişci 2000, 12; 1991a, 517.

[27] Stefan Berglund [Deputy UNHCR Representative in Turkey] to Head, Desk I, Regional Bureau for Europe and North America, 1 September 1988, *UNHCR Archives*, Fonds 11, Series 3, 100 TUR IRQ Refugee Situations—Special Groups of Refugees—Refugees from Iraq in Turkey [Volume A], Folio 7.

[28] UNHCR Branch Office in Ankara to Head, Desk I, Regional Bureau for Europe and North America, 11 September 1988, *UNHCR Archives*, Fonds 11, Series 3, 100 TUR IRQ Refugee Situations—Special Groups of Refugees—Refugees from Iraq in Turkey [Volume A], Folio 12.

[29] UNHCR Headquarters in Geneva to Turkish Permanent Mission in Geneva, 25 October 1988, "The Recent Influx into Turkey of Tens of Thousands of Iraqi National of Kurdish Origin who were Granted Asylum and Generously Assisted by the Turkish Authorities," *UNHCR Archives*, Fonds 11, Series 3, 100 TUR IRQ Refugee Situations—Special Groups of Refugees—Refugees from Iraq in Turkey [Volume A].

[30] 5 March 1991, "Briefing Note for the HC's Meeting with the Turkish Permanent Representative," *UNHCR Archives*, Fonds 11, Series 3, 10 TUR External Relations—Relations with Governments—Turkey [Volume B], Folio 31.

[31] Angelika Beer [Member of the German Parliament], 12 June 1989, "Anmerkungen zu einem Besuch in den Flüchtlingslagern der irakischen Kurden in der Türkei," *UNHCR Archives*, Fonds 11, Series 3, 100 TUR IRQ Refugee Situations—Special Groups of Refugees—Refugees from Iraq in Turkey [Volume B], Folio 33OA.

Meanwhile, a project to construct a new settlement in central Turkey with international funds was shelved by the prime minister "due to objections by the local Yozgat population to the introduction of Iraqi Kurds into their province." There was an additional "secret reason" that was "highly confidential" and would "not be made public": Turkish authorities were concerned about contacts between the PKK and Iraqi Kurds in the camps. They, therefore, preferred "to keep the Kurdish population located in one area, which is currently under martial law."[32]

In March 1990, UNHCR's representative in the country grew increasingly concerned about the risk of refoulement, reporting to headquarters that "[r]ecent events in Turkey and Iraq jeopardize the situation of Iraqi Kurds who have received temporary sanctuary in Turkey." He noted that the country seemed to have "advance knowledge" of an amnesty that had just been declared in Iraq.[33] An Iraqi delegation subsequently visited Mardin to discuss voluntary return with camp leaders.[34] It was "clear that Turkish officials . . . have been cooperating with Iraqi officials for several months in trying to persuade the TAC population, particularly at Mardin, to repatriate." Alongside this intensifying "persuasion effort," there were "veiled threats" that Iraqi Kurds who refused to return voluntarily would be forcibly repatriated.[35] UNHCR's branch office in Ankara inferred that "a Turkish-Iraqi deal is being worked out."[36] There were further reports of Turkish officials pressuring refugees to return that summer, along with police violence and arrests at Muş and Mardin camps.[37]

At the same time, Turkish authorities surveyed the camp populations on where they would like to be resettled. The survey results were transmitted to UNHCR

---

[32] Daniel E. Conway [UNHCR Representative in Turkey] to UN High Commissioner for Refugees, 4 May 1990, "Turkey: Follow-up Report on Cancellation of Yozgat Project," *UNHCR Archives*, Fonds 11, Series 3, 100 TUR IRQ Refugee Situations—Special Groups of Refugees—Refugees from Iraq in Turkey [Volume E], Folio 83.

[33] Daniel E. Conway to M.H. Khan [Head of Desk I, Regional Bureau for Europe and North America, UNHCR Headquarters in Geneva], 12 March 1990, "Threats to Future of Iraqis in Mardin Temporary Accommodation Center, and Possibly to All Iraqis in Turkey," *UNHCR Archives*, Fonds 11, Series 3, 100 TUR IRQ Refugee Situations—Special Groups of Refugees—Refugees from Iraq in Turkey [Volume D], Folio 68.

[34] UNHCR Branch Office in Ankara to M.H. Khan, 16 May 1990, "Current Situation in Mardin Temporary Accommodation Center," *UNHCR Archives*, Fonds 11, Series 3, 100 TUR IRQ Refugee Situations—Special Groups of Refugees—Refugees from Iraq in Turkey [Volume E], Folio 83.

[35] M.H. Khan, 18 May 1990, "Note for the High Commissioner: Turkey Protection Problems in TACs and Flight of Iraqis from TACs to Greece," *UNHCR Archives*, Fonds 11, Series 3, 100 TUR IRQ Refugee Situations—Special Groups of Refugees—Refugees from Iraq in Turkey [Volume E], Folio 85.

[36] Daniel E. Conway to M.H. Khan, 19 March 1990, "Threats to Future of Iraqis in Mardin Temporary Accommodation Center, and Possibly to All Iraqis in Turkey, Follow Up Report No. 2" *UNHCR Archives*, Fonds 11, Series 3, 100 TUR IRQ Refugee Situations—Special Groups of Refugees—Refugees from Iraq in Turkey [Volume D], Folio 70.

[37] Thorvald Stoltenberg [UN High Commissioner for Refugees], 12 June 1990, *UNHCR Archives*, Fonds 11, Series 3, 100 TUR IRQ Refugee Situations—Special Groups of Refugees—Refugees from Iraq in Turkey [Volume E], Folio 93.

by the Ministry of Foreign Affairs, along with the claim that the "expressed wishes of the Iraqis was the most important element." Resettling these refugees would make Turkey better off "politically and financially."[38] UNHCR foresaw that forced repatriation of the Iraqi Kurds would be justified by Turkey saying "[w]e asked Western governments to take the Iraqis on the basis of the Iraqis' expressed wishes but the Western Governments did not want them."[39] Western countries proved unreceptive to their resettlement in the following years, and the majority were repatriated through Operation Provide Comfort following the creation of a "safe haven" in northern Iraq.

During this time, the Kurdish refugee issue was debated in the Turkish parliament. In 1988, Cumhur Keskin (Sosyaldemokrat Halk Partisi), representing the Kurdish-majority Hakkâri District, decried conditions in the refugee camps and asserted that journalists were not permitted to write about them. Although the Kurds wanted refugee status, Turkish officials refused to receive their applications.[40] Two years later, the same representative emphasized that the Kurds still had no clear status. They were neither "refugees" nor "immigrants," and they did not receive the same treatment as other foreigners.[41] Mustafa Hilmi Özen (Anavatan Partisi), from the Turk-majority Istanbul District, countered that Turkey had no legal obligations to the Kurds, and in any case UNHCR had expressed its approval of the shelters established for them.[42]

The subsequent inflow from Iraq, in 1990, involved third-country nationals (most of whom were quickly repatriated) and a small number of Iraqis: after Iraq invaded Kuwait in August 1990, foreign workers fled both countries. Some 63,000 people entered Turkey, the majority of whom were Pakistanis and Bangladeshis, before being sent to their respective countries. Iraqi soldiers and civilians also began escaping to Turkey, particularly with the launch of Operation Desert Storm in January 1991. Between August 2, 1990, and April 2, 1991, almost 7,500 Iraqis were admitted, including about 1,800 military personnel. After processing in Hakkâri, Şırnak, Van, and Mardin, they were housed in the Turkish Coal Enterprises' plants at Kangal-Sivas, the Tatvan Guesthouse, and the Agriculture School hostel at Kayseri-Kuşçu.[43] A number of shooting incidents were reported at the Turkey-Iraq border during this period. UNHCR characterized the border

---

[38] Daniel E. Conway, 18 May 1990, "Yozgat Project Follow-up/Turkish Proposal to Resettle Iraqis from TACs," *UNHCR Archives*, Fonds 11, Series 3, 100 TUR IRQ Refugee Situations—Special Groups of Refugees—Refugees from Iraq in Turkey [Volume E], Folio 85A.

[39] Daniel E. Conway, 6 June 1990, *UNHCR Archives*, Fonds 11, Series 3, 100 TUR IRQ Refugee Situations—Special Groups of Refugees—Refugees from Iraq in Turkey [Volume E], Folio 87.

[40] Republic of Turkey 1988, 6: Cilt 18, Birleşim 93–94.

[41] Turkey 1990, 41: Cilt 79, Birleşim 147–48.

[42] Ibid., 150–51.

[43] Kaynak 1992, 27, 46, 68; Latif 2002, 11–12.

as an "extremely sensitive security area," since the PKK had "infiltrated from safe havens in Iraq in the past."[44]

When large numbers of Iraqi Kurds next entered Turkey in 1991, the country increased its calls for their return, culminating in the establishment of a safe haven in northern Iraq. With hundreds of thousands of Kurds attempting to escape the Iraqi military's crackdown in April 1991, the Turkish National Security Council initially decided to seal the country's borders. A letter was sent to the UN Security Council describing the situation as a threat to international peace and security. The government had decided not to repeat what it saw as its "mistake" in 1988 and may have been concerned about PKK infiltration. However, the Turkish military found it impossible to enforce the border closure and some 460,000 asylum-seekers had poured in by mid-April.[45] At the same time, Turkish authorities convened a meeting of UN agencies to announce that they had decided "to move all refugees back across the border into Iraq."[46]

Turkish president Turgut Özal called for the creation of a security zone on the Iraqi side of the border, where asylum-seekers could reside. May 3 saw the beginning of an extraordinarily rapid repatriation of these asylum-seekers to the safe haven north of the 36th parallel. By the end of May, the fewer than 14,000 who remained in Turkey were taken to Şırnak-Silopi pilgrimage accommodations. On October 29, 1991, only 4,000 of the asylum-seekers who had entered in April 1991 were still in Turkey. The total number of Iraqis from all influxes who remained in Turkey stood at around 25,000. The majority of those who did not want to be repatriated were later resettled in third countries.[47]

It is worth noting that when 50,000 Turkmen refugees entered Turkey as part of the mass influx from northern Iraq in 1991, they were permitted to reside in a special camp away from the border (and from the predominantly Kurdish refugees). Many were provided with residence permits.[48] Four years prior, some Iraqi asylum-seekers entering Turkey claimed to be of Turkmen origin "for fear of being deported" by Turkish authorities. This situation necessitated UNHCR interviews "to identify ethnic Kurds among [that] group."[49]

---

[44] Daniel E. Conway to M.H. Khan, 21 December 1990, "Shooting Incident on Turkish/Iraqi Border," UNHCR Archives, Fonds 11, Series 3, 100 TUR IRQ Refugee Situations—Special Groups of Refugees—Refugees from Iraq in Turkey [Volume F], Folio 115.

[45] Latif 2002, 12–14; Frelick 1997, 26; Kaynak 1992, 28.

[46] Daniel E. Conway, 11 April 1991, "Gulf Emergency," UNHCR Archives, Fonds 11, Series 3, 10 TUR External Relations—Relations with Governments—Turkey [Volume B], Folio 34.

[47] Latif 2002, 13–14; Kaynak 1992, 28, 49; Kirişci 2001, 77.

[48] Kirişci 1991a, 521–22; 1996b, 390, 99; 2000, 14.

[49] UNHCR Branch Office in Ankara to UNHCR Headquarters in Geneva, 2 September 1987, "Concerning Refugee Situation Kayseri," UNHCR Archives, Fonds 11, Series 3, 100 TUR IRQ Refugee Situations—Special Groups of Refugees—Refugees from Iraq in Turkey [Volume A], Folio 4.

The Turkish government proved unwilling to admit Iraqi asylum-seekers in subsequent years. Ministry of Interior officials said that there could be no genuine asylum-seekers because northern Iraq had been made safe by Operation Provide Comfort. In 1994, Amnesty International reported that authorities had systematically arrested and deported over 300 Iraqis, including asylum-seekers recognized by UNHCR who had been accepted for resettlement by third countries. In addition, hundreds of Iraqis who had been accepted for resettlement had trouble securing exit permits from the government.[50] A 1994 letter sent by Iraqi refugees in Turkey to UNHCR headquarters describes their predicament:

> What we suffer we're the Iraqi refugees from persecution in Turkey are more than what we have been experience under "Saddam ruling" . . . We are unable to find any legal status in Turkey, the police and security attack our houses day and night without any notification, we received ill-usage by them, arresting us even if we show them documents issued by "United Nations," they deport us as a group to North of Iraq "Zakho" monthly, they are forcing us to sign papers in Turkish language that we cannot understand what is written on . . . Besides that, Turkish Authorities issued a decision against Iraqi refugees to prevent us from departure, even if we have visa or departure date by the IOM . . . We appeal to you and ask for mercy to consult with the Turkish Government to put an end to our affliction and alleviate from our hard conditions by consider our cases by and large.[51]

In preparation for the 2003 Iraq War, Turkey planned refugee camps within Iraqi territory, but its fears of another mass influx proved unfounded.[52]

To summarize, Turkey designated ethnic Kurds from Iraq in 1988 as temporary guests. It refused international assistance and encamped them in difficult conditions while seeking their return or resettlement. After failing to keep its border closed in the face of hundreds of thousands of Iraqi Kurds in 1991, Turkey successfully pushed for the creation of a security zone on the Iraqi side of the border where they could reside. Concerns about Kurdish separatism appear to have influenced Turkey's responses in both cases. In contrast, Turkmen refugees from Iraq were granted residence permits.

---

[50] Amnesty International 1994, 12–13; Kirişci 2001, 77; Frelick 1997, 17–18.

[51] All Iraqi Refugees in Turkey to UNHCR Headquarters in Geneva, 12 August 1994, *UNHCR Archives*, Fonds 11, Series 3, 100 TUR IRQ Refugee Situations—Special Groups of Refugees—Refugees from Iraq in Turkey [Volume H], Folio 140.

[52] Kaya 2009, 1–2.

## Iranians

Following the 1979 revolution, Iranians began fleeing to Turkey to escape Ayatollah Khomeini's regime. The majority of these were members of the elite who had been allied with the deposed Shah, or supporters of leftist opposition groups like the Mojahedin-e-Khalq and the Tudeh Party. As Iranian security forces and Kurdish guerilla groups battled, Kurds began arriving as well. These included members of the Democratic Party of Iranian Kurdistan, the communist Komala party, and the Worker-Communist Party of Iran. Smaller groups of religious and ethnic minorities also fleeing to Turkey included Armenians, Assyrians, Azeris, Baha'is, Jews, and Zoroastrians.[53]

Thus, the majority of refugees from Iran belonged to the Persian and Kurdish ethnic groups, who lacked an ethnic tie with Turks. Moreover, Turkey cultivated a cordial relationship with Iran. During the Iran-Iraq war, Turkey declared "positive neutrality." Thereafter, despite ideological differences and the occasional diplomatic crisis, their relationship featured increasing trade and economic cooperation and multiple state visits on both sides. In 1997, Iranian ambassador Mohammed Reza Bagheri gave a provocative speech in the Turkish town of Sincan. Iranian and Turkish diplomats were subsequently expelled, but the "Sincan affair" was quickly resolved.[54]

With friendly bilateral relations and no ethnic tie, I expect Iranian refugees to be treated restrictively by Turkey, particularly after the end of the Iran-Iraq war in 1988. The discussion that follows demonstrates that as relations between Iran and Turkey got closer, conditions for Iranian refugees became more precarious. In the 1990s, the two countries increasingly coordinated their activities, resulting in increased deportations.

Anxious not to offend the Iranian government, Turkish officials continued to allow Iranians to enter the country under a preexisting visa-free regime but systematically discouraged them from applying for asylum. Instead of extending asylum-seeker status to these individuals, they permitted them to enter the country without a visa and reside there temporarily as tourists. Iranians who entered illegally, or without valid passports, were sentenced to symbolic fines in court then released. The majority moved on to third countries relying on their own means, with only a small proportion applying to UNHCR. Although there are no official statistics on how many Iranians benefited from this arrangement, a Turkish parliamentarian put the number at 1.5 million between 1980 and 1991.[55]

---

[53] Latif 2002, 8–9, 17–18; Frantz 2003, 25; Kirişci 2001, 76.
[54] "Turkey," 2010; Aras 2003; Hale 2000; Helsinki Citizens' Assembly 2011.
[55] Latif 2002, 9, 16–17; Kirişci 2001, 76–77; 1996a, 297–98.

An internal UNHCR document explained "Turkish policy vis-à-vis Iranian refugees" in 1984 by pointing to, among other factors, "the traditional close links which exist between Iran and Turkey." These relations had been "further strengthened after Khomeini's coming to power and the ensuing decline in [Iran's] relations with other states" since Turkey had become "an important transit country for the exchange of goods between Iran and other states." The confidential memo continues:

> The desire to maintain good relations with Iran explains why Turkey is not in a position to officially allow Iranian refugees to remain in the country, nor to withdraw its geographical limitation to the 1951 Convention . . . In order not to highlight the refugee problem, the Turkish authorities are in favor of asylum-seekers leaving the country as quickly as possible. Moreover, the authorities turn a blind eye to persons not having valid travel documents and/or visas leaving the country as well as the fact that those who wish to leave Turkey acquire false papers whilst in the country . . . The desire to maintain a good relationship with Iran also explains why Turkey has hitherto refused to accept funds from UNHCR in order to assist asylum-seekers from Iran and why collective accommodation for Iranians has not been established and finally, the relationship between Turkey and Iran explains why there is no visa obligation at present for Iranian citizens entering Turkey. In other words, *Turkey wishes above all to play down the refugee problem in order not to jeopardize her relations with Iran.*[56] (emphasis added)

In the context of a discussion with UNHCR about Iranian refugees in 1986, a foreign ministry official also remarked that the relationship between the two countries was "very good." In at least one instance, the Turkish government sent UNHCR a list of Iranian refugees who were "objectionable for political reasons," so that UNHCR could arrange their "early departure for a third country."[57]

Subsequent flows of Iranians faced somewhat riskier circumstances as the relationship between Iraq and Turkey got closer. Beginning in 1992, the Iranian and Turkish governments signed a series of agreements to cooperate for improved border security and the prevention of terrorist activities. A September 1992 protocol established a "Common Security Committee" and pledged measures to prevent illegal crossings and enforce extradition agreements. An October 1993

---

[56] Michael Peterson [Protection Officer, Europe Regional Section] to Michel Moussalli [Director of International Protection, UNHCR Headquarters in Geneva], 19 March 1984, "The Refugee Situation in Turkey," *UNHCR Archives*, Fonds 11, Series 2, Box 11, 10 TUR Relations with Governments—Turkey.

[57] Gary G. Troeller to Fügen Ok [Director, Department of Multilateral Political Affairs, Ministry of Foreign Affairs], 10 February 1987, "Note for the File," *UNHCR Archives*, Fonds 11, Series 3, 10 TUR External Relations—Relations with Governments—Turkey [Volume A], Folio 11.

protocol provided for regular meetings of the Common Security Committee. In December, Turkish police arrested and deported fifty Iranians, including four Iranian opposition activists who had sought asylum. The following month, Turkish police expelled two Iranian asylum-seekers and received four members of the PKK from Iran, in an apparent *quid pro quo*. Another agreement was signed in June 1994, after which the Turkish interior minister reportedly said: "No element acting against the Islamic Republic of Iran will be allowed to remain on Turkish territory."[58] The Iranian interior minister responded, "Tehran is well aware of Turkey's problems and regards Turkey's foes as its own."[59] After an April 1996 agreement reportedly called for the reciprocal exchange of opposition activists, refoulements of Iranian asylum-seekers jumped. Although the Turkish government refused to confirm or deny the signing of this agreement, Iranian officials were less circumspect. Other agreements were said to be in the works, and the Iranian government had reportedly requested the return of 600 dissidents from Turkey.[60]

UNHCR officials, for their part, expressed concern about the Iranian members of Mojahedin-e-Khalq who had fled Iraq for Turkey in 1992. In light of recent conversations between Turkey and Iran, these refugees ought to be "discouraged to come to Turkey."[61] Turkish authorities were unlikely to "accept the presence of a group . . . that is among the Iranian regime's most resolute adversaries."[62]

There are indications that agents of the Iranian government were active in pursuing politically active asylum-seekers and exiles on Turkish territory. In 1988, a car with Iranian diplomatic license plates crossing from Turkey into Iran was found to have a kidnapped Iranian dissident in its trunk. In June 1992, a member of the Mojahedin-e-Khalq was abducted in Istanbul and later found dead. In December of that year, a member of an Iranian monarchist group was abducted in Istanbul. The Kurdish Democratic Party of Iran saw two of its members killed in August 1993 and a third shot dead in January 1994. A member of the Paris-based National Council of Resistance of Iran, who was visiting Istanbul to assist Iranian asylum-seekers, was assassinated in February 1996.[63] UNHCR's

---

[58] Qtd. in Amnesty International 1997, 9.

[59] Qtd. in Frelick 1997, 24.

[60] Amnesty International 1994, 8; 1997, 9; Frelick 1997, 23–24.

[61] Patrick Tezier [Legal Unit, Protection Officer, UNHCR Branch Office in Turkey], 9 October 1992, *UNHCR Archives*, Fonds 11, Series 3, 100 TUR IRQ Refugee Situations—Special Groups of Refugees—Refugees from Iraq in Turkey [Volume H], Folio 138.

[62] John McCallin [UNHCR Representative in Turkey] to A.M. Demmer [Director, Regional Bureau for Europe, UNHCR Headquarters in Geneva], 3 November 1992, "Situation des membres et sympathisants (Irregular movers ex Iraq) du PMOI en Turquie," *UNHCR Archives*, Fonds 11, Series 3, 100 TUR IRQ Refugee Situations—Special Groups of Refugees—Refugees from Iraq in Turkey [Volume H], Folio 140. In the original French, this section reads: "Il n'est pas certain que les autorités accepteront la présence sur le territoire Turc, pour une période indéterminée d'un groupe de personnes qui ne cesse d'augmenter, qui bénéficiait de l'asile dans un autre pays et qui compte parmi les adversaires les plus résolus au régime Iranien."

[63] Frelick 1997, 24–25; Amnesty International 1994, 9.

representative in Turkey also noted that a Mojahedin-e-Khalq member had been murdered in 1993, "presumably by Iranian agents." He concluded that "all these opposition groups face major security problems, aggravated by recent agreements between Turkish and Iranian authorities."[64]

Iranian applicants for asylum reported that Turkish police used status determination interviews to gather information about other Iranians in Turkey. Police officers reportedly joked with some of these individuals that "[Iranian president, Akbar Hashemi] Rafsanjani is expecting them." In some cases, Turkish police officers escorted Iranian asylum-seekers recognized by UNHCR to the Iranian embassy for interrogation.[65]

Thus, during the Iran-Iraq war, Iranians were permitted to enter Turkey so long as they did not claim asylum and moved on quietly to other countries. Starting in the 1990s, as relations between Turkey and Iran got closer, deportations of Iranians were stepped up. Notably, the two countries appeared to be coordinating their activities regarding Iranian dissidents.

## Bosnians and Kosovars

The Bosnian War in 1992–1995 and the Kosovo War in 1998–1999 soured Turkey's relations with the Federal Republic of Yugoslavia. During the Bosnian War, Turkey adopted an embargo, froze assets, closed its airspace, and recalled its ambassador. It also helped enforce a no-fly zone over Bosnia in 1993. During the Kosovo War, Turkey supported North Atlantic Treaty Organization (NATO) action and contributed troops to the Kosovo Force. Neither the Bosniak Muslims nor the ethnic Albanians who fled these wars shared an ethnic tie with Turks.[66]

Therefore, I expect Bosnians and Kosovars to be treated similarly to each other by Turkish authorities. The combination of hostile sending country relations and no ethnic tie would predict that these refugees not be treated particularly inclusively or restrictively. In fact, the Turkish government allowed them to enter the country as tourists and did not forcibly encamp them. At the same time, Turkey declined to grant them refugee status, and the majority repatriated.

Starting in March and April 1992, over 20,000 Bosnian Muslims fled to Turkey. Turkish officials declined to grant them refugee status under the 1951 Refugee Convention. Although the 1934 Settlement Law might have covered them, it was

---

[64] John McCallin to Kamel Morjane [Director, Regional Bureau for South West Asia, North Africa, and the Middle East], 16 August 1993, "Irregular Movers," *UNHCR Archives*, Fonds 11, Series 3, 100 TUR IRQ Refugee Situations—Special Groups of Refugees—Refugees from Iraq in Turkey [Volume H], Folio 138.

[65] Frelick 1997, 14–15, 23.

[66] Müftüler-Bac 1997; Hale 2000.

not applied either. Despite pressure from Bosnian immigrant associations, the government considered them "guests" and gave them only temporary protection.[67] Whereas refugee status would have permitted them to work, they could not obtain work permits as guests.[68]

Under an agreement between Turkey and Yugoslavia, citizens of the latter could receive visa waivers for stays of up to two months. As a result, Bosnians were able to enter Turkey as tourists using their Yugoslav passports. Their stay was automatically extended for up to six months, and they could obtain renewable residence permits. Starting in November 1992, Bosnians were able to use Turkish hospitals and schools. Many stayed with family members in Istanbul, while others were housed in refugee camps. These were officially run by the Turkish government, although the Anatolian Development Foundation (a Turkish NGO and UNHCR implementing partner) was actively involved in managing them. Only 3,000 formally applied for asylum and the vast majority were repatriated after the Dayton Agreement was signed at the end of 1995.[69]

When about 18,000 Kosovars entered Turkey in late 1998 and 1999, they too were labeled guests rather than refugees. They were admitted as tourists and issued six-month residence permits. The majority lived in urban centers, with others staying at Kırklareli camp (formally, Gazi Osman Paşa Immigrant Guesthouse). This camp, in which Bosnians had also resided, was managed by the Turkish Red Crescent and received UNHCR-funded relief via the Anatolian Development Foundation. Similar provisions applied to a group of Albanians relocated from Macedonia as part of the Humanitarian Evacuation Program. Like the Bosnians, the vast majority of Kosovars were repatriated or resettled.[70]

To sum up, Bosnian and Kosovar refugees were permitted to enter Turkey, to reside where they wished, and to access public schools and hospitals. However, they were not granted refugee status nor was the 1934 Settlement Law applied to them. Ultimately, the majority repatriated or were resettled.

## Refugees from Soviet and Post-Soviet States

Turkey received small numbers of refugees from the Eastern Bloc throughout the Cold War and from post-Soviet states thereafter. Turkey was a NATO member and clearly opposed the Warsaw Pact during the Cold War, but it was quick to

---

[67] Latif 2002, 7; Frantz 2003, 23; Kirişci 1996b, 389; 2001, 76.

[68] UNHCR Branch Office in Ankara to UNHCR Branch Office in Zagreb, 21 April 1994, *UNHCR Archives*, Fonds 11, Series 3, 100 TUR BSN Refugee Situations—Special Groups of Refugees—Refugees from Bosnia in Turkey.

[69] Amnesty International 1994, 3; Kirişci 1996b, 297, 389, 400–01; Frantz 2003, 23; Kirişci 2001, 76.

[70] Kirişci 2001, 76; Frantz 2003, 23–24.

build a rapport with post-Soviet states. For example, Turkey's relations with Uzbekistan were excellent. Turkey and Russia also enjoyed a warm relationship and signed trade and defense agreements during the 2000s. At the same time, most refugees from the Eastern Bloc (and later, post-Soviet states) did not share an ethnic tie with Turks.[71]

Accordingly, I expect refugees from this region to experience more restrictive treatment in the post–Cold War period than during the Cold War. The evidence presented here shows that, at least starting in 1970, those fleeing the Eastern Bloc for Turkey were granted refugee status. In contrast, Turkey refused to recognize as refugees those who escaped post-Soviet states. Beginning in the 1990s, Chechens were denied access to RSD procedures and were not permitted to receive assistance from UNHCR or NGOs.

Turkey was initially reluctant to extend formal refugee status to Hungarians and Russians during the early years of the Cold War, but it nonetheless allowed them to reside safely in Turkey pending their resettlement. The 1956 Hungarian Uprising and subsequent mass displacement alarmed the Turkish government, which discussed with UNHCR "measures to solve the Hungarian refugee problem in Turkey."[72] Turkey initially insisted on excluding Hungarians from refugee status, based on the temporal limitation of the 1951 Refugee Convention to "events occurring in Europe before 1 January 1951."[73] Similarly, Turkey excluded Russian refugees under the convention's geographical limitation.[74] Even then, Turkish officials reassured UNHCR that those excluded from the convention "would get a certain legal status and in particular would be protected against deportation measures." In other words, "the matter could be solved in a pragmatic way."[75] Specifically, "Russian refugees would normally not be allowed to settle in Turkey but enabled to emigrate elsewhere."[76]

---

[71] Kirişci 1996a, 296–97; 2001, 75–76; "Turkey," 2010; Tanrısever 2003; Hale 2000.

[72] Assad Sadry to UN High Commissioner for Refugees, 30 August 1957, "UNHCR Representative in Greece to be Accredited in Turkey," *UNHCR Archives*, Fonds 11, Series 1, Box 77, 2/5/1/1 ACC/ TUR Branch Offices—Accreditation—Turkey, Folio 1.

[73] Prince Alfred zur Lippe-Weissenfeld [UNHCR Representative in Turkey] to A. Inhan [Deputy Director General, Ministry of Foreign Affairs], 5 November 1962, *UNHCR Archives*, Fonds 11, Series 1, Box 348, 22/1 TUR Eligibility—Turkey, Folio 22. This eligibility problem was definitely resolved in 1965. Eberhard Jahn to Paul Weis, 14 April 1965, "Protection Turkey—Report on Mission 19–20 March 1965," *UNHCR Archives*, Fonds 11, Series 1, Box 348, 22/1 TUR Eligibility—Turkey, Folio 45.

[74] Eberhard Jahn to Paul Weis, 14 April 1965, "Protection Turkey—Report on Mission 19–20 March 1965," *UNHCR Archives*, Fonds 11, Series 1, Box 348, 22/1 TUR Eligibility—Turkey, Folio 45. This interpretation was corrected in 1967. Heinz Schindler [UNHCR Representative in Turkey] to UNHCR Headquarters in Geneva, 22 December 1967, "1951 Convention: Refugees of Russian Origin," *UNHCR Archives*, Fonds 11, Series 1, Box 348, 22/1 TUR Eligibility—Turkey, Folio 70.

[75] 17 May 1966, "Note on Discussions with Mr. Idiz, Ankara, and Mr. Sirman of the Turkish Delegation in Geneva on 17 May 1966," *UNHCR Archives*, Fonds 11, Series 1, Box 348, 22/1 TUR Eligibility—Turkey, Folio 47.

[76] Eberhard Jahn to Heinz Schindler, 16 February 1967, *UNHCR Archives*, Fonds 11, Series 1, Box 348, 22/1 TUR Eligibility—Turkey, Folio 51.

In time, those fleeing Eastern Europe and the Soviet Union were recognized by Turkey as de jure refugees under the 1951 Convention. These refugee flows were never large, and it was fairly easy to secure resettlement for them elsewhere in the West. International agencies, like the International Catholic Migration Commission and UNHCR, generally met the costs of hosting and resettling these refugees. According to the Turkish government, 8,143 individuals were granted convention refugee status between 1970 and 1991. Few of these remained in Turkey permanently, however. Notably, treating this group of refugees favorably fit squarely with Turkey's anti-communist foreign policy orientation.[77]

With the end of the Cold War, the flow of refugees from Eastern Europe dwindled. At the same time, however, Turkey's policies toward refugees from this region had shifted. The former Soviet republics fell under the 1951 Convention's conception of Europe, so Turkey could not invoke the geographical limitation to exclude asylum-seekers from these post-Soviet states. Still, Turkey declined to grant refugee status to Azerbaijanis, Uzbekistanis, and Chechens.[78]

Turkey's desire not to offend friendly Azerbaijan, Uzbekistan, and Russia likely underlay this practice. Citizens of these countries were generally able to enter the country easily with the proper travel documents but were not granted refugee status. Between 1994 and 1996, 14 individuals from Uzbekistan, 6 from Bulgaria, 4 from Yugoslav successor states, 2 from Russia, and 2 from Ukraine applied for asylum. Other than the applications from the former Yugoslavia (which had been accepted), all the other cases had either been rejected or were still being processed in March 1996.[79]

Instead of granting them refugee status, Turkey either allowed individuals from those countries to remain in Turkey unofficially or permitted them to immigrate as ethnic Turks under the Settlement Law. For example, about 500 Meskhetian Turkish families from Uzbekistan were able to immigrate in 1992 and 1993 under the Law on Settlement, thereby relieving the Turkish government from having to decide on claims for asylum. A special law (Law 3835) was passed by the Turkish parliament in July 1992 to authorize the government to sponsor their resettlement, and the group was settled in Eastern Anatolia in government-provided housing.[80]

Refugees fleeing the Second Chechen War starting in 1999 were sometimes denied admission and uniformly excluded from RSD procedures. In February 2000, 100 Chechens appeared at the Turkish-Georgian border. The Turkish government insisted that they remain in Georgia and pledged to provide them with

77  Kirişci 1996a, 295–96; Latif 2002, 21; Kirişci 2001, 74–75; 2000, 11.
78  Kirişci 1991b, 549–50; 1996a, 296–97; 2001, 75.
79  Kirişci 1996a, 296–97; 2001, 75.
80  Kirişci 1996b, 390, 99–400.

humanitarian assistance. In 2003, there were about 2,000 Chechens living in Istanbul without residence permits. UNHCR had been forbidden from making contact with or assisting them, as were NGOs. The Turkish government may have wanted to avoid the repetition of previous charges by Russia that it was harboring Chechen rebels.[81]

Chechens ought to be considered "European" under the 1951 Convention, since Russia is a member of the Council of Europe. Despite this, they were denied access to status determination procedures. According to Amnesty International, of the 1,000 Chechens in Turkey in 2009, not one had been recognized as a refugee. Rather, officials at the Istanbul Directorate of Security refused to receive their asylum applications. Instead, the Ministry of Interior designated them as guests who may receive resident permits and remain in the country temporarily. The community also faced detentions at times "when their presence was politically sensitive," such as during a 2004 visit by President Vladimir Putin to Turkey.[82]

Several interviewees stressed the influence of bilateral Turkey-Russia relations on the treatment of Chechens in Turkey. One NGO worker explained that Turkey "does not want to process [asylum applications from] Chechens" because of concerns about its relationship with Russia.[83] An expert at the Ministry of Interior's Migration and Asylum Bureau also emphasized that, despite Russia's membership in the Council of Europe, Chechens were not granted refugee status due to "political reasons" linked to "Turkey-Russia relations."[84]

## Delegation

In chapter 2, I suggested that delegation poses few drawbacks for policymakers. UNHCR tends to be sensitive to the government's concerns and is easily punished if it oversteps its authority. Even while the government shifts blame to UNHCR, the Agency's access and influence are circumscribed. To provide context, this section begins by reviewing the history of UNHCR in Turkey. Next, I detail multiple episodes during which UNHCR bowed to government pressure and fashioned its behavior to please Turkish authorities. Finally, I show that the government claimed that UNHCR was responsible even while actively limiting its activities.

[81] Kirişci 2001, 75; Frantz 2003, 24; Kirişci 1996a, 296.
[82] Republic of Turkey 1988, 14.
[83] NGO worker. Personal interview by author. Istanbul, Turkey, February 2, 2012.
[84] Expert, Migration and Asylum Bureau, Ministry of Interior. Personal interview by author. Ankara, Turkey, February 21, 2012.

## Context

The Turkish government seemed cognizant from the outset that there were ben-efits to be reaped from having UNHCR representation in the country. Still, relations between the government and the Agency subsequently had their ups and downs. At times, the two parties had a good working relationship and coordinated their activities. At other times, the government ignored UNHCR's status determination decisions and deported recognized refugees. Further, in 1994, the adoption of an Asylum Regulation instituted parallel government and UNHCR status determination procedures.

UNHCR started reaching out to Turkish officials in the 1950s, but it was not successful in establishing a branch office until 1960. In 1952, the Turkish government had demurred on establishing UNHCR representation in the country, since there were no refugees other than the ethnic Turks arriving en masse from Bulgaria (the small number of other refugees in Turkey had already been naturalized).[85] In 1957, UNHCR officials sought to persuade Turkey of the "advantages, both to the Turkish Government and the refugees in having the [High Commissioner's] Office represented in Turkey." Indeed, having a UNHCR representative "on the spot" would have helped in "solving" the "Hungarian refugee problem in Turkey."[86] Moreover, a representative would facilitate the provision of refugee assistance and enable UNHCR to better coordinate its activities with the Turkish government.[87] Turkish authorities agreed.[88]

The government preferred that UNHCR run a dedicated branch office in the country, rather than place Turkey under the umbrella of a regional representative. When, as an interim measure in 1975, the Regional Representative in the Middle East took responsibility for operations in Turkey, Turkish officials emphasized that, "in the long run," they would prefer to have a representative in the country "on a more permanent basis." UNHCR personnel surmised that

[85] Permanent Delegation of Turkey to the European Office of the UN, 7 April 1952, *UNHCR Archives*, Fonds 11, Series 1, Box 354, 22/2 Refugees from Bulgaria in Turkey 22-2-I, Folio 15. The relevant section reads: "Quant à la question d'accréditer M. Knud Larsen à Ankara, le Gouvernement Turc est de l'avis suivant: Les réfugiés aidés par l'OIR, et se trouvent en Turquie en nombre restraint, ont plus ou moins tous acquis la nationalité turque. Comme il n'existe en Turquie pas d'autre catégories de réfugiés que ceux d'origine ethnique turque venant en grande masse en Bulgarie, le Gouvernement Turc juge utile la création de cette réprésentation après que le Haut Commissariat sera arrivé à une conclusion définitive concernant l'aide qu'il leur apportera."

[86] Assad Sadry to UN High Commissioner for Refugees, 30 August 1957, "UNHCR Representative in Greece to be Accredited in Turkey," *UNHCR Archives*, Fonds 11, Series 1, Box 77, 2/5/1/1 ACC/TUR Branch Offices—Accreditation—Turkey, Folio 1.

[87] A.R. Lindt to Turkish Minister of Foreign Affairs, 4 July 1960, *UNHCR Archives*, Fonds 11, Series 1, Box 77, 2/5/1/1 ACC/TUR Branch Offices—Accreditation—Turkey, Folio 3.

[88] Assad Sadry, 25 September 1957, "Extract from Mr. Sadry's Report on Trip to Turkey," *UNHCR Archives*, Fonds 11, Series 1, Box 77, 2/5/1/1 ACC/TUR Branch Offices—Accreditation—Turkey, Folio 2.

"[t]his desire may at least partly be connected with the efforts of Turkey to improve her relationships with certain Eastern European countries and with her interest in avoiding that refugee matters may lead to renewed tension." It may also have been connected, they speculated, to the recent arrival of refugees "from Arab countries, particularly Iraq."[89]

However, tensions surfaced between the Turkish government and UNHCR in the late 1980s and early 1990s. In particular, the working relationship between UNHCR and Turkey began to come under strain when the country experienced several mass influxes between 1988 and 1991. Until the mid-to-late 1980s, the Agency had focused on conducting RSD and processing resettlement for refugees from the Soviet Union and Eastern Europe. Under an informal arrangement, UNHCR had extended its status determination and protection to non-European asylum-seekers, who had begun arriving in large numbers chiefly from Iran and Iraq. However, after Kurdish asylum-seekers repatriated to the safe zone in northern Iraq, the government began deporting newly arrived asylum-seekers from the area regardless of whether they had secured recognition from UNHCR.[90] Internal UNHCR correspondence from 1994 contrasted the Agency's "relations of trust" with the Ministry of Foreign Affairs on the one hand with its "ambivalent (if not defiant on the Turkish side)" relationship with the Ministry of Interior's Department of Foreigners on the other hand.[91]

The adoption of the 1994 Asylum Regulation realigned the division of responsibilities between the government and the Agency.[92] Under the Asylum Regulation, Turkey still maintained the geographical limitation, and UNHCR continued to be responsible for non-European asylum-seekers. However, the Ministry of Interior would conduct first-instance status determination interviews. Turkish authorities first decided whether an individual was a "genuine" asylum-seeker, then UNHCR determined whether they qualified for protection and attempted to find a resettlement possibility for them. In effect, the regulation established two "parallel tracks" for status determination, one domestic and one conducted by UNHCR.[93]

---

[89] Eberhard Jahn to Michel Moussalli, 1 September 1976, "UNHCR Representation in Turkey," *UNHCR Archives*, Fonds 11, Series 2, Box 403, 203 TUR Privileges, Immunities, and Accreditations—Turkey, Folio 18.

[90] Latif 2002, 23; Kirişci 2001, 71, 76–77.

[91] Lina Sultani [Deputy UNHCR Representative in Turkey] and Patrick Tezier [Head of Legal Unit, UNHCR Branch Office in Ankara] to Head, Desk I, Regional Bureau for Europe, 20 January 1994, *UNHCR Archives*, Fonds 11, Series 3, 10 TUR External Relations—Relations with Governments—Turkey [Volume B], Folio 51. The exact wording is: "La délégation entretient des rapports de confiance avec le ministre de affaires étrangères, et ambivalents (pour ne pas dire defiants du cote turc) avec le département des étrangers au ministère de l'intérieur."

[92] "Regulation on the Procedures and Principles related to Mass Influxes and Foreigners Arriving in Turkey either as Individuals or in Groups Wishing to Seek Asylum either from Turkey or Requesting Residence Permission in order to Seek Asylum from Another Country" (No. 1994/6169).

[93] Zieck 2010, 610; Kirişci 1996a, 305; Frelick 1997, 9; Latif 2002, 24.

More specifically, the regulation instructed asylum-seekers to register with the Turkish police within five days of their arrival. Local police conducted an eligibility interview and forwarded the interview documents to the Ministry of Interior. Officials at the Ministry of Interior made a decision after, the regulation stipulated, consulting with the Ministry of Foreign Affairs and other relevant government bodies. In some cases, authorities were known to solicit UNHCR's opinion. Applicants who were rejected by the Turkish government were instructed to leave the country within 15 days, otherwise they became subject to arrest and deportation.[94]

Once the government recognized an asylum-seeker's eligibility, they were directed to apply to UNHCR and issued a renewable six-month residence permit. In the meantime, asylum-seekers were instructed to relocate to a designated "satellite city." At their assigned city, they were required to register with the police regularly (in some places, daily) in order to verify their continued presence. Vulnerable asylum-seekers and those who feared threats to their security (such as high-profile politicians and former military personnel) were sometimes sent to the Yozgat Refugee Guesthouse, a heavily guarded government facility located 150 miles from Ankara. The regulation accorded recognized asylum-seekers the right to work and to education. However, they had to leave the country if they were unable to secure resettlement within a "reasonable time."[95]

If an asylum-seeker was recognized by the UNHCR, meanwhile, the Agency issued them with a "letter of concern," their case was processed for resettlement, and the Agency informed the Ministry of Interior so that the asylum-seeker could extend their residence permit. UNHCR also informed the ministry if asylum-seekers were rejected (and their appeals were unsuccessful). In addition to conducting status determination and managing resettlement for non-European asylum-seekers, UNHCR also provided legal and social counseling, financial aid, and material assistance to asylum-seekers and refugees.[96]

After the 1994 Asylum Regulation came into force, Amnesty International reported that the government "increasingly refuses to cooperate with the UNHCR."[97] Perhaps the lowest point came in March 1997, when the Ministry of Interior issued deportation orders for over 600 people, including asylum-seekers who had been recognized by UNHCR or were awaiting the Agency's

[94] Frantz 2003, 16–18, 35–36; Kirişci 2001, 80; Latif 2002, 24–25; Frelick 1997, 9, 12, 16. Mass influxes were covered in the third and fourth sections of the regulation. In essence, the regulation stipulated that large-scale population movements be stopped at the border. Authorities were expected to take any "necessary and effective measures" to ensure that asylum-seekers were prevented from crossing into the country. Latif 2002, 24; Frantz 2003, 28; Frelick 1997, 26–27.

[95] The restriction that the satellite city system puts on asylum-seekers' freedom of movement is in line with Article 17 of the 1950 Law on the Residence and Movement of Aliens. Frantz 2003, 18, 29, 33–36; Kaya 2009, 5; Frelick 1997, 9, 11, 16, 25.

[96] Frantz 2003, 18–19; Latif 2002, 26–27.

[97] Amnesty International 1994, 1.

determination on their applications. It was also announced that anyone who was illegally present in Turkey would be denied an exit permit. The government only suspended the deportation order following a domestic and international outcry.[98]

Starting in 1997, deportations became less frequent and the government and UNHCR began to develop closer cooperative relations once again. According to Kirişci, government officials recognized that partnering with UNHCR would alleviate international criticism, while bringing about better implementation of the regulation. A UNHCR-funded publicity campaign was launched to inform potential asylum-seekers about the regulation. The Ministry of Interior instructed officials in border towns to direct asylum-seekers to UNHCR, and the Agency was permitted to open offices in border towns like Ağrı and Van.[99]

Relations between the UNHCR and Turkey continued to improve in the following months and years. In May 1997, UNHCR met with the interior and foreign ministries met to discuss the status of over 3,000 asylum-seekers who had entered the country before the asylum regulation came into force. Although they had received or were awaiting recognition from UNHCR, they were technically in violation of the regulation and feared deportation. By August, a "one-time solution" had been reached, which allowed recognized asylum-seekers to exit to their resettlement countries and gave UNHCR several months to reach a determination on remaining cases. By 1998, Turkish officials were attending seminars and conferences organized by UNHCR, and in January 1999, the government amended the asylum regulation to increase the five-day limit to ten days. The following year, the government and the Agency signed a three-year training and technical cooperation agreement.[100]

The government also began to rely on UNHCR in its own status determination decisions, suggesting a pattern of "informal" delegation. If the government and UNHCR did not reach the same determination independently, informal consultations resolved the differences. Government officials were willing to go along with positive UNHCR decisions, so long as the asylum-seekers registered with the police and were ultimately resettled.[101] Conversely, a foreign ministry official explained, "If they [UNHCR] do not accept the claim, we accept their judgment."[102] As mentioned earlier, the Agency routinely communicated its decisions on asylum applicants to the government.

The Turkish government's continued willingness to host asylum-seekers was premised on the assumption that their residence would be temporary, pending

[98]  Kirişci 2001, 72, 82.
[99]  Ibid., 72–73, 83–85, 87.
[100] Ibid., 82–83; Latif 2002, 25–26.
[101] Kirişci 2001, 86.
[102] Qtd. in Frelick 1997, 19.

resettlement by UNHCR. That UNHCR arranged resettlement for asylum-seekers was key. According to the head of the Foreigners Department at the Ministry of Interior, "When a refugee is not granted a visa to travel to a third country, this is the point where we feel our problem. If resettlement is guaranteed, then asylum-seekers present no problem."[103] Another Ministry of Interior official described extending rights to asylum-seekers until they are resettled as "a big concession."[104]

As alluded to in the earlier discussion of discrimination, delegation patterns in Turkey have not followed a simple dichotomy aligned with the country's geographical limitation to the 1951 Refugee Convention. In other words, it is not the case that the government consistently handled European refugees while UNHCR dealt with non-Europeans. For example, UNHCR conducted status determination and managed resettlement for, technically European, refugees from the Eastern Bloc during the Cold War. Meanwhile, non-European refugees from Iraq who fled to Turkey in the late 1980s were excluded from UNHCR's aegis.

Given the pattern of state-to-state hostility as well as the lack of ethnic ties, I would expect the government to delegate to UN agencies for Iraqis in 1990–1991, Bosnians in 1992–1995, Kosovars in 1998–1999, and Eastern Bloc refugees in 1970–1990. Delegation patterns in Turkey largely match my expectations, with one exception: Turkey declining to delegate for Iraqis in 1990–1991.

The remainder of this section shows that interactions between Turkey and UNHCR were shaped by the logic outlined in chapter 2. In particular, UNHCR sought to maintain a positive relationship with Turkish authorities and tempered its behavior to avoid riling them. Even as Turkey deflected blame by pointing to UNHCR, the Agency was hamstrung by the government and its own resource constraints.

## Assuaging the Authorities

I claimed in chapter 2 that, from the perspective of policymakers in refugee-receiving countries, the disadvantages of delegating to UNHCR are few. A good relationship with authorities is essential to the Agency's continued operation in the country. As a result, UNHCR is careful not to antagonize government officials and is easy to censure. The evidence presented next demonstrates that UNHCR tailored its activities to mollify Turkish officials and was punished when it refused to yield to Turkey's demands.

---

[103] Qtd. in ibid., 11.

[104] Aydoğan Asar (Chief Superintendent, Migration and Asylum Bureau, Ministry of Interior). Personal interview by author, with translator. Ministry of Interior, Ankara, Turkey, February 23, 2012.

The UNHCR archives contain multiple examples of its efforts to please the Turkish government. For example, in 1952, a UNHCR report concluded that naturalized Bulgarian Turks no longer fell under the Agency's scope for financial assistance, an outcome with which Turkey was reportedly "not very happy." This prompted UNHCR to consider ways to "make them happier," including a private promise by the High Commissioner to raise the issue of Bulgarian Turks in the UN General Assembly.[105] If UNHCR could also initiate a $50,000 project for refugees in Turkey, that would likely be viewed by Turkish officials as "very satisfactory."[106] In 1989, Turkey called on UNHCR to cover "travel costs and living expenses" of Bulgarian Turks in transit to Turkey from third countries.[107] UNHCR agreed to contribute to "the cost of care and maintenance" as well as "travel expenses" for this group.[108]

There is also evidence that UNHCR fashioned its resettlement activities to placate Turkish authorities. Judging that a 1984 refoulement of 62 Iranians might be intended "to give HCR a lesson in order to speed up resettlement," a UNHCR official underscored that "[t]he number of resettlement opportunities *must* be increased and resettlement procedures speeded up" (emphasis in original).[109] A similar conclusion was reached by UNHCR's representative in Ankara in 1986, saying "sooner rather than later UNHCR must be in a position to get many more people of concern out of Turkey more rapidly if we are to diminish the number of people being quietly returned."[110]

At the same time, UNHCR proved sensitive to government concerns about refugee arrivals from Iraq and Iran. With respect to Iraqi Kurds in 1990, UNHCR was "anxious that resettlement programs not become [a] pull factor for those who otherwise would stay in Iraq."[111] When a group of Iraqi refugees entered

[105] Amir Abbas Hoveyda to UN High Commissioner for Refugees, 8 August 1952, "Report from Dr. Weis on the Status and Situation of Bulgarian Refugees in Turkey," *UNHCR Archives*, Fonds 11, Series 1, Box 354, 22/2 Refugees from Bulgaria in Turkey 22-2-II, Folio 15.

[106] Amir Abbas Hoveyda to M.M. Pages, 30 October 1952, "Bulgarian Refugees of Ethnic Origin," *UNHCR Archives*, Fonds 11, Series 1, Box 354, 22/2 Refugees from Bulgaria in Turkey 22-2-II, Folio 25.

[107] Ercüment Yavuzalp to Jean-Pierre Hocké, 31 May 1989, *UNHCR Archives*, Fonds 11, Series 3, 100 TUR BUL Refugee Situations—Special Groups of Refugees—Bulgaria Refugees in Turkey [Volume A], Folio 2.

[108] Jean-Pierre Hocké to Ercüment Yavuzalp, 16 June 1989, *UNHCR Archives*, Fonds 11, Series 3, 100 TUR BUL Refugee Situations—Special Groups of Refugees—Bulgaria Refugees in Turkey [Volume A], Folio 2.

[109] Michael Peterson to Michel Moussalli, 19 March 1984, "The Refugee Situation in Turkey," *UNHCR Archives*, Fonds 11, Series 2, Box 11, 10 TUR Relations with Governments—Turkey.

[110] Gary G. Troeller to Fionella Cappelli [Head, Regional Bureau for Europe and North America], 28 November 1986, "Note for the File on Meeting at Ministry of Foreign Affairs on 25 November," *UNHCR Archives*, Fonds 11, Series 3, 10 TUR External Relations—Relations with Governments—Turkey [Volume A], Folio 9.

[111] Daniel E. Conway to Waldo Villapando [UNHCR Representative in Italy], 17 December 1990, "Iraqis in Van," *UNHCR Archives*, Fonds 11, Series 3, 100 TUR IRQ Refugee Situations—Special Groups of Refugees—Refugees from Iraq in Turkey [Volume F], Folio 115.

Turkey from Iran, UNHCR advised them to "return to Iran."[112] An internal cable explains that the branch office in Turkey adopted this policy due to "the significant and increasing number of arrivals" of refugees.[113] Moreover, UNHCR officials concluded that they must establish channels in Iraq for resettling Iranian Mojahedin-e-Khalq members, which would "indicate to the Turkish authorities that UNCHR is seeking [to] solve the existing problem."[114] If these Iranians continued leaving Iraq for Turkey, "their presence would not be tolerated anymore by the [Turkish] authorities."[115]

UNHCR engaged in self-censorship to preserve its relationship with Turkish authorities as well. For instance, if the government did not want to give refugee status to Russians in 1966 and thought "the matter could be solved in a pragmatic way," then UNHCR "would certainly not insist on a clarification in principle."[116] In 1994, the branch office in Turkey revealed that it engaged in "self-censorship." Specifically, it avoided using the terms "mandate" and "refugee" in its correspondence with Turkish officials because these terms had provoked a "negative reaction." Moreover, the branch office cautioned, some refugee groups had to be dealt with "on a case-by-case basis" rather than discussed in general conversation because of the "extreme sensitivity of the Turkish authorities to them."[117]

On occasion, Turkish authorities punished the Agency when it did not behave as they desired. At one point, for instance, Turkish authorities entrusted

---

[112] Daniel E. Conway, 13 April 1990, "Information Note: Background Information Related to Humanitarian Assistance to Iraqis in Turkey Who Had Previously Achieved Protection in Iran," *UNHCR Archives*, Fonds 11, Series 3, 100 TUR IRQ Refugee Situations—Special Groups of Refugees—Refugees from Iraq in Turkey [Volume E], Folio 78.

[113] UNHCR Branch Office in Ankara, 16 April 1990, *UNHCR Archives*, Fonds 11, Series 3, 100 TUR IRQ Refugee Situations—Special Groups of Refugees—Refugees from Iraq in Turkey [Volume E], Folio 79.

[114] Kaj Impola [Assistant Protection Officer, Department of International Protection/Regional Bureau for Europe], 14 December 1992, "Meeting with RBE and SWANAME on Dissidents and Irregular Movers of 'People's Mojahedin in Iran' ex Iraq," *UNHCR Archives*, Fonds 11, Series 3, 100 TUR IRQ Refugee Situations—Special Groups of Refugees—Refugees from Iraq in Turkey [Volume H], Folio 138.

[115] John McCallin to Kamel Morjane, 16 August 1993, "Irregular Movers," *UNHCR Archives*, Fonds 11, Series 3, 100 TUR IRQ Refugee Situations—Special Groups of Refugees—Refugees from Iraq in Turkey [Volume H], Folio 138.

[116] 17 May 1966, "Note on Discussions with Mr. Idiz, Ankara, and Mr. Sirman of the Turkish Delegation in Geneva on 17 May 1966," *UNHCR Archives*, Fonds 11, Series 1, Box 348, 22/1 TUR Eligibility—Turkey, Folio 47.

[117] Lina Sultani and Patrick Tezier to Head, Desk I, Regional Bureau for Europe, 20 January 1994, *UNHCR Archives*, Fonds 11, Series 3, 10 TUR External Relations—Relations with Governments—Turkey [Volume B], Folio 51. The branch office was referring specifically to Tunisians. The original text in French reads: "Dans les relations epistolaires, la delegation éviter d'utiliser le termes de `mandat', de réfugié, ces expressions avant suscite dans le passé une réaction négative des autorités turques. On peut d'ailleurs s'interroger sur les justifications de cette `auto censure.' . . . La situation des tunisiens reconnus sous le mandat n'est pas relevé . . . Eu égard à l'extrême sensibilité des autorités turques à leur endroit, nous pensons préférable de resoudre les problemes de protection et de reinstallation cas par cas. Invoquer cette question dans un débat d'ordre général risquerait de nuire au résultat des négociations."

UNHCR with raising funds from international donors to construct housing for Iraqi Kurdish refugees. In April 1989, UNHCR told the government that donor countries were "not interested" in the project. The response from Turkish officials was withering. UNHCR was told that the authorities were "extremely disappointed" because the Agency had only offered "immaterial advice, and little in the way of financial assistance." It had "sat" on Turkey's project proposal and handled fundraising in a "very 'cavalier' manner" while "moving with glacial speed." In approaching donors, UNHCR had "tampered with the project proposal," when it had "no business" negotiating the project. The upbraiding ended with the statement that "[f]rankly speaking, the Turkish Government fails to understand what services UNHCR can and will provide to the World's unfortunates."[118] As a result, the Turkish government "at the highest level" refused to sign an agreement with the Agency.[119] Moreover, UNHCR should not expect to gain access to the camps, since "this would not in any way . . . further the cause of the Iraqis in the least."[120]

There are examples of UNHCR bowing to government pressure as well. In 1986, Turkish authorities asked UNHCR to help them get "a full picture of all who called our office, whom we recognized and whom we rejected." In exchange for the government's "good cooperation," UNHCR was expected to reciprocate by providing information on a list of names compiled by Turkish authorities.[121] Officials were not interested only in "high ranking activists or particular opposition groups," but wanted to know the status of all asylum-seekers. UNHCR's representative saw this issue as "increasingly delicate" and did not want "to suddenly look 'uncooperative.' "[122] From Geneva, headquarters confirmed that pending asylum cases and accepted refugees could be named.[123] The branch office also felt that sharing information on recognized refugees would "enhance trust" between it and Turkish officials and prevent their refoulement without notifying

---

[118] G. Walzer [UNHCR Headquarters in Geneva] and Stefan Berglund [Acting UNHCR Representative in Turkey], 21 April 1989, "Note for the File," *UNHCR Archives*, Fonds 11, Series 3, 10 TUR External Relations—Relations with Governments—Turkey [Volume A], Folio 17.

[119] G. Walzer, 22 April 1989, "Note for the File," *UNHCR Archives*, Fonds 11, Series 3, 10 TUR External Relations—Relations with Governments—Turkey [Volume A], Folio 17.

[120] Stefan Berglund to Acting Head, Regional Bureau for Europe and North America, UNHCR Headquarters in Geneva, 26 April 1989, "Telephone Conversation with Mr. Sibay," *UNHCR Archives*, Fonds 11, Series 3, 100 TUR IRQ Refugee Situations—Special Groups of Refugees—Refugees from Iraq in Turkey [Volume B], Folio 28.

[121] Gary G. Troeller, 8 July 1986, "Note for the File," *UNHCR Archives*, Fonds 11, Series 3, 10 TUR External Relations—Relations with Governments—Turkey [Volume A], Folio 3.

[122] Gary G. Troeller to Fionella Cappelli, 14 November 1986, "Information Sharing with the Authorities," *UNHCR Archives*, Fonds 11, Series 3, 10 TUR External Relations—Relations with Governments—Turkey [Volume A], Folio 8.

[123] M.H. Khan to Gary G. Troeller, 15 December 1988, "Communications to the Ministry of Interior on Persons of Concern to UNHCR," *UNHCR Archives*, Fonds 11, Series 3, 10 TUR External Relations—Relations with Governments—Turkey [Volume A].

UNHCR.[124] Information sharing in this manner had "helped rather than hurt us."[125] After all, Turkish authorities had agreed not to return recognized refugees listed by UNHCR.[126]

When Turkey adopted a new asylum regulation in 1994, this seems to have come as a surprise to the UNHCR. However, the Agency's reaction was broadly in line with its tendency to prioritize good relations with Turkey. In December 1992, following discussions on "the possibility of introducing refugee legislation," UNHCR sent the Turkish foreign ministry two drafts (one maintaining the geographical limitation and one lifting it).[127] But the final document appears to have been put together by Ministry of Interior officials in consultation with the Ministry of Foreign Affairs. There was little or no consultation with other government agencies, UNHCR, refugee-related NGOs, or legal experts.[128] This was confirmed by an interviewee at UNHCR, who explained that the Agency had been "shocked," but decided to pursue persuasion and diplomacy instead of confrontation.[129] In fact, Zieck points out that UNHCR subsequently adjusted its eligibility criteria to match the government's, applying the narrow refugee definition from the 1951 Convention, rather than the more expansive one that appears in the Agency's documentation.[130]

Several NGO personnel I interviewed faulted UNHCR for prioritizing good relations with the Turkish government over advocating for refugee protection. One interviewee described UNHCR as "very docile" because it "likes to think the process is fragile and their support is critical." Although he thought the Agency should be "vocally critical," he conceded that "when tested, the government is willing to put UNHCR in its place."[131] These views were echoed by others. An NGO worker noted that UNHCR is "reluctant" to be "more active and fight with public authorities" because they "do not want to damage relations."[132] Another

[124] Stefan Berglund [Acting UNHCR Representative in Turkey] to M.H. Khan, 26 April 1989, "Communications to the Ministry of Interior on Persons of Concern to UNHCR," *UNHCR Archives*, Fonds 11, Series 3, 10 TUR External Relations—Relations with Governments—Turkey [Volume A], Folio 17.

[125] Gary G. Troeller to M.H. Khan, 4 August 1989, "Communications to the Ministry of Interior on Persons of Concern to UNHCR," *UNHCR Archives*, Fonds 11, Series 3, 10 TUR External Relations—Relations with Governments—Turkey [Volume A], Folio 17I.

[126] Gary G. Troeller to M.H. Khan, 29 September 1989, "Communications to the Ministry of Interior on Persons of Concern to UNHCR—Refoulement Statistics," *UNHCR Archives*, Fonds 11, Series 3, 10 TUR External Relations—Relations with Governments—Turkey [Volume A], Folio 21.

[127] John McCallin to Rıza Türmen [Director General for Multilateral Political Affairs, Ministry of Foreign Affairs], 4 December 1992, *UNHCR Archives*, Fonds 11, Series 3, 10 TUR External Relations—Relations with Governments—Turkey [Volume B], Folio 51.

[128] Kirişci 2001, 83; 1996a, 301.

[129] UNHCR Turkey official. Personal interview by author. Istanbul, Turkey, February 10, 2012.

[130] Zieck 2010, 610. The convention definition hinges on persecution, while the expanded definition allows for indiscriminate threats due to generalized violence.

[131] NGO worker. Personal interview by author. Istanbul, Turkey, February 2, 2012.

[132] Elçin Türkdoğan (Refugee Project Coordinator, Human Rights Foundation of Turkey). Personal interview by author. Human Rights Foundation of Turkey Office, Ankara, Turkey, February 20, 2012.

agreed that "UNHCR is too concerned with keeping good relations with the state to properly protect refugees."[133]

These episodes show that UNHCR adapted its refugee assistance and resettlement work to please the Turkish government. It even avoided using certain terms, including "refugee," for fear of alienating government officials. When Turkey's government became unsatisfied with the Agency, it refused to cooperate with it. UNHCR found it had no choice but to bow to government pressure, including providing information on refugees to the authorities. The following discussion demonstrates that the Agency's work was further constrained by its limited influence and finances.

## Capacity Constraints and Limited Leverage

In chapter 2, I argued that delegation to UNHCR is not a costly strategy because of the Agency's limited influence and funds. The analysis presented next shows that Turkey simultaneously shifted blame to UNHCR and restricted its access and activities. UNHCR was unable to influence government policy on a range of refugee groups and proved sensitive to cost considerations.

When the Turkish government received complaints about the treatment of refugees, it often redirected these to UNHCR. In March 1972, the branch office in Ankara received a visit from a Polish diplomat. He expressed his embassy's increasing concern that "Polish nationals seeking asylum are granted refugee status in Turkey." He had initially approached the Turkish foreign ministry, since his government viewed "the decision of granting the Convention status" to Polish citizens a "geste inamical" (unfriendly gesture) on the part of Turkey. Instead, he was referred to the branch office and told that "the matter was one within the competence of the UNHCR Representative in Turkey."[134] Similarly, the Turkish interior minister responded to parliamentarians' concerns about the deportation of Iranians in 1995 by emphasizing that UNHCR had denied them refugee status.[135]

But UNHCR's limited clout is betrayed by the fact that it was at the mercy of Turkish security personnel. During a 1986 mission to Turkey's eastern provinces of Ağrı and Van, UNHCR was "prevented . . . from interviewing asylum-seekers" and "followed by up to six plain-clothes policemen on foot and in two

[133] Volkan Görendağ (Refugee Affairs Coordinator, Amnesty International). Personal interview by author, with translator. Amnesty International Office, Ankara, Turkey, February 24, 2012.
[134] UNHCR Representative in Turkey to UNHCR Headquarters in Geneva, 22 March 1972, "Polish Démarche to the BO," *UNHCR Archives*, Fonds 11, Series 2, Box 1206, 630 TUR Protection and General Legal Matters—Eligibility—Turkey, Folio 4.
[135] Turkey 1995, 94: Cilt 12, Birleşim 598.

cars." When the Agency protested this "obstruction," it was told that "some of the refugees may have been drug traffickers or terrorists and that local authorities may not have wished UNHCR to interview those people for these reasons." Additionally, the Agency was told that "the fact that refugees are coming into Turkey and contacting UNHCR is proof that border guards are doing their job" because "if border guards did not wish to allow anyone into the country, no one would enter."[136] Later, refugees would pen a letter to the UNHCR representative complaining that Turkish police were arresting refugees in front of the branch office in Ankara.[137]

Indeed, UNHCR often struggled to gain access to asylum-seekers. Following the influx of Iraqi Kurds in 1988, the branch office requested access to the areas in which they were encamped, "but our trials have so far been in vain."[138] After the Iraqi invasion of Kuwait, the government "refused" to let UNHCR visit the border area, even though the United Nations Development Programme (UNDP), the International Organization for Migration (IOM), and the World Food Program were allowed to conduct an assessment mission. UNHCR was told "we aren't admitting any refugees, so UNHCR does not need to go to the border."[139]

Eventually, it appeared that UNHCR could only gain access to the camps by registering their residents for resettlement. The government had suggested that "UNHCR's primary role should be to assist in meeting the majority wish for resettlement." The Agency would be granted "full cooperation and access" in order to carry out resettlement processing.[140] Agency staff feared, though, that "if UNHCR allows linkage of resettlement with access to the TACs," then Turkey might "transfer to UNHCR . . . total responsibility for the TAC population" along with the associated "cost implications."[141] At the same time, it was important

---

[136] F. Galindo-Velez, 21 October 1986, "Note for the File: Meeting with Mrs. Fügen Ok, Ministry of Foreign Affairs," *UNHCR Archives*, Fonds 11, Series 3, 10 TUR External Relations—Relations with Governments—Turkey [Volume A], Folio 7.

[137] The Refugees Financial and Solidarity Box to Gary G. Troller, 9 September 1988, *UNHCR Archives*, Fonds 11, Series 3, 100 TUR GEN Refugee Situations—Special Groups of Refugees—Refugees in Turkey—General, Folio 2.

[138] Stefan Berglund to Head, Desk I, Regional Bureau for Europe and North America, 1 September 1988, *UNHCR Archives*, Fonds 11, Series 3, 100 TUR Refugee Situations—Special Groups of Refugees—Refugees from Iraq in Turkey [Volume A], Folio 7.

[139] UNHCR Branch Office in Ankara, 17 September 1989, "Re Tamils from Kuwait via Iraq," *UNHCR Archives*, undated, Fonds 11, Series 3, 100 TUR LKA Refugee Situations—Special Groups of Refugees—Sri Lankan Refugees in Turkey.

[140] "Resettlement of Iraqi Refugees from 'Temporary Accommodation Centers' (TACs) in South-East Turkey," *UNHCR Archives*, Fonds 11, Series 3, 100 TUR IRQ Refugee Situations—Special Groups of Refugees—Refugees from Iraq in Turkey [Volume F], Folio 110A.

[141] Daniel E. Conway to M.H. Khan, 10 July 1990, "Resettlement of Iraqi Kurds in the TACs," *UNHCR Archives*, Fonds 11, Series 3, 100 TUR IRQ Refugee Situations—Special Groups of Refugees—Refugees from Iraq in Turkey [Volume F], Folio 102.

to "clear the air" before the Gulf crisis sparked another inflow of refugees into Turkey. Agency personnel reasoned that "UNHCR's position would be strengthened by having already reached an understanding with the Turkish authorities on the TACs problem."[142] Subsequently, UNHCR's "government-recognized activities in the TACs [were] limited to resettlement processing."[143] An internal briefing note from 1991 complained that "UNHCR has no operational role in the establishment and running of new transit centers, which are under the authority of the Ministry of Interior. UNHCR has had very little access to the refugees under Government care in the south-east."[144] Turkish officials continued to "link" access with resettlement, however, expressing "disillusion on the inadequate response received for the resettlement of . . . the Iraqi Kurds who had arrived in 1988."[145]

Though UNHCR at times attempted to influence government policy, its efforts were often met with limited success. A confidential Agency document from 1984 surmises that "[i]t does not seem possible at the moment to modify Turkish refugee policy in order that Iranian asylum-seekers may stay in Turkey on a permanent basis." Moreover, UNHCR's policy recommendation was that Iranian asylum-seekers who departed from Turkey should not be returned because "such return might jeopardize our endeavors to get Turkey to accept the presence of certain asylum-seekers on a permanent basis."[146]

With respect to a possible expulsion of Iraqi refugees in 1990, the Agency concluded "[i]t is clear that UNHCR may not be in much of a position to influence events." UNHCR's "stock" with the government was "not high."[147] And in April 1991, UNHCR suspected that the Turkish government might try to transfer UNHCR-donated supplies to Iraqi territory, in order to keep refugees from crossing the border. The Agency should not attempt to prevent this handover

---

[142] UNHCR Headquarters in Geneva, 24 October 1990, "Iraqis Kurds in Turkey: US Resettlement and Assistance," *UNHCR Archives*, Fonds 11, Series 3, 100 TUR IRQ Refugee Situations—Special Groups of Refugees—Refugees from Iraq in Turkey [Volume F], Folio 110.

[143] UNHCR Headquarters in Geneva, 28 January 1991, "Iraqi Kurds ex-TACS/Turkey," *UNHCR Archives*, Fonds 11, Series 3, 100 TUR IRQ Refugee Situations—Special Groups of Refugees— Refugees from Iraq in Turkey [Volume F], Folio 115.

[144] 5 March 1991, "Briefing Note for the HC's Meeting with the Turkish Permanent Representative," *UNHCR Archives*, Fonds 11, Series 3, 10 TUR External Relations—Relations with Governments— Turkey [Volume B], Folio 31.

[145] Dario Carminati [Deputy UNHCR Representative in Turkey], 19 March 1991, "Note for the File," *UNHCR Archives*, Fonds 11, Series 3, 10 TUR External Relations—Relations with Governments—Turkey [Volume B], Folio 31.

[146] Michael Peterson to Michel Moussalli, 19 March 1984, "The Refugee Situation in Turkey," *UNHCR Archives*, Fonds 11, Series 2, Box 11, 10 TUR Relations with Governments—Turkey.

[147] Daniel E. Conway to M.H. Khan, 19 March 1990, "Threats to Future of Iraqis in Mardin Temporary Accommodation Center, and Possibly to All Iraqis in Turkey, Follow Up Report No. 3," *UNHCR Archives*, Fonds 11, Series 3, 100 TUR IRQ Refugee Situations—Special Groups of Refugees—Refugees from Iraq in Turkey [Volume D], Folio 71.

because "we will not be able to change Turkish policy on this matter in the next 24 hours."[148]

It is clear that the Agency was constrained in its dealings with the government. When Sri Lankan Tamils fled the Iraqi invasion of Kuwait, Turkey was willing to give them transit visas. But, UNHCR's branch office cautioned, it would not be "realistic" to assume that they would be allowed to stay in Turkey temporarily. Even if they were to be recognized by UNHCR, "any attempt to achieve this is certain to be unsuccessful."[149] Moreover, the branch office feared that even opening a discussion on this topic with the government "could aggravate the situation concerning Iraqi Kurds, which is already very sensitive."[150] And regarding Turkmen from Iraq, the UNHCR representative in Turkey informed his superiors that he was "not in a position to obtain available information about this group." He suggested, instead, that UNHCR headquarters "refrain from sending requests for information about these ICs [individual cases]."[151]

As a result of these dynamics, UNHCR sometimes found itself between a rock and a hard place. For instance, the government announced that Iraqi refugees would be moved back across the border in April 1991. The UN would not be able to dictate "the location" of the refugees, but it would be made "responsible to house, feed, protect, and provide medical care" for them. UNHCR's representative was apprehensive, saying:

We are approaching a political crisis. On the one hand, UNHCR will be offered responsibility for care of a highly visible and very needy refugee population. If we refuse, we will be blamed for the deaths that will occur (many will occur if we accept in any case). On the other hand, if we accept, we accept the movement of the refugees into Iraq.[152]

Finally, financial considerations figured into UNHCR's calculations. For example, the Agency became concerned in 1990 that the government would not

[148] Daniel E. Conway to A.M. Demmer, 7 April 1991, "Gulf Emergency," *UNHCR Archives*, Fonds 11, Series 3, 10 TUR External Relations—Relations with Governments—Turkey [Volume B], Folio 34.
[149] UNHCR Branch Office in Ankara, 17 September 1989, "Re Tamils from Kuwait via Iraq," *UNHCR Archives*, Fonds 11, Series 3, 100 TUR LKA Refugee Situations—Special Groups of Refugees—Sri Lankan Refugees in Turkey.
[150] UNHCR Branch Office in Ankara, 4 September 1989, "Re Tamils in Iraq," *UNHCR Archives*, Fonds 11, Series 3, 100 TUR LKA Refugee Situations—Special Groups of Refugees—Sri Lankan Refugees in Turkey.
[151] Daniel E. Conway [Representative] to UNHCR Headquarters, 28 January 1991, "Iraqi Draft Evader/Deserters," *UNHCR Archives*, Fonds 11, Series 3, 100 TUR IRQ Refugee Situations—Special Groups of Refugees—Refugees from Iraq in Turkey [Volume F], Folio 115.
[152] Daniel E. Conway [Representative], 11 April 1991, "Gulf Emergency," *UNHCR Archives*, Fonds 11, Series 3, 10 TUR External Relations—Relations with Governments—Turkey [Volume B], Folio 34.

allow UNHCR involvement in status determination for Eastern Europeans. This situation left the Agency "unaware of the criteria applied or procedures utilized by the Turkish authorities." That resettlement opportunities for Eastern Europeans were drying up was "cause for concern" for the Agency, because it might "find itself in the position of assisting persons for very long or even indefinite periods who were declared refugees by the Turkish authorities." The "cost implications" were clear.[153]

This evidence establishes that Turkish officials deflected responsibility to UNHCR even while Turkish security personnel circumscribed its activities. UNHCR was denied access to the Iraqi Kurdish refugees who entered Turkey in 1988 and subsequently instructed to focus on processing them for resettlement. In internal communications, Agency personnel matter-of-factly noted their helplessness in influencing government policy on Iranians and Iraqis, the futility of their advocating on behalf of Sri Lankan Tamils, and their inability to even gather information on Iraqi Turkmens in Turkey. UNHCR faced *faits accomplis* multiple times and, throughout, displayed a wariness of confronting the Turkish authorities alongside a concern with being saddled with untenable costs.

## Summary of Findings

Having analyzed the patterns of discrimination and delegation in Turkey, I focus in this section on the implications for my argument. First, I summarize the findings presented earlier. Then, I evaluate whether they align with my theoretical expectations. Overall, discrimination and delegation trends in Turkey are broadly consistent with my argument. Even though most scholars have emphasized a dichotomy between European refugees and non-European asylum-seekers, my analysis demonstrates that Turkish asylum policies are far more nuanced.

The earlier discussion demonstrated clear differences in treatment across refugee groups. This observation has not escaped the attention of domestic political actors in Turkey. In a parliamentary debate in 1992, Şevket Kazan (Refah Partisi-Kocaeli) noted that the government's policy toward refugees from Iraq and Iran had been different from its policy toward refugees from Bulgaria. While many Bulgarians were granted citizenship and remained in Turkey, the vast majority of Iraqis had been repatriated.[154]

Indeed, when hundreds of thousands of ethnic Turks crossed the border in 1989 to flee Bulgaria's assimilation campaign, Turkey responded by opening its

[153] Daniel E. Conway to Fionella Cappelli, 26 June 1990, "Need for Comprehensive Policy Concerning Eastern Europeans," *UNHCR Archives*, Fonds 11, Series 3, 100 TUR GEN Refugee Situations—Special Groups of Refugees—Refugees in Turkey—General, Folio 9.
[154] Turkey 1992, 9: Cilt, 63, Birleşim, 76.

border to them. Legislation was passed to designate them as immigrants under the 1934 Law on Settlement. Accordingly, they received state sponsorship and assistance, including access to government-funded housing and employment. In addition, they were able to apply for Turkish citizenship. While many of these refugees returned to Bulgaria after its regime change the following year, about half were naturalized and remained in Turkey. In all, this group experienced the most inclusive asylum policy relative to other refugee groups.

In contrast, Turkey sought to encamp and repatriate the mass influx of Kurds from Iraq in 1988 and 1991. In 1988, the government restricted Iraqi Kurds to camps in southeastern Turkey. In lieu of granting them refugee status, they were designated as temporary guests. The country was unable to enforce a border closure policy in the face of an inflow of hundreds of thousands in 1991. Still, the government successfully advocated for the creation of a "security zone" in northern Iraq and, through Operation Provide Comfort, was able to repatriate the vast majority of Kurds who had fled to Turkey in both waves.

It is worth noting that these refugee flows happened within a fairly short time frame. Bulgarian refugees arrived in Turkey in 1989 and Iraqis in 1988 and 1991. Even within the span of a few years, the government varied its treatment of these refugee groups considerably. The hundreds of thousands of Bulgarian refugees received far more inclusive treatment, with the government adopting a range of measures to ensure their easy and quick integration. Not only were they fleeing a hostile regime, but they were ethnic Turks who could quickly become voting citizens. The government's response to Iraqi refugees, though the size of that flow was comparable, was markedly different. Turkish policymakers were not predisposed to grant Iraqi Kurds a warm welcome, particularly in light of security concerns involving Turkey's own Kurdish minority. It is possible that this group of refugees was singled out because they share an affinity with an excluded minority in Turkey. At any rate, and in contrast to the assistance and privileges granted to Bulgarian refugees, Iraqi refugees were restricted to camps and quickly repatriated. Even UNHCR observed that "Turkey offers few possibilities for local integration of refugees, with the notable exception of ethnic Turks from Asian and European countries."[155] In short, the treatment of Iraqi refugees was strikingly different from that of Bulgarian Turks.

Turkey's relationship with Iran appears to have directly shaped the experience of Iranian refugees in Turkey. Iranians were initially able to enter Turkey and reside there temporarily until they could move on, but were discouraged from applying for asylum. As security cooperation between Iran and Turkey

---

[155] 5 March 1991, "Briefing Note for the HC's Meeting with the Turkish Permanent Representative," *UNHCR Archives*, Fonds 11, Series 3, 10 TUR External Relations—Relations with Governments—Turkey [Volume B], Folio 31.

increased, arrests and deportations also increased. This security cooperation be-tween the two countries seems to have involved the reciprocal exchange of dis-sidents as well. Iranian asylum-seekers found themselves escorted to the Iranian embassy by the Turkish police. Agents of the Iranian government also appeared to be active on Turkish territory, abducting and killing dissidents.

Meanwhile, Bosnian and Kosovar refugees were designated as guests. However, they faced no difficulty entering the country in 1992 and 1998, respec-tively. They were permitted to reside in urban areas and could access Turkish schools and hospitals. The majority of these refugees returned home, or were resettled elsewhere.

Turkey's allegiances during and after the Cold War likely influenced its re-sponse to Eastern Bloc and Chechen refugees. The small number of individuals fleeing Eastern Europe and the Soviet Union for Turkey during the Cold War were granted refugee status under the 1951 Convention, and international or-ganizations met the costs associated with hosting them. The majority of these refugees were resettled, and few remained in Turkey permanently. This posi-tion was in line with Turkey's alignment with NATO and the West. After the end of the Cold War, and as relations with Russia became cordial, Chechens were refused refugee status. In some cases, the country refused admission to Chechens appearing at the border. In other cases, the government refused to accept their asylum applications. Instead, they were designated as guests and allowed to remain in the country temporarily. UNHCR and NGOs were forbidden from assisting Chechens, who also occasionally experienced detention. As detailed earlier, interviewees from NGOs as well as from within the Turkish government have attributed this pattern to Turkey's desire to avoid antagonizing Russia.

With regard to UNHCR, the Turkish government was selective as to when and where it would be involved in refugee affairs. For example, the Agency was in charge of status determination and resettlement for Eastern Bloc refu-gees. However, the government distanced UNHCR from Chechens. Moreover, the government sometimes maintained a good relationship with UNHCR and at other times ignored its determinations by deporting recognized refugees. As mentioned earlier, though the 1994 Asylum Regulation created a "parallel track" system of government and UNHCR status determination procedures, the gov-ernment often informally coordinated its decisions with the Agency. Finally, there is evidence that UNHCR carefully moderated its language and behavior and even narrowed its eligibility criteria in order to maintain good relations with the government. Turkish officials simultaneously deflected blame to UNHCR and circumscribed its access to refugees, and the Agency proved keenly aware of its limited ability to influence government policy.

Table 5.1 summarizes Turkey's asylum policy by group, with those groups and time periods that match my theoretical predictions marked in bold. My

Table 5.1 Predicted asylum policies in Turkey

| | | Sending Country Relations | |
| --- | --- | --- | --- |
| | | Hostile | Friendly |
| *Affinity with Refugee Group* | Co-Ethnic | Inclusive (Bul 1989–1990) | Delegation |
| | No Ethnic Tie | Delegation (Irq 1990–1991) (EB 1970–1990) (Bos 1992–1995) (Kos 1998–1999) | Restrictive (Irq 1988–1989) (Irn 1979–2010) (FSU 1999–2010) |

Note: EB=Eastern Bloc; FSU=Former Soviet Union

argument predicts inclusiveness and restrictiveness accurately, with only one exception (Iraqis in 1990–1991). Moreover, Turkey delegated to the UN for Iranian refugees in 1979–2010 and did not delegate for Iraqi refugees in 1990–1991. For Bosnian and Kosovar refugees, UNHCR was involved in assistance, if not in status determination.

This discussion also allows a comparison of refugee groups' treatment relative to each other. Iraqis, Iranians, and refugees from the former Soviet Union received the most restrictive treatment. Turkey initially attempted to stop Iraqis from entering the country and repatriated them at the earliest opportunity. Iranians experienced detentions and deportations, and were pursued by agents of their home government in Turkey. And Chechens were denied refugee status and could not receive assistance from UNHCR or NGOs. I place Eastern Bloc refugees and Bosnians/Kosovars in the intermediate category. Asylum-seekers from the Eastern Bloc received refugee status, but the government had no interest in integrating them as it did the Bulgarian Turks. Bosnians and Kosovars, though not given refugee status, were able to enter the country and access social services until they repatriated.

In Turkey's case, in contrast with Egypt, there are several instances where bilateral relations were shaped by events that also produced a refugee flow. For example, Bulgaria's treatment of its ethnic Turkish minority both soured relations with Turkey and sparked the flow of Bulgarian Turk refugees. Similarly, the 1990–1991 Gulf War, the Bosnian War, and the Kosovo War generated refugee flows into Turkey, and concurrently triggered a shift in Turkish relations with Iraq and Yugoslavia. However, it is important to note that in none of these cases did sending country relations change because of the refugee flow itself or because of Turkey's response to that flow. In other words, it is true that Bulgaria's assimilation policies resulted in hostile bilateral relations as well as a flow of refugees into Turkey. However, this hostility cannot be attributed to the flow of refugees from Bulgaria nor to the quality of their reception by Turkey. In short, sending country relations influenced refugee policies and not vice versa.

It also appears that the Turkish government's distrust of Turkish Kurds may have shaped its response to ethnic Kurds from Iraq. In both 1988 and 1991, Turkish officials hesitated to admit large numbers of Iraqi Kurds, at least in part due to concerns about Kurdish separatism. Moreover, Iraqi Kurds may have been restricted to closely monitored camps in order to prevent contact between these refugees and the PKK. These dynamics might explain why there was no shift in asylum policy in 1990 to coincide with the change in Iraqi-Turkish relations.

To summarize, this chapter's analysis reveals how Turkey's asylum policies were shaped by foreign policy and ethnic politics. By and large, the findings about discrimination and delegation are in line with my argument. In the following section, I explore possible alternative explanations, such as economic considerations, security concerns, and humanitarianism, that might account for asylum policy in Turkey.

## Alternative Explanations

Of the alternative explanations that I have drawn from the literature on refugees, only national security calculations appear to have played a role in shaping Turkey's asylum policy. First, it is important to stress that Turkey's policies toward the different refugee groups discussed earlier appear to be systematic and deliberate. Moreover, pivotal decisions appear to be taken at the top, in some cases by the prime minister or cabinet officials.

Economic explanations do not adequately account for the patterns in Turkish asylum policies. Shifts in policy do not seem to match changes in economic performance. Between 1970 and 2010, Turkey's real GDP per capita grew from about US$4,300 to over US$10,400.[156] In fact, Turkey is considered one of the fastest growing economies in the world. However, I do not observe uniformly more inclusive policies over time.

Resource constraints are not a compelling explanation, moreover, even when Turkey was faced with large refugee flows. The government was willing to expend significant resources in order to integrate hundreds of thousands of Bulgarian refugees, for example. International assistance, which the government did not seek, did not underlie this response. There is also no evidence that factors related to the "desirability" of refugees' labor skills were part of Turkish officials' calculus.

---

[156] GDP per capita is reported at 2005 constant prices. Heston, Summers, and Aten 2012.

On the other hand, national security considerations likely played a role in shaping Turkey's responses to Iraqi Kurds. The country's refusal to integrate Iraqi Kurds appears to have been linked to concerns related to Kurdish separatism. Turkish government officials were concerned about possible contact between the PKK and Iraqi Kurdish refugees. It is worth noting that the Iraqi Kurds' identity as ethnic others was a crucial part of these fears. At the same time, security concerns cannot explain differences in the treatment of other refugee groups.

Still, as the comparison between Bulgarian Turks and Iraqi Kurds demonstrates, large refugee movements did not automatically generate a restrictive response by Turkish authorities. Rather, foreign policy and ethnic identity account for Turkey's welcoming response to Bulgarian Turks and its inimical response to Iraqi Kurds. In addition, there was no evidence that Turkey was strategically fashioning its asylum policies in line with the behavior of other receiving countries in the region.

Moreover, Turkey was a multiparty democracy throughout the period under study. The Turkish military intervened in Turkish politics multiple times, including via coups d'etat in 1960, 1971, and 1980. However, none of these episodes marked a reversal in Turkish asylum policies. Turkey's patterns of discrimination and delegation, as well as its at times turbulent relationship with UNHCR, belie the influence of path dependence.

There is also no evidence that policies were shaped by humanitarian concerns, the cause of refugee flows, or the conditions of refugees. For example, both the Bulgarian Turks and the Iraqi Kurds were minorities fleeing repression. Still, differences in the government's treatment of each group were stark. Neither does the compassion fatigue argument hold up, since not all groups received an initial welcome that gradually wore off.

Finally, regional considerations are often invoked to explain Turkey's asylum policy, particularly the country's repeated efforts to accede to the European Union (EU). In 2001, the EU adopted an Accession Partnership Document that set out reforms for Turkey to undertake, and which included a discussion of Turkey's legislation on asylum. That same year, Turkey issued the National Program for the Adoption of the European Union Acquis, which also addressed forced migration.[157] However, this harmonization process cannot explain the variation in policies across refugee groups described in this chapter. For instance, it does not appear to be linked to improved treatment for Chechen and Iranian refugees over time. While it is likely that these factors influenced the drafting

---

[157] Turkish Ministry for EU Affairs 2001. In addition, since the year 2000, the European Court of Human Rights has issued a number of judgments against Turkey, relating to its treatment of non-European asylum-seekers. These cases included: Jabari v. Turkey (2000), D. and others v. Turkey (2006), Abdolkhani and Karimnia v. Turkey (2009), Z.N.S. v. Turkey (2010), Charahili v. Turkey (2010), Keshmiri v. Turkey (2010), and Tehrani and others v. Turkey (2010). Zieck 2010, 601–02.

and passing of a new asylum law in 2013 as well as the EU-Turkey agreement regarding Syrian refugees in 2016, they do not apply to much of the period under study in this chapter. Thus, with the partial exception of national security considerations, these alternative explanations cannot fully explain the patterns and shifts in Turkey's asylum policy.

## Conclusion

The most common explanation for Turkey's asylum policies is the country's geographical limitation, whereby it only grants Europeans refugee status. Accordingly, most studies have contrasted Turkey's treatment of European asylum-seekers and refugees with its responses to non-Europeans. However, the analysis in this chapter demonstrates that the variation in Turkey's group-specific asylum policies does not fit neatly within a European/non-European dichotomy. For instance, Bulgarians, Chechens, and Bosnians/Kosovars should all be considered "European" under the 1951 Refugee Convention. However, there is significant variation in treatment between these different refugee groups.

Much of the variation in Turkey's asylum policies is explained by the combined influence of foreign policy and ethnic politics. These factors explain the country's inclusiveness and restrictiveness in the face of certain refugee groups, as well as decisions to shift responsibility to the UN. At the same time, alternative explanations related to material, humanitarian, or other concerns do not fully and persuasively explain the variation in this case.

The ongoing Syrian crisis is unprecedented for Turkey in terms of the sheer size of the displaced population. Thus far, Turkey has admitted 3.6 million Syrian refugees and allowed the vast majority to reside outside camps, even while limiting UNHCR involvement. Syrian refugees in Turkey have some access to social services, and a small number have even been granted Turkish citizenship. Recent scholarship suggests that Turkey's inclusive treatment of Syrian refugees has been shaped by its anti-Assad stance, as well as the ruling Justice and Development Party's (AKP) affinity with the predominantly Sunni Muslim Syrians. Meanwhile, the government's persecution of Turkey's own ethnic Kurdish minority is linked with the singling out of ethnic Kurdish refugees from Syria for harsher treatment.[158] Despite significant legal developments in the country, and particularly the formalization of a temporary protection regime, Turkey's policymaking toward Syrian refugees continues to be shaped by foreign policy and ethnic politics.

[158] Abdelaaty 2019; Bélanger and Saraçoğlu 2019; Saraçoğlu and Demirkol 2015; Polat 2018.

Turkey stands apart from most other countries in that it has been on the receiving end of several large refugee inflows and in that it maintains a geographical limitation to the 1951 Refugee Convention. Still, and similar to a more typical refugee recipient like Egypt, its patterns of discrimination and delegation are largely in line with the argument I outlined in chapter 2. The next chapter moves the analysis to Kenya. There, I delve into within-country dynamics by examining parliamentary debates to demonstrate that asylum policy is indeed shaped by competing demands voiced by parliamentarians and diplomats.

# 6

# Refugee Debates in Kenya

Kenya is often considered a crucial case in the field of refugee studies. In 2019, the country hosted one of the world's largest refugee populations, at over 400,000 refugees.[1] It was home to one of the biggest refugee camps in the world. And third-generation refugees from Somalia resided in its nearly 30-year-old Dadaab refugee complex. For these reasons, it is valuable to verify that my arguments regarding discrimination and delegation hold for this important case.

Most studies on refugees in Kenya begin with the assertion that the country had a liberal asylum regime throughout the 1960s, 1970s, and 1980s. Ethiopian, Rwandan, Sudanese, and Ugandan refugees could move freely, access social services, and even integrate if they so chose. These accounts then note that there was a sharp reversal in the early 1990s, with the sudden influx of hundreds of thousands of Somali refugees. The government suspended its status determination procedures, adopted an unofficial "encampment" policy, and handed over all refugee affairs to UNHCR. Observers have suggested many reasons for this shift, including the magnitude of the refugee flow, the drying up of international aid, Kenya's democratization process, and the economic pressures associated with structural adjustment.

What these existing accounts mask is the disparity in treatment across refugee groups, whether they arrived before or after 1991. In this chapter, I compare Kenya's responses toward major refugee groups and examine the government's relationship with UNHCR from the country's independence until the 2010 constitutional reform. To do so, I present evidence from archival sources containing correspondence between UNHCR officials in Kenya and the Agency's headquarters in Geneva. I also draw on interviews at a number of refugee-related NGOs.

Where the previous two chapters analyzed discrimination and delegation, this chapter goes a step further by also examining within-country mechanisms suggested by my argument. Specifically, I focus on two sets of domestic actors in Kenya with divergent incentives: legislators and diplomats. While parliamentarians who represent domestic constituencies are most concerned about ethnic affinity with refugees, members of the foreign policy establishment are more attune to relations with the refugee-sending country. Here, I rely on qualitative data analysis of Kenyan parliamentary proceedings. My dataset includes every

---

[1] UNHCR 2020.

*Discrimination and Delegation*. Lamis Elmy Abdelaaty, Oxford University Press (2021). © Oxford University Press.
DOI: 10.1093/oso/9780197530061.003.0006

mention of the keywords refugee, asylum, and the Swahili verb root -*kimbi*- (to run or escape) in the proceedings of the Kenyan parliament between 1963 and 2010.

This chapter proceeds in six sections. The first focuses on discrimination and chronicles Kenya's policy responses to different refugee groups over time. The second section examines delegation, describing the government's interactions with UNHCR. The third section then shifts to within-country dynamics by analyzing parliamentary statements made by Kenyan legislators and foreign policy personnel. The next section summarizes my findings and gauges whether they fit my theoretical expectations. The fifth section considers alternative explanations before the sixth and final section concludes.

## Discrimination

The common narrative about Kenya's refugee policies is that the country moved abruptly from hospitality to hostility in 1991 in response to massive refugee influxes from Sudan, Ethiopia, and especially Somalia. According to this account, the country had long been welcoming toward the relatively small number of refugees who fled to it. Kenya's attitude was essentially laissez-faire, in that there was no national refugee legislation, but refugees faced few obstacles to local integration. They were permitted to access social services, enter the labor market, open businesses, and reside wherever they wished. However, this common narrative continues, the mass influxes of the early 1990s brought with them political, economic, social, and environmental problems. Refugees were detained and forcibly deported. High-level officials began to link refugees with crime, terrorism, and arms trafficking.[2]

One version of this account asserts that the government was more accommodating toward the first wave of refugees in Nairobi and Mombasa because these were largely urban businesspeople, intellectuals, and professionals. While subsequent waves of refugees (poorer and rural) were restricted to camps, the authorities had seen fit to close their eyes and reap the economic benefits of allowing educated and skilled refugees to participate in the urban economy.[3]

Accordingly, some authors distinguish between two "classes" of refugees. On the one hand, there are refugees who had been recognized by the government before 1991, called convention refugees. On the other hand there are mandate refugees whether they underwent individual RSD or were recognized on a prima facie basis after 1991. There are a number of differences in treatment between

---

[2]  Mogire 2009, 16–17; Veney 2007, 93–94; Verdirame 1999, 57; Milner 2009, 86.
[3]  Kagwanja 1998, 53; Veney 2007, 132–33; Pérouse de Montclos 1998b, 9.

pre- and post-1991 refugees. In contrast with mandate refugees, convention refugees may reside wherever they wish and some have even been naturalized.[4]

These broad-brush accounts are belied by evidence from the UNHCR archives, however. In 1970, less than a thousand refugees were living in Kenya, according to the Agency's statistics. Still, a foreign ministry official said the country was "in a difficult position." It could not host "a considerable number" because there were insufficient jobs and no land for establishing settlements. He was concerned that "too favorable treatment" would lead to an influx of refugees.[5] This evidence casts doubt on the portrayal of pre-1990s Kenya as a welcoming destination for refugees.

The remainder of this section demonstrates that Kenya's responses to refugee groups were far more nuanced than the common narrative suggests. In it, I provide some background information before discussing five refugee groups: Somalis, Sudanese, Ethiopians, Ugandans, and Rwandans. Kenya's policies were not uniformly inclusive prior to 1990, nor were they restrictive across the board after that year. Rather, the variation in Kenya's treatment of different refugee groups lines up more closely with bilateral relations and ethnic affinity.

## Context

Kenya has ratified the 1951 Refugee Convention, its 1967 Protocol, and the 1969 OAU Convention. The problem, as Hyndman and Nylund note, "is the deficiency in the implementation of the international treaties . . . on a domestic level."[6] Indeed, until 2006 (when a Refugee Act was passed), Kenya lacked national legislation governing refugees. Instead, refugees were regulated by general provisions on immigration and non-citizens, like the Immigration Act (cap. 172) and the Aliens Restrictions Act (cap. 173).[7]

Despite the apparent lack of domestic legislation, Kenyan government officials long asserted that refugee affairs were carefully regulated. As the deputy secretary of the Ministry of Home Affairs, Heritage, and Sports explained: the lack of a "written refugee policy per se . . . does not mean that refugee issues are not coordinated. The ad hoc policy on refugee affairs adopted by the Government is managed by an elaborate administrative mechanism."[8]

---

[4] Verdirame and Harrell-Bond 2005, 216; RCK 2012, 20; Moret, Baglioni, and Efionayi-Mäder 2006, 38; UNHCR 2005, 8.

[5] Carsten Brink-Peterson [UNHCR Representative in Kenya], 13 March 1970, "Note for the File: Discussions with Mr. Gachui, Ministry of Foreign Affairs on 12 March 1970," *UNHCR Archives*, Fonds 11, Series 2, Box 400, 203 KEN Privileges, Immunities, and Accreditations—Kenya, Folio 10A.

[6] Hyndman and Nylund 1998, 29.

[7] International Commission of Jurists (Kenya Section) 1998, 16.

[8] Lomongin 2001, 1.

National refugee legislation was drafted in the 1980s in what was, according to one interviewee, a response to the Ugandan influx.[9] However, by June 1989, the permanent secretary of foreign affairs was acknowledging that "the political atmosphere" might delay submitting a finalized draft of the legislation to parliament.[10] In 1992, the under-secretary from the refugee secretariat in the Office of the President said that it would soon be brought before parliament. This did not occur, however, perhaps because policymakers wanted to maintain flexibility in dealing with refugees. A 2006 Refugee Act and a set of accompanying regulations issued in 2009 seemed to signal a shift in responsibility for refugee affairs, but these were not fully implemented. By 2010, the passing of a new constitution had prompted the drafting of a new Refugees Bill.[11]

Though Kenya has received refugees since its independence in 1963, these were generally few in number and only exceeded 10,000 in 1987. In the early 1990s, with increasing flows of Somalis and Sudanese, Kenya's refugee population jumped from about 14,000 in 1990 to over 400,000 in 1992. At the end of 2010, Kenya hosted 402,900 refugees, making it the sixth largest refugee-hosting country in the world. Somalis represented the largest share at 87%, followed by Sudanese and Ethiopian refugees at 5% each.[12]

Before the early 1990s, there were no camps in Kenya and refugees often self-settled in urban areas. Asylum-seekers whose applications were being processed had the option of residing at the Thika Reception Center. With the mass influx in the early 1990s, however, the population of the Thika Reception Center grew to 8,000, though it had been originally set up for 350 asylum-seekers. President Daniel arap Moi requested UNHCR's assistance and refugee camps were built.[13]

Starting in 1991, camps were established for Somalis and Ethiopians in the North Eastern Province (Liboi, Mandera, Banissa, El-Wak) and Coast Province (Utange, Marafa, St. Annes, Hatimy, Jomvu). Ifo also opened in 1991, followed by Dagahaley and Hagadera in 1992 (together, the three comprise the Dadaab complex). Kakuma, located in Turkana district, was set up in 1992 to receive unaccompanied minors from Sudan.[14]

[9] NGO worker. Personal interview by author. Nairobi, Kenya, May 4, 2012.

[10] Ernest Chipman [Head, Desk V, Regional Bureau for Africa] to C. Kpénou [Head, Regional Bureau for Africa], 1 June 1989, "DHC's Mission to Kenya: 16–17 May 1989," *UNHCR Archives*, Fonds 11, Series 3, 10 KEN External Relations—Relations with Governments—Kenya [Volume A], Folio 4.

[11] Sakataka 1992, 1; Milner 2009, 89; Verdirame 1999, 56; Mogire 2009, 20; Kenya 2009; Lindley 2011, 21.

[12] UNHCR n.d; UNHCR 2011c.

[13] Campbell, Crisp, and Kiragu 2011, 5; Verdirame and Harrell-Bond 2005, 31; Veney 2007, 95, 97–98.

[14] Campbell, Crisp, and Kiragu 2011, 5; Veney 2007, 95, 97–98; Verdirame and Harrell-Bond 2005, 31, 33; Milner 2009, 86.

Within a few years, the Kenyan government began closing a number of refugee camps in the North Eastern Province (NEP), Coast Province, and Central Province. Liboi was closed in 1994 and its mainly Somali and Ethiopian inhabitants moved to Dadaab. The Thika Reception Center was closed the followed year, and residents transferred to border camps. By 1998, all urban camps had been closed, and remaining refugees had been relocated to Kakuma or Dadaab.[15]

As a matter of official policy, Kenya became a "transit country" in the early 1990s. Refugees were hosted on a temporary basis: they could reside in a camp and receive UNHCR assistance until they were repatriated back home or resettled to another country. For recognized refugees, getting Kenyan citizenship was almost impossible. Although the constitution allowed for the naturalization of long-standing residents who could speak Swahili and were economically self-reliant, it also required that individuals have entered Kenya legally. Offering citizenship to refugees remained out of the question, not only because of their sheer number, but also because the majority of them were from Somalia.[16]

In practice, and despite Kenya's self-designation as a transit country, the majority of refugees tended to stay in Kenya rather than relocate to a third country or return home. Although Kenya was the target of the largest refugee resettlement program out of Africa, at its peak this only amounted to 5,000 refugees on average per year.[17] Repatriation programs for Somali refugees, though in some cases returning tens of thousands, also had a small effect compared to the sheer size of that refugee population.

The analysis that follows covers five of Kenya's major refugee groups in turn: Somalis, Sudanese, Ethiopians, Ugandans, and Rwandans. According to the argument I presented in chapter 2, differences in treatment between these refugee groups should match relations with the sending country and ethnic affinity. In addition, changes in treatment over time should coincide with shifts in relations with the sending country.

## Somalis

The armed rebellion in Somalia generated a flow of refugees into Kenya starting in 1988, but it was only around the fall of Siad Barre in 1991 that hundreds of thousands began crossing the border. Somalia's renunciation of its irredentist project in Kenya had enabled the two countries to build friendly ties over time.

[15] Veney 2007, 97–08, 100, 09, 72; Kagwanja and Juma 2008, 224.
[16] Campbell, Crisp, and Kiragu 2011, 40; Lindley 2011, 36; Verdirame 1999, 58; Pavanello, Elhawary, and Pantuliano 2010, 28.
[17] Milner 2009, 39.

However, the fall of the Barre regime and the outbreak of civil war in Somalia left that country without a functioning central government. The majority of refugees were ethnically Somali and Somali Bantu. Meanwhile, the Kenyan ruling elite was Kikuyu under presidents Jomo Kenyatta (1964–1978) and Mwai Kibaki (2003–2010) and Kalenjin under Moi (1979–2002). In other words, the refugees fleeing Somalia did not share an affinity with the dominant ethnic group in Kenya.[18]

Given the argument laid out in chapter 2, I would expect Somali refugees to experience especially restrictive treatment when they fled the friendly Barre regime. In the post-1991 period, and in the absence of a functioning government in Somalia, I expect that the lack of an ethnic tie alone will result in restrictive policies toward Somali refugees. The evidence presented here indicates that Kenya only opened its border to Somali refugees after Barre's government collapsed. Thereafter, Somali refugees were encamped in harsh conditions and subjected to expulsions. Similar to ethnic Kurds in Turkey, ethnic Somalis in Kenya have long experienced discrimination. It seems certain that Kenya's exclusionary approach to Kenyan Somalis shaped its responses to Somali refugees as well.

From 1988 and up until the fall of the Barre regime, Kenya attempted to prevent the flow of Somali refugees. The government maintained a large presence at the border and off the coast, forcibly pushing back thousands of refugees. Somali refugees were not allowed to disembark, even as their boats capsized. Refugees who had established makeshift camps in the NEP were forced across the border, and thousands of refugees remained in no man's land. Africa Watch described incidents where refugees were arrested, interrogated, beaten, starved, or handed to Somali forces. In April and July 1989, some 5,000 Somalis who were suspected of supporting Somali Patriotic Movement guerillas were arrested. In November, a group of 3,000 refugees were forced across the border by the Kenyan military at gunpoint after high-level Somali officials visited Nairobi and the border area. Sixty of these were delivered to Somali authorities, and 18 were executed immediately.[19]

Cooperative relations with Somalia seem to have shaped Kenya's decision to block these refugees and deny them access to humanitarian assistance. In exchange for sending back Somali refugees, Kenya was reportedly to receive policing rights extending to Dobley in Somalia and the ability to inspect Somali military hardware. Only former government and military officials allied with Barre were granted entry. They flew into the country and booked themselves into Nairobi hotels. Meanwhile, humanitarian agencies were barred from assisting

---

[18] Tóth 2011; Chau 2010.
[19] Milner 2009, 84, 86; Veney 2007, 94, 95, 170; Africa Watch 1991, 343, 45–46, 50, 52; Pérouse de Montclos 1998a, 157.

ordinary Somalis.[20] The government did not want UNHCR to visit them and "risk having the Office declare them as refugee[s]."[21]

Publicly, Kenya even denied that the Somalis were refugees on some occasions. A press statement issued by the Kenyan government described a group that had "crossed temporarily" and claimed they themselves "did not wish to be considered as refugees." As "pastoralists who periodically move from [one] place to the other in search of pasture for their animals," most had "been able to return to Somalia." The press statement emphasized that Kenyan and Somali authorities were "in touch" regarding this group.[22]

That Kenya initially prevented Somali refugees from entering is very likely connected to Moi's good relations with Barre. According to Human Rights Watch, the two governments had a long-standing agreement to cooperate against opposition factions in the border zone. Forces who attempted to use Kenyan territory to launch guerrilla attacks in southern Somalia were repelled. Back in 1989, the Kenyan chief of defense staff had assured the Barre government that Ogadeni refugees (from the ethnically Somali region of Ethiopia) would not be permitted to remain in Kenya. Only after the Barre regime collapsed did Moi bend to international pressure and open the border. Even then, Kenya allowed its territory to be used to supply arms and other *matériel* to the ex-dictator's militias.[23]

Once the Barre regime fell in early 1991, President Moi opened the borders, although the number of refugees seeking entry had risen substantially by this point.[24] The Kenyan government would not recognize Somalis as "full status" refugees, however, calling them "asylum-seekers" instead. In internal documents, UNHCR reasoned that Somalis had long moved in and out of Kenya. While they might return to Somalia despite its instability, officials feared that recognizing them as refugees would "tie them down" in Kenya.[25]

Having admitted them, the Kenyan government decided to confine Somali refugees to under-resourced and insecure camps located in the country's

[20]  Africa Watch 1991, 343, 50, 52; Pérouse de Montclos 1998a, 157; Veney 2007, 95; Kagwanja and Juma 2008, 219–20.

[21]  Ernest Chipman to C. Kpénou [Head, Regional Bureau for Africa], 1 June 1989, "DHC's Mission to Kenya: 16–17 May 1989," *UNHCR Archives*, Fonds 11, Series 3, 10 KEN External Relations—Relations with Governments—Kenya [Volume A], Folio 4.

[22]  Thomas A. Ogada [Representative, Mission of the Republic of Kenya to the United Nations] to UNHCR Headquarters in Geneva, 6 November 1989, "Press Statement by the Ministry of Foreign Affairs and International Co-operation on the Alleged Somali Refugees at Liboi," *UNHCR Archives*, Fonds 11, Series 3, 100 KEN SOM Refugee Situations—Special Groups of Refugees—Somalian Refugees in Kenya [Volume A], Folio 1.

[23]  Tóth 2011, 184, fn. 8; Human Rights Watch 1990, 1; Lawyers Committee for Human Rights 1995, 65.

[24]  Milner 2009, 84, 86, 104.

[25]  Sylvester Awuye [UNHCR Representative to Kenya] to Peter Meijer [Head, Desk II, Regional Bureau for Africa, UNHCR Headquarters in Geneva], 30 October 1991, "Mr. Ronald Ward of the Baptist of Canada's Mission Report," *UNHCR Archives*, Fonds 11, Series 3, 100 KEN GEN Refugee Situations—Special Groups of Refugees—Refugees in Kenya [Volume A], Folio 14.

periphery. The government had initially established camps for Somalis (some-times called "Africa's first boat people") surrounding Mombasa and nearby Malindi, at Utange, Marafa, St. Annes, Hatimy, Jomvu, and Swaleh Nguru. Many were forced into these camps in Coast Province, while others were able to self-settle. As described in more detail below, these coastal camps were closed in the 1990s and their populations transferred elsewhere. In the NEP, three camps were established for Somalis in Dadaab (Ifo in 1991 and Hagadera and Dagahaley in 1992). These camps are located less than 100 kilometers from the border with Somalia, and their location in the NEP is telling. The NEP is a marginalized prov-ince in which the central government has invested little for economic develop-ment and growth. In 1992, UNHCR and Kenyan officials reportedly withheld assistance to two camps in the northeast to force Somali refugees residing there to move to Dadaab.[26] Within Dadaab, moreover, budgetary restrictions often limited food rations resulting in rising malnutrition rates. An evaluation by Médecins Sans Frontières wondered whether there was a deliberate strategy to "starve the refugee back to Somalia."[27]

Once in Dadaab, it was very difficult for refugees to leave. Movement passes authorized traveling for certain reasons like pursuing higher education or med-ical treatment, conducting trade or business, resettlement, or fleeing a security threat in the camp. There were significant delays in processing applications, and they could be declined arbitrarily. In 2009, only about 2% of Dadaab residents were issued passes.[28]

Chronic insecurity in and around camps in the NEP became brazen starting in 1993, and the area was rife with robberies, killing, and rapes for most of the 1990s. The government declined to improve security in and around the camps, citing insufficient funds even after the refugee crisis had stabilized. Instead, UNHCR took it upon itself to construct fences and provide Kenyan security per-sonnel with vehicles and communications equipment.[29]

Somali refugees who managed to evade the camps are concentrated in the bus-tling but perilous Eastleigh neighborhood of Nairobi. In the 1990s, Eastleigh was transformed by Somalis from a residential area into a commercial center with a booming informal economy. The area hosts a number of retail malls, import-export businesses, real-estate agencies, hotels and lodges, cafes and restaurants, and money transfer and exchange services.[30] Eastleigh is aptly described by Lindley as "a place of deprivation, failing infrastructure, and frequent crime, as

[26] Verdirame 1999, 68–69; Veney 2007, 97, 110; Kagwanja and Juma 2008, 224; Lindley 2011, 20, 41; Wagacha and Guiney 2008, 92.

[27] Qtd.in Verdirame and Harrell-Bond 2005, 249.

[28] Lindley 2011, 37; Pavanello, Elhawary, and Pantuliano 2010, 23.

[29] Veney 2007, 96, 171–72.

[30] Campbell 2006, 402–03; Pavanello, Elhawary, and Pantuliano 2010, 23; Lindley 2011, 41; Veney 2007, 131.

well as vibrant informal trade and impressive entrepreneurial wealth."[31] During a trip to the Eastleigh suburb for a scheduled interview, I was forced to turn back when I encountered a large protest by Somali traders complaining about insecurity.[32]

For its part, the Kenyan government sought to enforce its encampment policy by launching frequent raids to round up Somali refugees in urban areas. In May 1989, police raids were conducted around Nairobi. Somalis were reportedly targeted based on their physical appearance, and individuals who could neither speak Swahili nor prove their Kenyan citizenship were deported. During the weekend of August 15, 1992, police in Nairobi and Mombasa arrested anyone with "Somali features" who did not have a Kenyan ID card. In December 1995, Somalis were transported to Thika where their families could come retrieve them.[33]

Of course, Kenya's long-standing discriminatory policies toward its domestic population of ethnic Somalis likely shaped the country's responses to Somali refugees. In 1991, Africa Watch claimed that "refugees at the border were vetted according to their ethnic group, rather than on the basis that they were civilians at risk."[34] Pérouse de Montclos argues that Somali refugees receive the worst treatment, not due to a genuine fear of secession, but because the political and economic marginalization of Kenyan Somalis prevented them from influencing ruling elites in Nairobi.[35]

Political competition between ethnic groups in Kenya partially explains the repression of Kenyan Somalis, and by extension, Somali refugees. Whereas Kenyatta had been a member of the Kikuyu, Kenya's largest ethnic group, Moi was a Kalenjin. When a coup was attempted against Moi by the Kenyan Air Force while he was out of the country in August 1982, he came to see himself as stranded on a "political island" surrounded by Kenyatta's Kikuyu supporters. He sought to ensure the rise of his ethnic group and adopted a range of repressive measures, which included campaigns in the NEP.[36]

As a result, the NEP, where ethnic Somalis are concentrated, has witnessed significant government repression since Kenyan independence in 1963. Following Barre's invasion of the Ogaden in Ethiopia in 1977, the NEP saw massive human rights abuses, including massacres in Garissa (1980), Modogashe (1982), Pokot (1984), and Wajir (1984 and 1987).[37] Minister of Internal Security Godfrey

[31] Lindley 2011, 38.
[32] See news coverage of this protest here: http://allafrica.com/stories/201205090091.html
[33] African Rights 1993, 7; Pérouse de Montclos 1998b, 22–23.
[34] Africa Watch 1991, 349.
[35] Pérouse de Montclos 1998a, 168.
[36] Hyndman 1997, 165–66; Milner 2009, 103.
[37] Hyndman 1997, 165–66; Lawyers Committee for Human Rights 1995, 65; Otunnu 1992, 25; Milner 2009, 101–03; Tóth 2011, 179.

Kariuki quipped "the only good Somali is a dead one."[38] Under a state of emergency which lasted until 1991, Kenyan authorities could restrict travel into and out of the province, detain suspects without charge or trial, and set up special courts.[39] In 1993, Africa Watch described Kenyan Somalis as "second-class citizens," who faced routine and institutionalized abuse and discrimination by the government and the public. They were frequently blamed for gun-running, cattle-rustling, and poaching. In official statements, the word "Somali" was often used synonymously with *shifta*, meaning bandit.[40]

The Kenyan government's contempt for Kenyan Somalis translated into scorn for Somali refugees. Particularly with a large influx of refugees, it was difficult to distinguish Somali refugees from Kenyan Somalis. The history of Somali irredentism in the region, however, meant that the Kenyan government treated both groups with resentment.[41] As Hyndman puts it: "The Government of Kenya has not hidden its disdain for Somali refugees living in Kenya, nor for its own Kenyan nationals of Somali ethnicity."[42]

As a consequence, the Kenyan government engaged in the surveillance and expulsion of Somali refugees and Kenyan Somalis alike. The government began screening all ethnic Somalis in November 1989, ostensibly to prevent Somalis from infiltrating Kenya. The following month, 500 ethnic Somalis (of whom some were Kenyan Somalis) without proper identification were sent to Mogadishu.[43] Hundreds of Kenyan Somalis were judged to have "fraudulent" papers and expelled. Even Kenyan Somalis "found to have sympathy with Somalia" were to be deported.[44] On June 16, 1991, hundreds of ethnic Somalis were rounded up for screening, and some 3,500 Kenyan Somalis were deported that year. In fact, the influx of Somali refugees may have been used to justify screening Kenyan Somalis.[45]

Indeed, security operations in Dadaab and surrounding areas subjected Somali refugees and Kenyan Somalis alike to substantial violence and abuse. In August 1992, following the killing of four policemen south of Dadaab, there was a major security operation in the area. The military apparently conducted a pogrom, killing hundreds of refugees, whose bodies were found around Dadaab four days after the army left. In 1993, Kenyan security forces intervened in

---

[38] Qtd. in Africa Watch 1991, 273.

[39] Hyndman 1997, 165–66; Lawyers Committee for Human Rights 1995, 65; Otunnu 1992, 25; Milner 2009, 101–03; Tóth 2011, 179.

[40] African Rights 1993, 8; Milner 2009, 104.

[41] Veney 2007, 109.

[42] Hyndman 1997, 161.

[43] Ibid., 164, 66; Otunnu 1992, 25; Human Rights Watch 1990, 1; Lawyers Committee for Human Rights 1995, 65.

[44] Veney 2007, 9; Human Rights Watch 2012, 15; Human Rights Watch 1990, 1; Lawyers Committee for Human Rights 1995, 65.

[45] Hyndman and Nylund 1998, 40; Otunnu 1992, 25; Veney 2007, 10.

Mandera and El-Wak, causing some 2,000 deaths. Outside the camps, Kenyan Somalis experienced violent raids as well. For instance, in October 2008 a police-military operation in Mandera sought to disarm rival Somali militias; hundreds of local residents were beaten, tortured, and raped by security agents. No investigation was launched, despite promises from the minister of state for internal security. Two years later, in October 2010, two Somali chiefs were tortured because they were suspected of harboring Ethiopian rebels.[46]

Many observers have also pointed to the securitization of Somali refugees in Kenya, whereby they have been cast as security threats and associated with crime, arms trafficking, and terrorism. In parliament, Minister for Home Affairs and National Heritage Francis Lotodo had this to say in April 1996: "we did not know how to handle refugees and that is why we had put them near the urban areas like Mombasa and Marafa, but when we realized that they were a security threat, we had to take them away."[47] Connections have been drawn between terrorist organizations (such as al-Ittihaad al-Islami) and Dadaab refugee camp. Kenyan Somalis and Somali refugees alike experienced stepped up repression and were targeted by counter-terrorism legislation and a new counter-terrorism unit established in February 2003. Kenyan government officials also expressed concerns that refugees contributed to small arms proliferation.[48] On July 13, 2010, member of parliament Boni Khalwale (FORD-K, Ikolomani) from Western Province expressed concern about the increase in Somali nationals living in Eastleigh "who can pose a threat even to the children of Mr. Deputy Speaker."[49]

Indeed, Kenya invoked security concerns on several occasions in order to close its border with Somalia. In 1999, after President Moi gave a speech linking refugees with crime and the spread of illicit arms, the border was closed. In 2001, the border was closed again. In early 2007, the border was closed after Ethiopia pushed the Union of Islamic Courts out of south-central Somalia. The minister for foreign affairs justified another border closure by noting that Kenya was unable to distinguish genuine refugees from Islamist fighters.[50] Still, according to Amnesty International, the government ignored offers to provide added capacity to screen asylum-seekers from Somalia.[51]

That the Kenyan government has linked Somalis with insecurity is inextricable from ethnic politics. Similar flows of non-Somali refugees would not, and indeed have not, sparked comparable references to insecurity on the part of the Kenyan government. For Milner, this association between Somalis and insecurity

---

[46] Wagacha and Guiney 2008, 93; Human Rights Watch 2012, 16.
[47] Kenya 1996, 487.
[48] Milner 2009, 97–98; Kagwanja and Juma 2008, 224–25.
[49] Kenya, 2010, 37.
[50] Burns 2010, 8; Milner 2009, 96.
[51] Amnesty International 2007, 9.

has more to do with historical factors than with actual evidence linking the two. In particular, he argues that memories, like those of the 1963–1967 *shifta* wars (in which Kenyan Somalis waged a guerrilla campaign with support from the Somali government) have resulted in a perception that all Somalis (whether Kenyan citizens or refugees) are security threats.[52]

For these reasons, Somali refugees in Kenya are often described as a case apart. One interviewee underscored that policies take on a different character when Somalis are involved. They are the reason the approach toward refugees has become securitized; border control with Uganda and Sudan is less strict than with Somalia.[53] NGO personnel who work regularly with refugees emphasize the unfavorable treatment that Somalis receive, compared with other refugee groups. The "legal framework may not reflect differences in treatment, but in reality, there are" differences between Somalis and other refugees. For example, "no one cares" if there are Congolese refugees in Nairobi, and "no one would actively harass [them if they did not have] papers, any more than they would a Kenyan." In contrast, "Kenya has never liked Somalis."[54] Another interviewee underscored that South Sudanese without documentation face very few problems, in contrast to Somalis who bear the brunt of police harassment.[55] According to Pérouse de Montclos, the treatment reserved for these refugees is the most severe.[56]

Legislators from the NEP decried this situation on multiple occasions. On July 28, 1993, Abdullahi Sheikh Ahmed (PICK-Mandera East Constituency) asked the Minister of State, Office of the President, about "Harassing of Somali Refugees." He insisted that "The Assistant Minister knows that helpless people are suffering. Women are raped, tortured and sometimes beaten even shot to death. We heard the other day that in Mandera that over 1000 refugees were repatriated forcibly without one single gun or anything recovered. I am wondering why we have to invite these people in the first place to stay in this country if we cannot respect their dignity."[57]

Legislators from other provinces, meanwhile, were more concerned about Somali refugees posing a security threat. On 28 March 1991, Boy Juma Boy (KANU-Matuga Constituency) from Coast Province complained about "those political refugees from Somalia" escaping tribalism (*ukabila*) who flocked

[52] Milner 2009, 85, 96. Similarly, Otunnu has argued that the long history of conflict between Kenya and Somalia is to blame for the government's unstated policy of "refugee deterrence." Otunnu 1992, 21, 25.

[53] NGO worker. Personal interview by author. Nairobi, Kenya, May 4, 2012.

[54] Roel Debruyne (Regional Protection and Migration Adviser, Danish Refugee Council—Horn of Africa & Yemen). Personal interview by author. Danish Refugee Council Office, Nairobi, Kenya, May 10, 2012.

[55] Grace Omweri (Legal Program Officer, Kituo Cha Sheria). Personal interview by author. Kituo Cha Sheria Branch Office—Eastleigh, Nairobi, Kenya, May 11, 2012.

[56] Pérouse de Montclos 1998a, 155.

[57] Kenya 1993, 1634.

(*wamejazana*) to Mombasa. He expressed a fear that the conflict in Somalia would spread if Kenya was not careful (*ikiwa hatutakuwa macho shida hii itafika ama italetwa hapa*).[58] Probably recalling the *shifta* wars, Richard Maoka Maore (KANU-Ntonyiri Constituency) from the Eastern Province wondered whether "given the history of the expansion programme by Somalia and the fact that there have been territorial claims on Kenya . . . there is a well-calculated take-over programme for the future."[59]

To summarize, Kenya braved international criticism and turned back Somali refugees so long as the friendly Barre regime was in power in Somalia. Once Barre fell, a large number of Somali refugees were admitted. However, these ethnic others were encamped in harsh conditions in the marginalized NEP, where they experienced multiple screenings, deportations, and violent attacks. This restrictive response, along with the frequent invocation of security concerns by Kenyan officials, is linked to the government's discriminatory outlook toward Kenyan Somalis.

## Sudanese

Sudanese refugees constituted Kenya's second largest refugee group starting in 1991, when some 23,000 Sudanese refugees arrived in Kenya, of whom around 7,000 were unaccompanied minors. Known as "walking boys" or "lost boys," these refugees had been forced back to Sudan from Ethiopia with the fall of Mengistu and then had walked into Kenya. In response, Kakuma camp was founded in Turkana district in July 1992. This remote district, officially recognized as the poorest in Kenya, is both economically and politically marginalized, as are the Turkana ethnic minority who inhabit it. The high temperatures make agriculture difficult in the area, and famines and droughts are common. Remarkably, the refugee population stood at 83,000 compared to 10,000 locals in 2003.[60]

Kenya was officially neutral during the Sudanese civil war, mediating between the Sudan People's Liberation Army (SPLA) and the Sudanese government.[61]

---

[58] Kenya 1991, D.1. In the original Swahili, his statement reads: "Ingefaa wao waende katika uwanja wa maonyesho ya kilimo huko Mombasa ili wajionee, vile wakimbizi wa kisiasa kutoka Somalia wamejazana huko kwa sababu kwao kuna taabu. Taabu hiyo haiwezi kuondolewa haraka kwa sababu ya ukabila na mambo yote yamekuwa ni fujo tupu ambayo wanataka kuileta hapa na ikiwa hatutakuwa macho shida hii itafika ama italetwa hapa. Wao wanatafuta mahali pa kupenya. Kama tundu halizipwi, watu hawa wataingia hapa na itakuwa shida kuirekebisha nchi hii. Itakuwa ni shida kwa sababu watu wetu wana matatizo."

[59] Kenya 2006, 3472.

[60] Verdirame 1999, 62; Jamal 2000, 37; Veney 2007, 100; Aukot 2003, 74; Pérouse de Montclos 2008, 201.

[61] South Sudan gained its independence in 2011.

In practice, however, the Kenyan government was accommodating toward the SPLA and ambivalent toward the Sudanese government in Khartoum. Relations between Kenya and Sudan were tense, because the latter had an explicit goal of exporting radical Islam to neighboring countries. In addition, the two countries were engaged in a territorial dispute over the Elemi triangle on the border between them. Meanwhile, Kenya hosted SPLA's leader John Garang, allowed the SPLA to have an office in Nairobi in the 1990s, and supported humanitarian organizations associated with the Sudan People's Liberation Movement, as well as Operation Lifeline Sudan, which the Sudanese government claimed was part of SPLA's supply chain. Most Sudanese refugees in Kenya are Dinka and Nuer.[62]

With these patterns in ethnic identity and foreign policy, my expectation is that Kenya would be more welcoming of refugees fleeing the Sudanese government than of those escaping the SPLA. The evidence presented in this section bears out this theoretical prediction. SPLA fighters who fled to Kenya were effectively given free rein. They were able to take up leadership positions in Kakuma refugee camp and to use the camp to recuperate and round up additional recruits. Meanwhile, refugees fleeing the SPLA encountered closed borders and violence.

Parliamentarians expressed unhappiness with the presence of Sudanese refugees in the country. Following a spillover of tensions between Southern Sudanese generals Kerubino Kuanyin and Garang onto Kenyan territory, Mukhisa Kituyi (FORD-K, Kimilili Constituency) from Western Province asked on December 9, 1998, why the government was "not able to regulate the conduct of Sudanese refugees in Kenya?"[63]

Still, they were well treated by the government. When two Sudanese asylum-seekers were denied refugee status as far back as February 1971, UNHCR's officer in Nairobi said that was "astonishing against the background of the reportedly positive attitude taken by the Government to the Southern Sudanese cause."[64]

When Kenya became one of the major destinations for refugees from southern Sudan in 1991, these included SPLA fighters.[65] Among Dinka refugees in particular, SPLA officers sometimes became self-appointed leaders. Human Rights Watch reported that they were told that "in some parts of Kakuma the chairmen are appointed by [Sudanese rebel leader] Garang."[66]

---

[62] Mogire 2011, 43, 60; Verdirame and Harrell-Bond 2005, 97, 276; Hornsby 2012.

[63] Kenya 1998, 2800.

[64] Carsten Brink-Peterson [UNHCR Legal Officer for East and Southern Africa] to UNHCR Headquarters in Geneva, 15 February 1971, "Eligibility—Kenya," *UNHCR Archives*, Fonds 11, Series 2, Box 1197, 630 KEN Protection and General Legal Matters—Eligibility—Kenya [Volume 1], Folio 5.

[65] Burns 2010, 7; Veney 2007, 123; Mogire 2011, 60.

[66] Human Rights Watch 2002, 128.

In vain, Sudan's government sought to enlist Kenya's "cooperation" in preventing refugee militarization and cross-border attacks. Expecting a new movement of Sudanese refugees into Kenya, Sudan requested the Kenyan authorities collect "[a]rms and ammunition," lodge refugees "at least 50 miles away from the border," and transmit asylum-seekers' names to the Sudanese embassy in Nairobi. Finally, Sudan hoped that "the Kenyan Government would not allow the refugees to carry [out] any political or military activity against the Sudan."[67]

Rather, the SPLA was able to engage in forcible recruitment and to divert aid supplies at Kakuma camp, located only 75 kilometers from the Sudanese border. SPLA commanders entered the camp and met with community leaders, who were required to produce a certain number of recruits. In 1996, an SPLA mobilization team enlisted 500 refugees from the camp. In 2000–2001, only 3,800 minors remained in Kakuma, and thousands of others were believed to have been sent to the warfront. Sudanese refugees reported that there was an SPLA training camp close to Kakuma for new recruits from the camp. The SPLA used some refugee settlements for "R&R" (rest and recuperation) and installed their families there. In northern Kenya, there was at least one camp where SPLA soldiers received food and logistical support from the Kenyan government. The SPLA also diverted food aid to rebels in southern Sudan.[68]

Meanwhile, refugees fleeing the SPLA (rather than the Sudanese government) were not secure in Kenya. Refugees fleeing SPLA-held areas were unable to enter the country, blocked by Home Guards and security forces at the border. At Lokichokio, SPLA security officers monitored cross-border traffic and refugees who escaped their notice were taken to them. Refugees were threatened, harassed, and even abducted, and former SPLA members risked reprisals by the organization.[69]

A Sudanese lawyer and former SPLA officer explained: "Sudanese refugees are honestly in a better position than other refugees. Kenya is sympathetic to our cause, and the treatment they reserve for us is not the same [as for other refugees]," though he was probably referring specifically to SPLA commanders.[70] For these reasons, the government may have been willing to overlook the group's recruitment and other activities in the Kakuma camps. Notably, the camp was reportedly infiltrated by Ethiopian security forces in addition to the SPLA, but the Kenyan government did not respond to these interventions with a reprisal as with al-Shabaab in Dadaab.[71]

---

[67] Embassy of Sudan in Nairobi to Kenya Ministry of Foreign Affairs and International Cooperation, 28 April 1992, UNHCR Archives, Fonds 11, Series 3, 100 KEN GEN Refugee Situations—Special Groups of Refugees—Refugees in Kenya [Volume A].

[68] Verdirame and Harrell-Bond 2005, 174–75, 261; Mogire 2011, 37; Kaiser 2008, 264; Africa Watch 1991, 347; Burns 2010, 8; Crisp 2000, 623.

[69] Africa Watch 1991, 347; Verdirame and Harrell-Bond 2005, 175, 77.

[70] Qtd. in Verdirame and Harrell-Bond 2005, 97.

[71] Mogire 2011, 43; Burns 2010, 8; Human Rights Watch 2002, 128.

In short, Kenya admitted refugees who fled Sudan's government, including members of the SPLA. Despite entreaties from Sudan's government, Kenyan officials turned a blind eye as SPLA fighters installed themselves in leadership roles at Kakuma camp and rounded up recruits and aid supplies. In contrast, refugees attempting to escape the SPLA were turned back or mistreated.

## Ethiopians

There have long been Ethiopian refugees in Kenya, particularly in urban areas. The first wave came as a result of the conflict over Eritrean secession in the 1960s, followed by a second wave of students, intellectuals, businesspeople, and former government officials after the overthrow of Emperor Haile Selassie in 1974. A third wave was caused by the "Red Terror" of 1977 and 1978. However, it was the fall of the Mengistu regime in May 1991, accompanied by drought and famine the following year, that sent a considerable number of refugees into Kenya. In 1992, the number of Ethiopian refugees reached 40,000, but that declined to just 5,000 a mere four years later. Ethiopians were housed mainly in Walda camp until it was closed, and later mostly resided in Ifo.[72]

Bilateral relations with Ethiopia were friendly. The two countries concluded multiple treaties and pacts, starting with a mutual defense pact in 1964. Kenya also supported Ethiopia during the 1977 Ogaden war with Somalia. An Ethiopian border incursion in 1999 was smoothed over quickly and a joint communiqué issued soon thereafter. The majority ethnicities of Ethiopian refugees are Oromo and Amhara.[73]

Refugees from Ethiopia were escaping a friendly regime and lacked an ethnic tie; therefore, I expect Kenya's government to treat them restrictively. Although there is not much information about this refugee group, the evidence seems to align with my theoretical expectations.

There are indications that the Kenyan government was less than receptive to asylum-seekers from Ethiopia. In January 1982, Ethiopians over the age of thirty were considered "education seekers" and not bona fide refugees.[74] By 1991, the government was denying that there were any refugees or asylum-seekers at Mandera. When UNHCR conveyed recurring requests for entry, local authorities rejected them.[75] The following year, the Kenyan government refused

---

[72] Ndege, Kagwanja, and Odiyo 2002, 6; Kagwanja 1998, 55; Hyndman and Nylund 1998, 24.

[73] Tekle 1996; Makinda 1985; "Kenya," 2010.

[74] Shinga-Vele Lukika [Program Officer, UNHCR Branch Office in Nairobi], 14 January 1982, "Note for the File: Eligibility Procedure in Kenya," *UNHCR Archives*, Fonds 11, Series 2, Box 1198, 630 KEN Protection and General Legal Matters—Eligibility—Kenya [Volume 2], Folio 137.

[75] UNHCR Branch Office in Nairobi to UNHCR Headquarters in Geneva, 30 March 1991, "Incoming Cable," *UNHCR Archives*, Fonds 11, Series 3, 100 KEN SOM Refugee Situations—Special Groups of Refugees—Somalian Refugees in Kenya [Volume A], Folio 8.

UNHCR's proposal to recognize Ethiopian (and Somali) refugees on a prima facie basis. Reneging on a prior agreement with UNHCR, authorities suggested that "asylum-seeker identity cards" be issued to refugees in camps, instead of "refugee identity cards."[76]

In addition, Ethiopian refugees reported being harassed by agents of the Ethiopian government operating in Kenya. Ethiopian refugees in Nairobi reportedly feared abduction and forcible repatriation, or being injured and killed, by Ethiopian intelligence officials active in Eastleigh. Indeed, the Refugee Consortium of Kenya (RCK) reported that Ethiopians were the group of refugees most often seeking advice on security threats originating from their home governments.[77] Ethiopian agents were widely known to operate in Nairobi, and Human Rights Watch quoted an NGO worker as saying that the "Ethiopian government is active in Nairobi."[78] Refugees claiming to have been tailed gave NGOs license plate numbers, which were subsequently traced to the Ethiopian embassy. In 1992, Ethiopian security agents engaged in a widely reported, politically motivated killing in Nairobi.[79]

In parliament, statements by representatives were typically unwelcoming of these non-co-ethnic refugees. On November 20, 2003, Abdi Tari Sasura (KANU-Saku Constituency) from Eastern Province wondered why Ethiopian refugees who had fled Mengistu's regime were still in Kenya after his departure. Why does the Kenyan government not "tell them to go back to their country" he wondered?[80]

Thus, Kenyan authorities appear to have been loath to designate Ethiopians as refugees or permit them to receive UNHCR assistance. Ethiopian refugees also faced harassment by agents of the Ethiopian government, likely with Kenya's tacit approval.

## Ugandans

The Ugandan presence in Kenya has a long history. Ugandan refugees began arriving in Kenya with the 1966 constitutional crisis and Milton Obote's assumption of absolute power, followed by his overthrow by Idi Amin in 1971, the fall of Amin in 1979, the second rise of Obote in 1980, his overthrow in a 1985 coup, and the war bringing Yoweri Museveni to power. The largest flows were in

---

[76] Sylvester Awuye, 13 February 1992, "Incoming Cable," *UNHCR Archives*, Fonds 11, Series 3, 10 KEN External Relations—Relations with Governments—Kenya [Volume B], Folio 18.

[77] Pavanello, Elhawary, and Pantuliano 2010, 19.

[78] Human Rights Watch 2002, 39.

[79] Ibid., 40.

[80] Kenya 2003, 3987.

the 1960s and 1970s and were mostly composed of teachers, doctors, and other skilled and educated urban professionals.[81]

Relations with Uganda fluctuated several times between 1966 and 2010. Initially, warm ties were manifested in both countries joining the East African Community (EAC), but relations deteriorated as Uganda laid claim to large swaths of Kenyan territory in 1976, and the EAC fell apart. Obote's return to power in 1980 allowed for a rapprochement, but relations soured again after he was deposed in 1985. Soon after assuming power, Museveni claimed that Kenya was harboring rebels, and there were border clashes between the two countries. Moi and Museveni reconciled in 1990, however, and continued cordial relations allowed the EAC to be eventually revived. There is no information on the ethnicity of Ugandan refugees in Kenya; though it is certain they are not Kikuyu or Kalenjin.[82]

My theoretical argument would expect Ugandan refugees to experience several shifts in treatment, coinciding with shifts in relations between Kenya and Uganda. Indeed, when bilateral relations were cordial (roughly 1966–1975, 1981–1985, and 1990–2010), Ugandan refugees experienced more restrictive responses such as increased expulsions. In contrast, they experienced less restrictive responses, including the ability to establish resistance organizations, as relations soured (roughly 1976–1980 and 1986–1989).

Observers have often assumed that Ugandan refugees faced a hospitable reception because of their skills and the contribution they made to Kenya's economy and development. Indeed, many were quickly absorbed into the public sector. Ugandan refugees, unlike those of other nationalities, may have been able to take advantage of the EAC.[83]

But contrary to this widespread claim, this group faced repressive policies that coincided with friendly relations between Kenya and Uganda. After the coup that brought Amin to power in 1971, Kenya made it difficult for Ugandans to set up resistance organizations. On some occasions, Kenya expelled refugees to Uganda who were subsequently executed by Amin. In 1973, three refugees were handed over to the Amin regime and were immediately executed.[84]

During this time, Ugandans were deemed ineligible for refugee status by Kenyan authorities. Internal UNHCR documents from this period remark on this issue multiple times. Ugandans were "not formally treated as refugees" by Kenya.[85] In UNHCR's evaluation, Kenya's "legal background and administrative

---

[81] Ndege, Kagwanja, and Odiyo 2002, 4; Campbell, Crisp, and Kiragu 2011, 5.

[82] Hornsby 2012; "Kenya," 2010.

[83] Lomongin 2001, 2; Pérouse de Montclos 1998b, 28. For examples of this sort of argument, see, Milner 2009, 86; Veney 2007, 8.

[84] Mogire 2011, 58.

[85] J. Terlin, "Note for the File," *UNHCR Archives*, Fonds 11, Series 2, Box 1197, 630 KEN Protection and General Legal Matters—Eligibility—Kenya [Volume 1], Folio 32.

practice" excluded citizens from EAC countries from recognition as refugees.[86] Government officials confirmed that EAC countries "do not as a rule allow refugees of one state in another and do not accept requests for political asylum from citizens of these states." In Kenya, it was "not our policy to grant refugee asylum to nationals from neighboring states." Ugandan citizens may be granted de facto asylum, but de jure recognition was denied.[87] This trend persisted despite the fact that the Treaty for East African Cooperation contained no stipulations on the movement of citizens between its member countries.[88]

After a meeting with Kenyan officials, UNHCR concluded that "If the Government (i.e., the Cabinet) considers the presence on their territory of any individual from a friendly neighboring country . . . as embarrassing, undesirable or unwanted, such [a] person is not recognized as a refugee" regardless of the validity of his or her claim.[89]

Tensions between the two governments surfaced in the 1970s, however, when Uganda claimed part of Kenyan territory, authorized military incursions across the border, and supported a Popular Front for the Liberation of Palestine (PFLP) plot to shoot down an El Al airplane in Nairobi. Amin was also close with Somalia, which had irredentist claims on Kenyan territory. Now Ugandans were able to discreetly set up several resistance organizations, including the Ugandan Liberation Movement, the Nairobi Discussion Group, and the Ugandan Nationalist Organization.[90]

Former high-level Ugandan officials, like the former minister of industry and minister of housing, fled Uganda for Kenya. The Kenyan government was willing to accept these asylum-seekers.[91] Still, when diplomatic relations between Kenya and Uganda were repaired briefly in 1978, Ugandan refugees were "very afraid of refoulement as a result."[92]

---

[86] G. Kaellenius [UNHCR Regional Liaison Representative for Africa in Addis Ababa] to UNHCR Representative in Nairobi, 27 February 1974, "IC J.L. Opira," *UNHCR Archives*, Fonds 11, Series 2, Box 1197, 630 KEN Protection and General Legal Matters—Eligibility—Kenya [Volume 1], Folio 21B.

[87] R. Seeger [Regional Protection Officer, East and Southern African Section, UNHCR Headquarters in Geneva], 17 October 1974, "Note for the File," *UNHCR Archives*, Fonds 11, Series 2, Box 1197, 630 KEN Protection and General Legal Matters—Eligibility—Kenya [Volume 1], Folio 27.

[88] R. Seeger to E.K. Dadzie [Director of Protection], 15 October 1974, "Eligibility with the East African Union," *UNHCR Archives*, Fonds 11, Series 2, Box 1197, 630 KEN Protection and General Legal Matters—Eligibility—Kenya [Volume 1], Folio 26.

[89] UNHCR Representative to Uganda to UNHCR Headquarters in Geneva, 7 March 1975, "Memorandum: Eligibility Procedure in Kenya," *UNHCR Archives*, Fonds 11, Series 2, Box 1197, 630 KEN Protection and General Legal Matters—Eligibility—Kenya [Volume 1], Folio 30.

[90] Mogire 2011, 58.

[91] UNHCR Branch Office in Nairobi to UNHCR Headquarters in Geneva, 16 April 1979, "Incoming Cable," *UNHCR Archives*, Fonds 11, Series 2, Box 1198, 630 KEN Protection and General Legal Matters—Eligibility—Kenya [Volume 2], Folio 114.

[92] Martin Ennals [Secretary General, Amnesty International], 24 April 1978, "Incoming Cable: Re Ugandan Refugees in Kenya," *UNHCR Archives*, Fonds 11, Series 2, Box 1198, 630 KEN Protection and General Legal Matters—Eligibility—Kenya [Volume 2], Folio 98.

With another shift in bilateral relations, Kenya cooperated with Obote, returning politically active exiles to Uganda between 1980 and 1985. In September 1982, the government announced that Ugandans required a work permit. Refugees who tried to obtain refugee status from UNHCR were deported.[93] As far as Kenyan authorities were concerned, most Ugandans were "now considered to be economic migrants and not refugees."[94]

Although some of these crackdowns have been attributed to economic conditions, they actually preceded the adoption of economic liberalization policies. The Special Branch (an intelligence department of the police) took a "restrictive stand" that applied "especially to Ugandans," rejecting every asylum application. UNHCR's inquiries indicated that this position had "motives . . . of a political nature." The Ugandan government had exerted "continuous pressure" on Kenya to "return certain prominent Ugandan exiles, including those who are registered as refugees."[95] In some cases, the Special Branch reversed a determination that had been made by the Immigration Department (at the Ministry of Home Affairs) in cooperation with UNHCR, concluding that asylum applications were "not genuine."[96] This "new approach" was attributed to "a decision by the National Security Council" and President Moi.[97]

Relations soured once again, however, when Museveni's government was accused by Moi of trying to destabilize Kenya by supporting dissidents and rebels, as well as permitting armed incursions. Beginning in 1985, Ugandan exiles received encouragement, and sometimes outright sponsorship, from the Kenyan government. Occasional roundups continued to occur, however.[98]

When 1,600 Ugandans escaped to Kenya in November 1986, the Kenyan government built them a temporary shelter and provided assistance.[99] With military personnel guarding them, Moi announced that the government would take care

---

[93] Africa Watch 1991, 347–48; Kagwanja 2002, 98.

[94] Shinga-Vele Lukika, 14 January 1982, "Note for the File: Eligibility Procedure in Kenya," *UNHCR Archives*, Fonds 11, Series 2, Box 1198, 630 KEN Protection and General Legal Matters—Eligibility—Kenya [Volume 2], Folio 137.

[95] Ilunga Ngandu [UNHCR Representative to Kenya] to UNHCR Headquarters in Geneva, 11 January 1982, "Memorandum: Determination of Refugee Status," *UNHCR Archives*, Fonds 11, Series 2, Box 1198, 630 KEN Protection and General Legal Matters—Eligibility—Kenya [Volume 2], Folio 136.

[96] I. Ngandu to UNHCR Headquarters, 11 January 1982, "Memorandum: Procedure for Determination of Refugee Status," *UNHCR Archives*, Fonds 11, Series 2, Box 1198, 630 KEN Protection and General Legal Matters—Eligibility—Kenya [Volume 2], Folio 135.

[97] Shinga-Vele Lukika, 14 January 1982, "Note for the File: Eligibility Procedure in Kenya," *UNHCR Archives*, Fonds 11, Series 2, Box 1198, 630 KEN Protection and General Legal Matters—Eligibility—Kenya [Volume 2], Folio 137.

[98] Africa Watch 1991, 347–48; African Rights 1993, 4; Verdirame and Harrell-Bond 2005, 32; Pérouse de Montclos 1998b, 28; Ndege, Kagwanja, and Odiyo 2002, 17.

[99] P.M. Kinyanjui [Office of the Vice-President and Ministry of Home Affairs] to UNHCR Representative in Kenya, 17 November 1986, "Assistance for Ugandan Refugees in Suam Camp," *UNHCR Archives*, Fonds 11, Series 3, 100 KEN UGA Refugee Situations—Special Groups of Refugees—Ugandan Refugees in Kenya, Folio 3.

of these refugees. These refugees received "treatment . . . so good" that UNHCR feared it would "act as a pull factor and thereby generate more refugee-like situations or alternatively create a dependency syndrome."[100]

During this time, Kenyan officials asked UNHCR to move Ugandan refugees who were staying close to the border at Busia to other locations in Kenya. They were reportedly concerned about border incursions from Uganda.[101] These concerns were heightened "especially as the relationship between the two countries has deteriorated," and Uganda accused Kenya of harboring rebels.[102]

Meanwhile, Kenya's foreign minister emphasized that Ugandans in Kenya were genuine refugees who had fled difficult conditions. Minister of Foreign Affairs Zachariah T. Onyonka (KANU-Kitutu West Constituency) noted on December 16, 1987, that "we have experienced a typical case . . . of what we call provocation." Defending Kenya's hosting of Ugandan refugees, he continued, "the truth of the matter is that we do not wish to be party to the genocide that is being committed in that country, and it is also true that the only Ugandans that we have here are genuine cases of refugees who have sought asylum in camps simply because they are running away from the terrible situation prevailing across the border."[103]

Finally, after the Rwandan Patriotic Front invaded Rwanda from Uganda, Moi issued a November 1990 directive ordering all Ugandan and Rwandan refugees to leave the country. Police sweeps followed in major towns including Nairobi, Nakuru, and Eldoret.[104] Following a meeting at the Kenyan Ministry of Home Affairs, UNHCR's representative reported to headquarters that "while Kenya would tolerate other nationals, be they ordinary aliens or refugees, Ugandans evoke great suspicion."[105]

Meanwhile, responses in parliament were decidedly hostile toward Ugandan refugees. Edward Eric Khasakhala (KANU-Emuhaya Constituency) from Western Province objected on July 2, 1980 that "we have very many refugees from Uganda who are crowded in our towns looking for jobs when we have

---

[100] G.T. Chaponda [Deputy Representative, UNHCR Branch Office in Kenya], 18 November 1986, "Mission Report: Suam Border Area, Kitale, Kenya 13–16 November, 1986," *UNHCR Archives*, Fonds 11, Series 3, 100 KEN UGA Refugee Situations—Special Groups of Refugees—Ugandan Refugees in Kenya, Folio 3.

[101] UNHCR Branch Office in Kenya, 24 September 1986, "Incoming Cable," *UNHCR Archives*, Fonds 11, Series 3, 100 KEN UGA Refugee Situations—Special Groups of Refugees—Ugandan Refugees in Kenya, Folio 2.

[102] G.T. Chaponda, 7 October 1987, "Note for the File," *UNHCR Archives*, Fonds 11, Series 3, 100 KEN UGA Refugee Situations—Special Groups of Refugees—Ugandan Refugees in Kenya, Folio 5.

[103] Kenya 1987, DD.2.

[104] Africa Watch 1991, 355, 57; Veney 2007, 96, 101.

[105] Sylvester Awuye, 14 December 1990, "Report on Representative's Meeting with Permanent Secretary, Ministry of Home Affairs and National Heritage (MHA), Mr. L. Arap Sawe, 10 December 1990," *UNHCR Archives*, Fonds 11, Series 3, 10 KEN External Relations—Relations with Governments—Kenya [Volume B], Folio 11.

our own people who are jobless."[106] Years later, on November 20, 2003, James Viscount Kimathi (KANU-Lari Constituency) noted that Ugandan refugees could go home since "[t]here is no more fighting in that country."[107]

In short, Kenya shifted its treatment of Ugandan refugees multiple times, each coinciding with a change in bilateral relations with Uganda. Relations were cordial during 1966–1975, and during this time Ugandan refugees were unable to set up resistance organizations, faced expulsions, and were denied refugee status. When relations deteriorated in 1976–1980, Ugandan refugees were permitted to establish resistance organizations, and former Ugandan government officials were admitted as asylum-seekers. An improvement in Kenyan-Ugandan relations in 1981–1985 brought along with it refugee expulsions, the imposition of a new work permit requirement, and rejections of asylum applications. The souring of bilateral relations in 1986–1989, in turn, led Kenya to sponsor Ugandan rebels and provide assistance to refugees. Expulsions and police sweeps resumed, however, when relations improved in 1990–2010.

## Rwandans

The year 1994 saw an inflow of refugees, predominantly Hutu, fleeing the aftermath of the Rwandan genocide. Kenya's warm relations with Rwandan president Juvénal Habyarimana translated into hostility for the Rwandan Patriotic Front (RPF) when the latter seized power in 1994. Only in 1997 was there a rapprochement between the two governments.[108]

According to my theoretical argument, I would expect that Kenya improve its treatment of Rwandan refugees once the RPF seized power and worsen its treatment following the rapprochement in 1997. As the following discussion shows, Rwandan refugees experienced roundups during Habyarimana's tenure, but even *génocidaires* (those guilty of mass killings) could find safety in Kenya once the RPF replaced him. Only when relations between the two countries improved in 1997 were suspected *génocidaires* rounded up and turned over.

Kenya refused to let the International Criminal Tribunal for Rwanda (ICTR) access *génocidaires* in 1995. A dismayed parliamentarian James Aggrey B. Orengo (KANU-Ugenya Constituency) demanded to know why the government allowed "more than 400 suspects, those suspected of having committed crimes in Rwanda to stay here?" on October 25, 1995.[109] For his part, Minister

---

[106] Kenya 1980, 428.
[107] Kenya 2003, 3992.
[108] Verdirame and Harrell-Bond 2005; "Kenya," 2010.
[109] Kenya 1995, 2165. Indeed, a particularly telling incident has to do with a group of 105 Rwandans from the Tingi camp in eastern Zaire. These individuals arrived at Wilson airport in Nairobi at the end of February 1997. UNHCR refused to recognize the group en masse because they suspected

of Foreign Affairs and International Co-operation Stephen Kalonzo Musyoka (KANU-Kitui North Constituency) delivered a Ministerial Statement on Rwanda on November 2, 1995, expressing consternation that "the Government of Rwanda . . . has outrageously and unashamedly attacked His Excellency the President claiming that our Head of State is harboring perpetrators of the genocide." He emphasized that "Kenya has hosted refugees from all parts of this region for decades including Rwanda even during the most difficult periods in the economy of our country; and we will continue to do so in keeping with the international obligations."[110]

This situation was markedly better than the treatment of Rwandan refugees when friendly Habyarimana was in power. For example, after Kenyan police were ordered to round up Rwandan refugees for repatriation in October 1990, the Committee for Human Rights and Democracy in Rwanda decried the indifference (la légèreté) which saw Rwandan refugees denied basic rights in Kenya and other neighboring countries.[111]

In 1996, the contentious relationship between the two countries worsened when the Kenyan government accused the Rwandan embassy of organizing an assassination attempt on former RPF minister Seth Sendashonga, who had defected to Kenya. Diplomatic ties between the two countries were severed, and the Rwandan embassy in Nairobi closed.[112]

There was a dramatic shift in 1997 following a rapprochement between the two countries. In July, Rwandan vice-president Paul Kagame visited Nairobi and insisted that Kenya turn over suspected génocidaires. That same month, "Operation Alien" kicked off, ostensibly to round up illegal aliens and foreign criminals. Refugees from all countries experienced arbitrary arrest and detention, but Hutu refugees were primary targets, including recognized Rwandans and Burundians authorized to reside in Nairobi. Seven Rwandans were arrested and transferred to the ICTR. In July 1997, Kenya also stopped admitting asylum-seekers traveling with old passports (the Rwandan government had changed its passports in 1995/1996).[113]

---

some of the adults could be génocidaires. The Rwandans insisted on coming under the protection of the Kenyan government. After four weeks, and upon the request of the Kenyan government, the group was transferred to Kakuma. Verdirame and Harrell-Bond 2005, 66–67.

[110] Kenya 1995, 2397.

[111] Pierre Karemera [Comité pour les droits de l'homme et la democratie au Rwanda] to UN High Commissioner for Refugees, 23 October 1990, UNHCR Archives, Fonds 11, Series 3, 100 KEN RWA Refugee Situations—Special Groups of Refugees—Rwandan Refugees in Kenya, Folio 1. In the original French, this portion of the letter reads: "Encore une fois, Excellence Monsieur le Haut Commissaire, nous constatons avec consternation la légèreté avec laquelle les droit les plus élémentaires sont déniés aux réfugiés rwandais essentiellement et la précarité de leur protection dans certain pays limitrophes du Rwanda."

[112] O'Neill, Rutinwa, and Verdirame 2000, 154–55; Verdirame and Harrell-Bond 2005, 126.

[113] Verdirame and Harrell-Bond 2005, 59.

The analysis in this section reveals that, contrary to the conventional wisdom, Kenya's asylum policies did not experience a simple shift in 1990. Far from being uniformly welcoming, Kenya cracked down on some refugee groups prior to 1990, such as Ethiopians and (during certain periods) Ugandans. Further, rather than restricting all refugee groups after 1990, Kenya extended more inclusive treatment to Sudanese and (at times) Rwandan refugees. For each of the refugee groups discussed in this section, Kenya's responses appear to more closely align with bilateral relations and ethnic identity.

## Delegation

Chapter 2 asserted that delegation poses few drawbacks from the perspective of the host country's policymakers. UNHCR wields little influence and is constrained by its limited funding. It is also sensitive to government sanction and tends to adhere to government demands. This section first provides background information about the division of responsibilities between the Kenyan government and UNHCR. Then, I show that the Agency's capacity and means were constrained regarding RSD, encampment, and the ability to access asylum-seekers in Kenya. Finally, I discuss several incidents in which the Agency bowed to government censure.

## Context

Though Kenya recognized the advantages of hosting a UNHCR representative early on, the government retained responsibility for refugees until 1991. At that point, the transfer of responsibility to UNHCR was associated with a deceleration in the processing of individual asylum claims and a shift to recognizing refugees on a group basis. When the government decided to adopt a refugee encampment policy, UNHCR went along by undertaking camp management, dissuading refugees from residing in the capital, and launching a massive repatriation operation in Somalia.

UNHCR's presence in Kenya began with a 1969 decision to move the office of the Legal Adviser for East and Southern Africa from Dar es Salaam to Nairobi. According to correspondence from the UNHCR archives, High Commissioner Sadruddin Aga Khan proposed the move to Kenyan attorney general Charles Mugane Njonjo, following a "discussion of refugee problems."[114] Njonjo seemed

---

[114] Sadruddin Aga Khan [UN High Commissioner for Refugees] to Charles Njonjo [Attorney General of Kenya], 30 June 1969, *UNHCR Archives*, Fonds 11, Series 1, Box 76, 2/5/1/1 ACC/KEN Branch Offices—Accreditation—Kenya, Folio 4.

pleased, responding that it was "an excellent idea" and saying he was "sure it will help us immensely in dealing with this problem of refugees."[115]

For some time thereafter, refugee affairs were handled by the National Refugee Secretariat (NRS), which was based at the Ministry of Home Affairs and National Heritage until 1990/1991. An Eligibility Committee—which included representatives of the Ministry of Home Affairs, Office of the Vice-President, and the Immigration Department—conducted status determination, with UNHCR in an advisory role. Decisions were subject to final clearance by the Special Branch, an arm of Kenya's security apparatus. During this time, foreign aid agencies were largely uninvolved in refugee affairs in Kenya.[116]

However, when some 400,000 Somali refugees arrived along with about 7,000 "walking boys" from Sudan, the Eligibility Committee stopped functioning. By 1991, UNHCR had set up an office in Nairobi, called "Wood Avenue," where status determination interviews were administered by the Jesuit Refugee Service (JRS). This office issued protection letters, an A4 sheet with the individual's name and photo that identified him or her as a refugee recognized by UNHCR, and directed refugees to live in a particular camp.[117] According to a JRS publication, through 1992, refugees were interviewed at a rate of 100 to 250 per day.[118]

Some observers have implied that shifting RSD to an overburdened UNHCR stemmed from an aim to slow down asylum claims. Indeed, this system proved fairly slow, with asylum-seekers facing delays of up to two years for a decision on their application.[119]

As a result, the delegation of refugee affairs to UNHCR came along with granting refugee status on a group basis and offering these prima facie refugees temporary protection. As described earlier, individual RSD became untenable with the mass influx of refugees in the early 1990s. Rather than submit individual applications, asylum-seekers from Somalia and Sudan (and for a time Ethiopia) were considered by UNHCR on a group (i.e., prima facie) basis. Getting prima facie status proved fairly easy for Somali asylum-seekers, provided they could demonstrate that they came from Mogadishu and south-central parts of the country. Only those suspected of involvement in violence underwent individual RSD.[120]

[115] Charles Njonjo to Sadruddin Aga Khan, 10 July 1969, *UNHCR Archives*, Fonds 11, Series 1, Box 76, 2/5/1/1 ACC/KEN Branch Offices—Accreditation—Kenya, Folio 4A.

[116] Verdirame and Harrell-Bond 2005, 31, 80–81; International Commission of Jurists (Kenya Section) 1998, 26; Verdirame 1999, 56–57; Kenyan Ministry of State for Immigration and Registration of Persons 2009, 27; O'Neill, Rutinwa, and Verdirame 2000, 153.

[117] Veney 2007, 93; Milner 2009, 84; African Rights 1993, 3; Verdirame 1999, 59; O'Neill, Rutinwa, and Verdirame 2000, 154.

[118] JRS 1993.

[119] African Rights 1993, 4; Pavanello, Elhawary, and Pantuliano 2010, 15; Campbell, Crisp, and Kiragu 2011, 16.

[120] Moret, Baglioni, and Efionayi-Mäder 2006, 38; Verdirame and Harrell-Bond 2005, 33, 87; Verdirame 1999, 57; Hyndman and Nylund 1998, 29; Pavanello, Elhawary, and Pantuliano 2010, 15;

In September 1998, the government revived its own RSD procedures by establishing a National Eligibility Committee (NEC) with UNHCR's assistance.[121] The NEC only met sporadically, however, and by 2000, the RCK was once again calling status determination "the preserve of UNHCR."[122] As late as 2004, a senior government official said that the state bureaucracy saw refugees as "UNHCR's responsibility, not ours."[123]

Throughout this period, the government retained the NRS. This was upgraded to a department starting in 2003 and in 2005 was placed under the Ministry for Immigration and Registration of Persons, which worked under the Office of the President. These units had small staffs and focused largely on liaising between UNHCR and other parts of the Kenyan government, like the Department of Immigration, the Police Department, the National Registration Bureau, the Intelligence Service, and the Kenyan Human Rights Commission.[124]

Delegation to UNHCR was also accompanied by a decision to require refugees to reside in camps. Archival evidence seems to indicate that the encampment decision was made by the government. If these flows were seen as temporary, then border camps would make it possible to provide quick assistance while safeguarding Kenya's security and making eventual repatriation easier.[125] For its part, UNHCR agreed that asylum-seekers, with limited exceptions, "may be confined to specific places of residence."[126] Other accounts suggest that UNHCR sees encampment in the face of mass influxes as an acceptable compromise that both mollifies host governments and enables the Agency to assist refugees.[127]

Concurrently, UNHCR became responsible for managing camp operations, and substantial donor funds began to pour in. NGOs, as implementing partners, were subcontracted to provide social, health, and community services in the camps. The scope of UNHCR activities included constructing and repairing infrastructure like roads, boreholes, and medical and educational facilities. The Agency was also responsible for distributing supplies to refugees including plastic sheeting, blankets, firewood, and soap. This meant that UNHCR funds

---

Pérouse de Montclos 1998a, 156–57; Lomongin 2001, 5; Campbell, Crisp, and Kiragu 2011, 5, 16; Lindley 2011, 20, 32; Odhiambo-Abuya 2004, 188.

[121] Verdirame and Harrell-Bond 2005, 83.
[122] Qtd. in ibid., 36.
[123] Qtd. in Milner 2009, 88.
[124] Verdirame and Harrell-Bond 2005, 31; Kagwanja and Juma 2008, 220; Kenyan Ministry of State for Immigration and Registration of Persons 2009, 27; UNHCR 2005, 8–9.
[125] Campbell, Crisp, and Kiragu 2011, 5.
[126] UNHCR Branch Office in Kenya to UNHCR Headquarters in Geneva, 30 March 1991, "Incoming Cable," UNHCR Archives, Fonds 11, Series 3, 100 KEN SOM Refugee Situations—Special Groups of Refugees—Somalian Refugees in Kenya [Volume A], Folio 8.
[127] Jamal 2000, 8; Verdirame 1999, 57; Veney 2007, 94.

were overstretched, and funding reductions translated into overburdened infrastructure and fewer relief items for refugees.[128]

UNHCR went along with the government's policy in other ways through the 1990s and into the early 2000s. Refugees who reached the Agency's branch office in Nairobi were told to head to Dadaab or Kakuma. Few refugees were given authorization to reside in Nairobi, with assistance provided there only to the most vulnerable. One reason for this neglect of urban refugees was, according to a UNHCR report, because "for many years, the operation was hampered by chronic under-funding and under-staffing." Only in 2005 did the Agency launch an urban refugee program, the Nairobi Initiative.[129]

In December 1992, newly elected President Moi announced that refugees would be sent back to Somalia immediately. In response, UNHCR launched the Cross Border Operation (CBO), a massive rehabilitation and resettlement program in Somalia. The CBO aimed to enable Somali refugees in Kenya to return, as well as to dissuade further flows, by rehabilitating parts of Southern Somalia and creating a "preventive zone." By 1993, some 30,000 Somali refugees had returned from Kenya. That said, some refugees (having received the repatriation package) subsequently returned to camps in Kenya. At the same time, new arrivals from Somalia dramatically decreased in 1993 and 1994, though it is unclear whether this is due to the preventive zone or de-escalation of violence in the area.[130] Indeed, at one point, Kenyan authorities declined to develop new refugee campsites, since "the CBO would result in massive returns."[131]

According to my theoretical argument regarding foreign policy and ethnic politics, I would expect the Kenyan government to delegate to the UN for Sudanese refugees, for Ugandan refugees in the mid-1970s and again in the mid-1980s, and for Rwandan refugees until the mid-1990s. Kenya's delegation patterns do not perfectly match these expectations, since the government transferred responsibility for all refugees in the early 1990s.

Still, the evidence in the remainder of this section shows that many of the mechanisms I laid out in chapter 2 seem to influence interactions between Kenya's government and UNHCR. Specifically, the Agency's activities were limited due to restricted funds and influence. UNHCR also proved sensitive to sanction by Kenya and sought to conform to the government's preferences.

[128] Milner 2009, 87; Lindley 2011, 20; Verdirame 1999, 57; Hyndman and Nylund 1998, 28; Veney 2007, 154, 57, 67.

[129] Campbell, Crisp, and Kiragu 2011, 8; Lindley 2011, 38–39.

[130] Hyndman and Nylund 1998, 27; Lindley 2011, 24–29; Hyndman 2003, 177; Kirkby et al. 1997, 182–85.

[131] Musa Abiriga, 21 October 1992, "Note for the File: Meeting with Kenya Delegation to ExCom— 14 October 1992," *UNHCR Archives*, Fonds 11, Series 3, 10 KEN External Relations—Relations with Governments—Kenya [Volume B], Folio 24.

## Limited Resources and Power

Chapter 2 argued that by delegating to UNHCR, policymakers can shift blame for policies while ensuring that the Agency will not treat refugees too generously. In this section, internal communications reveal how its limited resources shaped UNHCR's advocacy and activities. The Agency was powerless to convince Kenya to establish a governmental status determination process, unable to handle the resource and resettlement demands of running its own process, and incapable of ensuring its decisions would be respected by Kenyan officials. While UNHCR may have appeared to be in control of the refugee camps, it was dependent on the government for permission and access.

During the 1970s, Kenya rebuffed UNHCR's repeated requests to establish an official process for RSD. In 1971, a process suggested by the Agency was deemed "too formal."[132] The following year a UNHCR official met with Kenyan authorities and reported back that they did not appear to be "even toying with the idea of establishing a consultative machinery."[133] The Agency was concerned about the procedures followed by the Kenyan government because there was "no provision for cooperation between the authorities and UNHCR" (even though the branch office was often consulted in practice).[134] There seemed to be a window of opportunity in 1978, and UNHCR approached the acting coordinator for an interministerial National Standing Committee on Refugees.[135] Once again, Kenyan authorities declined to set up an eligibility committee, a decision that "must have been taken at a higher level."[136] In 1980, UNHCR was informed that "the formation of the Eligibility Committee is no longer considered necessary nor useful." It had been envisioned when the numbers of Ugandans seeking asylum in Kenya was large.[137]

---

[132] Carsten Brink-Peterson, 9 June 1971, "Note for the File: Discussions with Mr. N.M. Mugo, Undersecretary, Ministry of Foreign Affairs, 17 May 1971," *UNHCR Archives*, Fonds 11, Series 2, Box 1197, 630 KEN Protection and General Legal Matters—Eligibility—Kenya [Volume 1], Folio 13.

[133] "Mission of Mr. E.K. Dadzie to Kenya, Tanzania, Zambia, Botswana, from 26 May 1972 to 19 June 1972," *UNHCR Archives*, Fonds 11, Series 2, Box 1197, 630 KEN Protection and General Legal Matters—Eligibility—Kenya [Volume 1], Folio 18.

[134] Eberhard Jahn, 7 April 1978, "Report on Dr. Jahn's Mission to the Sudan, Kenya, and Uganda, 4–18 March 1978," *UNHCR Archives*, Fonds 11, Series 2, Box 1198, 630 KEN Protection and General Legal Matters—Eligibility—Kenya [Volume 2], Folio 94.

[135] Shinga-Vele Lukika, 14 April 1978, "Note for the File: Meeting with Mr. M.H. Motiga re Refused Cases," *UNHCR Archives*, Fonds 11, Series 2, Box 1198, 630 KEN Protection and General Legal Matters—Eligibility—Kenya [Volume 2], Folio 96.

[136] Shinga-Vele Lukika to UNHCR Headquarters in Geneva, 27 April 1978, "Asylum Seekers Refused Refugee Status in Kenya," *UNHCR Archives*, Fonds 11, Series 2, Box 1198, 630 KEN Protection and General Legal Matters—Eligibility—Kenya [Volume 2], Folio 99.

[137] K.O. Doherty [Deputy Representative BO Kenya], 1 February 1980, "Meeting with Mr. D. Kaniaru of the Office of the President," *UNHCR Archives*, Fonds 11, Series 2, Box 1198, 630 KEN Protection and General Legal Matters—Eligibility—Kenya [Volume 2], Folio 123.

During this time, UNHCR decided internally that it would not expend much effort trying to persuade Kenya's government to establish a status determination procedure. It was going to be "very difficult" to set up an "autonomous and independent" eligibility body as well as an appeals process. In the meantime, the status quo was "not unsatisfactory" since there were no detentions or expulsions. The establishment of a status determination process with "more formal participation" by the Agency would require "the presence of qualified UNHCR staff . . . practically indefinitely." Accordingly, it might not be "good policy . . . to take more energetic action in this field."[138]

Kenya later transferred responsibility for refugees to UNHCR, and the Agency was eventually forced to adjust its activities in the face of dwindling resources. With the end of the "emergency phase" of the refugee crisis in 1997, UNHCR came under pressure to reduce spending in Kenya. It reportedly responded by rejecting cases and thereby keeping recognition rates low. The Agency tried to persuade the government to take over RSD again, only to be told that "refugees are UNHCR's problem."[139]

Even though UNHCR was put nominally in charge of RSD, the Kenyan government never *officially* conceded that it would recognize the Agency's decisions. Thus, after the US embassy bombing in August 1998, the minister of home affairs announced that UNHCR had no authority to grant refugee status, and its protection letters would not be recognized by the government. Refugees who complied with a directive to turn over their papers to the Immigration Department were issued with a "Notice to Prohibited Immigrant," which instructed them to leave Kenya within fourteen days.[140]

UNHCR's RSD operation was further limited by concerns, on the part of the Agency itself, that it would be charged with the difficult task of resettling any refugees that it recognized. An internal document from 1976 cautioned that "[one] must also bear in mind . . . that the Kenyan authorities would certainly not look with favor on mass positive eligibility decisions by UNHCR on Mozambicans." The Kenyan government would "almost certainly" expect UNHCR to resettle them, and this would be "extremely difficult." As such, UNHCR had to adopt "a very careful approach to the Kenyan authorities."[141] Earlier, UNHCR officials had noted the importance of clarifying that the resettlement of African refugees was, in principle though not always in practice, the responsibility of the OAU

---

[138] J. Terlin, "Note for the File," *UNHCR Archives*, Fonds 11, Series 2, Box 1197, 630 KEN Protection and General Legal Matters—Eligibility—Kenya [Volume 1], Folio 32.

[139] Verdirame and Harrell-Bond 2005, 34–35; Verdirame 1999, 57.

[140] Verdirame and Harrell-Bond 2005, 34, 82; Verdirame 1999, 57–58; O'Neill, Rutinwa, and Verdirame 2000, 154.

[141] J.D.R. Kelly, 2 June 1976, "Note for the File: Mozambicans in Kenya," *UNHCR Archives*, Fonds 11, Series 2, Box 1197, 630 KEN Protection and General Legal Matters—Eligibility—Kenya [Volume 1], Folio 58A.

Bureau. Otherwise, it was feared, "we shall be held responsible for moving these persons, a situation we wish to avoid."[142]

To the casual observer, UNHCR appeared to be in full control with regard to refugee camps. Inside the camps, the Kenyan government's "hands-off" approach made it seem largely and visibly absent: "Here, the government is spoken of in the past tense."[143] The Refugee Directorate did not have representatives in the camps, and district officers were uninvolved in refugee affairs. Indeed, the governmental district officer in Kakuma town had such limited involvement with the camp that he had to rely on UNHCR for transportation in order to sign travel passes. An NGO subcontracted by UNHCR, the Lutheran World Federation, was responsible for security and hired Kenyans and refugees to patrol the camp. Security issues were referred, depending on their gravity, to UNHCR or a refugee leaders' "court." Occasionally, government officials and members of parliament even complained that visits to the camps had to be negotiated with UNHCR.[144]

In some important respects, however, the Kenyan government was fully in control of encampment. UNHCR's activities could not take place without the government's permission and support—for example, the government provided land for the construction of camps. Crucially, the government decided where camps would be located and which camps would remain open or be closed.[145]

Indeed, archival documents confirm that camp closure decisions were made by Kenyan authorities. A 1992 letter from the home affairs ministry informed the UNHCR branch office that "[t]he Government has decided that the Refugee Camp at Utange, Mombasa be closed with immediate effect. The Refugees currently in that camp should be distributed to other Refugee camps existing in the country. Hence, you are kindly requested to facilitate the move."[146] UNHCR attempted to negotiate the terms of this move, such as that relocation should be voluntary.[147] The response from Home Affairs was to advise that "the relocation

---

[142] Robert Muller [Chief, Resettlement Section, UNHCR Headquarters in Geneva] to Carsten Brink-Peterson, "Interim procedure for the determination of refugee status," *UNHCR Archives*, Fonds 11, Series 2, Box 1197, 630 KEN Protection and General Legal Matters—Eligibility—Kenya [Volume 1], Folio 14.

[143] Catholic priest qtd. in Kagwanja 2002, 102.

[144] Aukot 2003, 74; Verdirame 1999, 62–63; Jamal 2000, 37; Veney 2007, 100; Kagwanja 2002, 102; UNHCR 2005, 22.

[145] Veney 2007, 174.

[146] Z.J. Kamencu [Permanent Secretary, Ministry of Home Affairs and National Heritage] to Carrol Faubert [UNHCR Representative in Kenya], 19 June 1992, *UNHCR Archives*, Fonds 11, Series 3, 100 KEN GEN Refugee Situations—Special Groups of Refugees—Refugees in Kenya [Volume A], Folio 17.

[147] Carol Faubert to Abudi Kobai [Deputy Secretary, Ministry of Home Affairs and National Heritage], 22 June 1992, *UNHCR Archives*, Fonds 11, Series 3, 100 KEN GEN Refugee Situations—Special Groups of Refugees—Refugees in Kenya [Volume A], Folio 17.

of the refugees from Mombasa and Utange camps to Hagadera camp should begin not later than 29 June 1992," that is, within days.[148] UNHCR was warned that "the decision to move the refugees from Mombasa and Utange is a cabinet decision and is not negotiable."[149] The Kenyan government also set a deadline, stressing that refugees ought to be moved from Utange by the end of August.[150] The urgency of relocation was reiterated the following year, along with a request to conduct a country-wide refugee headcount.[151] Once again, the government emphasized that the "closure is non-negotiable."[152] For its part, UNHCR said "[w]e certainly agree with the concept of closing camps located too near the border and consolidating refugee populations in areas formally allocated by" the government.[153]

UNHCR went along with these camp closures and refugee transfers. For example, it screened refugees at Thika to determine who should be allowed to remain. When the government decided to close the coastal camps in 1994, UNHCR organized the relocation of refugees to Dadaab and Kakuma. Veney says that the UNHCR "made it appear" as though the closures were due to voluntary repatriation rather than forced relocation.[154] From the Agency's perspective, it may have been preferable to have refugees relocated rather than refouled. The Agency could also reason that refugees would receive some protection in the camps.

The Agency was keenly aware that the government could impede its ability to operate. For instance, despite repeated requests in 1989, UNHCR was denied access to thousands of Somalis in Liboi.[155] The Agency had even proposed that the Kenya Red Cross be given access, "should the government not wish UNHCR

[148] Abudi Kobai to Representative UNHCR Representative to Kenya, 24 June 1992, "Relocation of Refugees from Mombasa and Utange Camp," UNHCR Archives, Fonds 11, Series 3, 100 KEN GEN Refugee Situations—Special Groups of Refugees—Refugees in Kenya [Volume A], Folio 17.

[149] G. Guebre-Christos [Deputy UNHCR Representative in Kenya], 29 July 1992, "Note for the File," UNHCR Archives, Fonds 11, Series 3, 10 KEN External Relations—Relations with Governments—Kenya [Volume B], Folio 20.

[150] Mbuo R. Waganagwa [Provincial Commissioner of Coast Province] to UNHCR Sub-Office in Mombasa, 29 July 1992, "Marafa Site," UNHCR Archives, Fonds 11, Series 3, 10 KEN External Relations—Relations with Governments—Kenya [Volume B], Folio 23.

[151] F.L. Abuje [Permanent Secretary, Ministry of Home Affairs and National Heritage] to Ebrima Camara [Deputy UNHCR Representative to Kenya], 7 September 1993, "Security in the Refugee Camps," UNHCR Archives, Fonds 11, Series 3, 10 KEN External Relations—Relations with Governments—Kenya [Volume C], Folio 28.

[152] Ebrima Camara to Karen AbuZayd [Chief, Kenya Unit, UNHCR Headquarters in Geneva], 8 September 1993, "Utange Camp—Relocation of Camp Population," UNHCR Archives, Fonds 11, Series 3, 10 KEN External Relations—Relations with Governments—Kenya [Volume C], Folio 28.

[153] Carol Faubert to Peter L.N. Kiilu [Provincial Commissioner, North Eastern Province], 14 December 1993, "Relocation of Liboi Refugee Transit Camp," UNHCR Archives, Fonds 11, Series 3, 10 KEN External Relations—Relations with Governments—Kenya [Volume C], Folio 31.

[154] Veney 2007, 173.

[155] Ernest Chipman to UNHCR Representative in Kenya, 20 October 1989, "Issues Arising from the 40th Session of ExCom," UNHCR Archives, Fonds 11, Series 3, 10 KEN External Relations—Relations with Governments—Kenya [Volume A], Folio 7.

to go itself."[156] Kenyan authorities held the Somalis under guard and refused to allow any international or national organizations access.[157]

This evidence depicts a UNHCR that was, despite appearances to the contrary, largely powerless and cash-strapped. With regard to RSD, the Agency could not persuade Kenya to set up an eligibility procedure. Conducting status determination itself proved demanding for UNHCR, and its decisions were sometimes ignored by the government. At the refugee camps, UNHCR appeared dominant but actually had no choice but to toe the line when the government decided to undertake a series of camp closures. Finally, UNHCR was forced to plead with the government, with limited success, in order to access groups of refugees. As the following discussion shows, UNHCR was also easily sanctioned by the Kenyan government and was therefore eager to follow Kenyan officials' directives.

## Punishment and Compliance

In chapter 2, I claimed that delegation to UNHCR imposes few costs on policymakers. The Agency is careful not to antagonize governments because it cannot operate on their territory without their approval. As a result, it tends to align itself with government preferences. Moreover, it is fairly easy for policymakers to punish UNHCR. In this section, I consider a number of vignettes that uncover these dynamics in Kenya.

When UNHCR officials were initially denied diplomatic status by the Kenyan government, their superiors in Geneva cautioned against making a fuss. The government was "dragging its feet" on officially recognizing him, reported Legal Adviser Kwame Adoo-Adare immediately after establishing a presence in Kenya in 1969.[158] "My status had never been completely cleared," complained his successor Carsten Brink-Peterson after several unsuccessful attempts to meet with the attorney general.[159]

This state of affairs resulted from "a compromise formula," said the response from UNHCR headquarters, which "[made] it possible to have a UNHCR

[156] Tessa Williams, 23 November 1989, "Note for the File," *UNHCR Archives*, Fonds 11, Series 3, 100 KEN GEN Refugee Situations—Special Groups of Refugees—Refugees in Kenya [Volume A], Folio 9.

[157] Amnesty International, 9 November 1989, "Fear of Refoulement: 2,500 Somali Asylum-Seekers in Northeastern Kenya," *UNHCR Archives*, Fonds 11, Series 3, 100 KEN SOM Refugee Situations—Special Groups of Refugees—Somalian Refugees in Kenya [Volume A], Folio 2.

[158] Kwame A. Amoo-Adare [UNHCR Legal Adviser for Eastern and Southern Africa] to Sadruddin Aga Khan, 25 November 1969, *UNHCR Archives*, Fonds 11, Series 2, Box 400, 203 KEN Privileges, Immunities, and Accreditations—Kenya, Folio 4.

[159] Carsten Brink-Peterson, 10 March 1970, "Note for the File: Discussions with the UNDP Resident Representative, Mr. Bruce Stedman in Nairobi," *UNHCR Archives*, Fonds 11, Series 2, Box 400, 203 KEN Privileges, Immunities, and Accreditations—Kenya, Folio 10B.

presence in Nairobi." Kenya's foreign ministry had "warned . . . very clearly" that the country was sensitive to criticism from the OAU that it was "promoting dissidence from political liberation parties . . ." Kenyan authorities were concerned that allowing the establishment of a full-fledged UNHCR branch office "would attract more refugees and thus lead to more criticism." Brink-Peterson was cautioned against pursuing official diplomatic status for himself: "if you make an issue of the status matter with the authorities, you will be heading for a lot of trouble." UNHCR in Kenya was "not comparable to . . . a normal UNHCR Branch Office." Instead, "refugees must be helped quietly and discreetly and . . . legal protection must also be done tactfully but firmly."[160] The matter was finally settled in 1972. The Kenyan government granted diplomatic recognition to Brink-Peterson's successor, but only following clarification that he would deal only with refugees in Kenya, as well as a title change from "Legal Adviser for East and Southern Africa" to "UNHCR Representative in Kenya."[161]

When UNHCR's behavior was deemed out of bounds, the government was quick to sanction it, as an incident that took place in 1989 reveals. A group of Ugandan refugees, including followers of Alice Lakwena, rioted at Thika Reception Center. Local press reported that Lakwena, who had led a rebellion against Museveni, had escaped from the center. President Moi was "embarrassed" because the Kenyan government had "consistently denied" that Lakwena was "being harbored" in the country. When they had entered the country in December 1987, UNHCR advocated for this group be released by police and transferred to Thika. So Moi ordered UNHCR's deputy representative to leave the country immediately, or else be declared persona non grata.[162]

Kenya was not done punishing UNHCR for the Lakwena incident, however. Shortly afterward, UNHCR's branch office in Kenya organized a meeting to discuss voluntary repatriation and invited Kenyan and Ugandan officials along with Ugandan refugee elders from Thika.[163] Less than 24 hours later, Kenya forcibly returned 238 Ugandans "without HCR knowledge or coordination."[164] The minister of home affairs said they did not consider this group to "be refugees, but

---

[160] Thomas Jamieson [Director of Operations, UNHCR Headquarters in Geneva] to Carsten Brink-Peterson, 20 March 1970, *UNHCR Archives*, Fonds 11, Series 2, Box 400, 203 KEN Privileges, Immunities, and Accreditations—Kenya, Folio 12.

[161] Carsten Brink-Peterson to UNHCR Headquarters in Geneva, 19 April 1971, "Memorandum: Status of Legal Adviser," *UNHCR Archives*, Fonds 11, Series 2, Box 400, 203 KEN Privileges, Immunities, and Accreditations—Kenya, Folio 30.

[162] G.T. Chaponda, 28 March 1989, "Note for the File," *UNHCR Archives*, Fonds 11, Series 3, 10 KEN External Relations—Relations with Governments—Kenya [Volume A], Folio 3.

[163] N. Obi [Associate Protection Officer, UNHCR Branch Office in Kenya], 4 April 1989, "Note for the File," *UNHCR Archives*, Fonds 11, Series 3, 10 KEN External Relations—Relations with Governments—Kenya [Volume A], Folio 3.

[164] Canh Nguyen-Tang [UNHCR Representative in Kenya], 6 April 1989, *UNHCR Archives*, Fonds 11, Series 3, 10 KEN External Relations—Relations with Governments—Kenya [Volume A], Folio 3.

merely people displaced during border problems."[165] An "administrative error was made in taking the group to Thika," but it was "a sovereign decision" to return them once hostilities had stopped."[166]

Sometimes the government's sanctioning of UNHCR was more subtle. When several hundred Somalis were forcibly returned from Mandera in July 1993, UNHCR issued a press release. Two days later, the Office of the President summoned UNHCR's representative to a meeting to express their regret "that at a time when the working relations between the Government and UNHCR was so positive, UNHCR should have gone public ... blaming the Kenya Government without even discussing the issue with Government Officers." Since this group had "activities linked to banditry ... this particular group is not a refugee group." UNHCR was told that "more results could be obtained through a quiet approach."[167]

UNHCR often proved eager to be responsive to the government's demands. In 1993, the government communicated that it "would rather expect visible progress in UNHCR repatriation efforts ... from Coastal refugee camps." In response, UNHCR explored expediting the first group of returnees "as [a] tangible indication vis-à-vis the GoK [Government of Kenya] that UNHCR is facilitating [voluntary repatriation] to the maximum extent possible."[168]

When the government decided to launch the occasional large-scale police roundup in the capital to enforce its encampment policy, UNHCR was not kept abreast but obliged by relocating refugees nonetheless. With one such round-up in August 1992, as with others, UNHCR was not "informed in advance of the operation nor did it take part in it."[169] However, the Department of Immigration was claiming that UNHCR had given too many refugees permission to remain in Nairobi.[170] So, according to Verdirame and Harrell-Bond, UNHCR's response was to forcibly transport refugees to the camps with a police escort, though it was "keen to do this out of the public eye."[171]

---

[165] Ernest Chipman to C. Kpénou, 1 June 1989, "DHC's Mission to Kenya: 16–17 May 1989," *UNHCR Archives*, Fonds 11, Series 3, 10 KEN External Relations—Relations with Governments—Kenya [Volume A], Folio 4.

[166] Canh Nguyen-Tang to Leonard Arap Sawe [Permanent Secretary, Ministry of Home Affairs and National Heritage], 20 July 1989, "Meeting of 7th July 1989 at MOHA&NH," *UNHCR Archives*, Fonds 11, Series 3, 10 KEN External Relations—Relations with Governments—Kenya [Volume A], Folio 4.

[167] Carol Faubert to Karen AbuZayd, 27 July 1993, "Note Verbale to GoK," *UNHCR Archives*, Fonds 11, Series 3, 10 KEN External Relations—Relations with Governments—Kenya [Volume C], Folio 28.

[168] Bart Leerschool [OIC, UNHCR Sub-Office in Mombasa] to Ebrima Camara, 3 November 1993, "New Arrival of Asylum seekers, Mombasa Old Port," *UNHCR Archives*, Fonds 11, Series 3, 100 KEN SOM Refugee Situations—Special Groups of Refugees—Somalian Refugees in Kenya [Volume B], Folio 26.

[169] *UNHCR Archives*, Fonds 11, Series 3, 100 KEN GEN Refugee Situations—Special Groups of Refugees—Refugees in Kenya [Volume A].

[170] Verdirame 1999, 72–75.

[171] Verdirame and Harrell-Bond 2005, 303.

UNHCR is frequently criticized by refugees and NGOs for emphasizing "soft diplomacy" with the Kenyan government in the face of border closures, refoulement, and difficult camp conditions. Observers note that UNHCR prioritizes continued engagement with the government; the Agency relies on the government for continued access and therefore cannot hold it truly accountable. UNHCR also refrained from issuing legal challenges when security forces have abused refugees.[172] According to an interviewee at an international NGO, the Agency does not push for improvements in the asylum system because it is concerned that "the entire house of cards could come crashing down."[173] At the same time, the Agency has been criticized for keeping its distance from refugees themselves, meeting with community representatives only after intercession by NGOs.[174] This may be the reason why the government and UNHCR reportedly enjoyed an "excellent" relationship in 2005.[175]

These examples show that UNHCR fell in line in response to Kenya's demands and was vulnerable to censure by the government. Early on, UNHCR representatives to the country were forced to accept their lack of diplomatic status and operate discreetly lest they anger the government. Later, when the Lakwena incident embarrassed Kenya, its government retaliated against UNHCR by threatening to declare one of its officials persona non grata and returning Ugandan refugees without coordinating with the agency. UNHCR was also warned that publicly criticizing the government would not yield results. For its part, UNHCR expedited refugee returns in response to government demands and went along with police roundups in the capital.

## Diplomats and Legislators

The previous sections explored delegation and discrimination, decisions essentially made by the executive. However, domestic actors in the receiving country can also influence decisions regarding asylum policy. For instance, in 1978, Kenyan authorities were considering allocating land for refugees in Kibwezi. Eight parliamentarians from Machakos district in Eastern Province objected, however. They expressed "fear" that "refugees will create social problems if integrated with nationals." They also voiced concerns about security, given that the allocated land would cut through a Mombasa-Nairobi "lifeline . . . for road,

---

[172] Lindley 2011, 22; African Rights 1993, 4; Lawyers Committee for Human Rights 1995, 69.
[173] NGO worker. Personal interview by author. Nairobi, Kenya, May 10, 2012.
[174] RCK 2003, 18.
[175] UNHCR 2005, 10.

railway, oil pipeline, and telephone." In response, authorities endeavored to select another site instead.[176]

In line with my argument in chapter 2, this section shows that members of the
Kenyan foreign policy bureaucracy advocated for inclusive asylum policies for
refugees from rivals and restrictive policies for refugees from friendly countries.
Meanwhile, members of parliament called for inclusive policies for ethnic kin
and restrictive policies for ethnic others. Legislators referenced ethnicity, while
diplomats referenced relations with sending countries.

There were divergences among legislators as well. In general, legislators
expressed hostility toward refugee groups with whom their constituents did not
share an ethnic affinity. A common sentiment was expressed by David Ekwee
Ethuro (NARC-Turkana Central Constituency) on November 20, 2003, when
he said regarding his non-co-ethnics: "I do not see why we still have refugees
from Uganda, Burundi, Rwanda and Ethiopia in our camps. These are fairly
stable countries."[177] Finally, government officials and domestic actors referred to
UNHCR's neutrality and its application of international standards.

This section begins by describing the database I constructed from the proceedings of the Kenyan parliament. Then, it compares statements made by legislators and by diplomats, demonstrating that there are divergent patterns in the
refugee groups they advocated for and that they justified their preferred policies
differently. Next, it explores variation among legislators, depending on the majority ethnicity of the district they represent. Finally, it examines references to
UNHCR and speakers' views of delegation to that Agency.

## Data

I examined the proceedings of the Kenyan parliament to create a database of
content related to foreign asylum-seekers and refugees. Searching issues released
between 1963, when Kenya gained its independence, and 2010, I located every
instance in which the keywords "refugee" or "asylum" were used. I also searched
for the Swahili verb root -kimbi- (to run or escape), to capture instances where
references were being made to refugees (m-/wa-kimbizi), asylum (kimbilio), and
asylum-seeking (-kimbilia).

[176] UNHCR Branch Office in Kenya, 10 May 1978, "Incoming Cable," UNHCR Archives, Fonds 11,
Series 2, Box 1198, 630 KEN Protection and General Legal Matters—Eligibility—Kenya [Volume 2],
Folio 101.
[177] Kenya 2003, 3999.

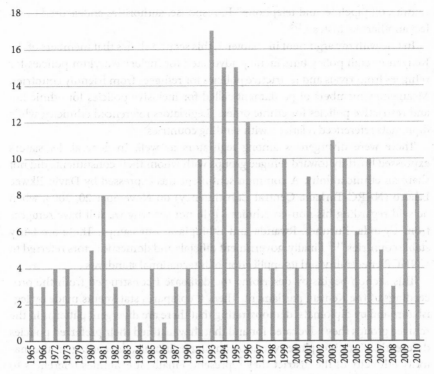

**Figure 6.1** Temporal distribution of Kenyan parliamentary documents referencing refugees

Note: Each document corresponds to one agenda item discussed on a particular day. In total, the database contains 216 documents with 249 unique speakers. The following years were missing from the online archive of the Kenya National Assembly Official Record (Hansard): 1967–1969, 1975, 1977–1978, and 1992.

The database comprises 216 documents and 249 unique participants. Each document collects statements by participants debating a distinct agenda item on a particular day. Figure 6.1 charts the frequency distribution of these units over time.[178] Appendix II provides additional details.

The following discussion presents my findings based on qualitative and quantitative analysis of this dataset. It focuses on Kenya's five largest refugee groups: Somalis, Sudanese, Ethiopians, Ugandans, and Rwandans.

---

[178] For the analysis presented here, I identified speakers who represented a district and were not members of the cabinet as "legislators." I considered the minister and assistant minister for foreign affairs as "diplomats." The database contains statements by 177 unique legislators and 12 diplomats.

## Divergence between Legislators and Diplomats

The first implication of my theoretical argument requires a comparison of statements by parliamentarians on the one hand and diplomats on the other. Legislators should demand inclusive refugee policies for ethnic kin and restrictive policies for ethnic others. Members of the foreign policy bureaucracy, meanwhile, should demand inclusive policies for refugees fleeing rivals and restrictive policies for refugees fleeing friendly regimes.

I first examine "co-occurrences," that is situations in which two codes are present anywhere in a particular statement. Specifically, I focus on statements that refer to a particular country or refugee group *and* indicate a preferred refugee policy. Figure 6.2 compares co-occurrences for members of parliament (MP) and foreign policy (FP) personnel. It plots Jaccard's coefficients, which measure the degree of shared overlap, for five countries (Somalia, Sudan, Ethiopia/Eritrea, Uganda, and Rwanda) and three tiers of refugee policy (inclusive, intermediate, and restrictive).

As shown in Figure 6.2, there were divergences between parliamentarians and diplomats across the different refugee groups. When parliamentarians mentioned refugee groups, they more commonly advocated for inclusive policies. In

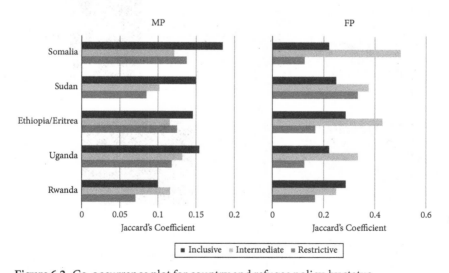

**Figure 6.2** Co-occurrence plot for country and refugee policy, by status

Note: Co-occurrences take into account the presence or absence of codes, but not their frequency, within each statement. Jaccard's coefficient, a similarity measure that ranges from 0 to 1, calculates the intersection of two sets divided by their union. MP=member of parliament, FP=foreign policy personnel.

contrast, diplomats more commonly called for intermediate policies when they spoke of refugee groups.

Still, a statement may contain a reference to a particular refugee group and advocate for, say, an inclusive refugee policy, without those two occurrences being necessarily related to each other. To overcome this problem, we can investigate statements that indicate support for an inclusive asylum policy and reference a particular country, *within a single text segment*. Figure 6.3 displays the proportion of such statements by country, for MPs and FP personnel.

These results indicate that there are differences in the policies advocated for each refugee group, depending on whether speakers were legislators or diplomats. For example, parliamentarians were more likely than diplomats to advocate inclusive policies for Somali refugees, while diplomats were more likely than parliamentarians to advocate inclusive policies for Ugandan refugees.

Of course, these figures aggregate across all parliamentarians (among whom some shared an ethnicity with refugees while others did not) and across all time periods analyzed (in which bilateral relations fluctuated between friendly and hostile). It is worth noting that while refugees from Somalia share a kinship

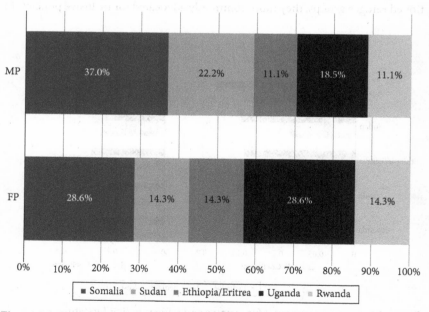

**Figure 6.3** Statements advocating inclusive refugee policies, by country and status
Note: This graph displays the proportion of statements in which, within a single text segment, a speaker indicated support for an inclusive asylum policy *and* mentioned Somalia/Somalis, Sudan/Sudanese/Darfuris, Ethiopia/Eritrea/Ethiopians, Uganda/Ugandans, or Rwanda/Rwandans. In total, 27 MP statements and 7 FP statements fulfilled these conditions. MP=member of parliament, FP=foreign policy personnel.

with Kenyan Somalis, this is not the case for refugees from Sudan, Ethiopia/ Eritrea, Uganda, and Rwanda.[179] This kinship may explain why parliamentarians advocated inclusive policies for Somali refugees more often than other refugee groups. Disaggregation by district (Somali and non-Somali) lends support to this reasoning.

Thus, quantitatively comparing parliamentarians' and diplomats' statements reveals that there are divergences in the policies they advocated for different refugee groups. While these findings match my theoretical expectations, strong conclusions should not be drawn from these figures, especially given the small sample sizes in Figure 6.3. The following analyses present additional and more detailed evidence.

## References to Ethnicity by Legislators and Foreign Policy by Diplomats

The second observable implication relates to how speakers justified their preferred asylum policies. Specifically, I expect legislators to emphasize ethnicity and diplomats to emphasize foreign policy. Of course, candid reasoning is more likely to be found in private communications than in public statements. Still, there is evidence in Kenyan parliamentary proceedings that is consistent with this observable implication.

Table 6.1 reports the percentage of statements by MPs and FP personnel that cite ethnicity and foreign policy as factors influencing their preferred refugee policy. Both legislators and diplomats cited foreign policy concerns more often than ethnic identity. However, 25% of MP statements referenced ethnicity, compared to 15% of FP personnel statements. Further, 85% of FP personnel

Table 6.1 Factors justifying refugee policy, by status

|  | MP | FP |
| --- | --- | --- |
| Ethnicity | 25.4% | 15.4% |
| Foreign Policy | 74.6% | 84.6% |

Note: Cells report column percentages. A reference to ethnicity or foreign policy appeared in 67 MP statements and 13 FP statements. MP=member of parliament, FP=foreign policy personnel.

[179] The majority ethnicity is "Somali and Somali Bantu" for refugees from Somalia, "Dinka and Nuer" for Sudanese refugees, "Oromo and Amhara" for Ethiopians, and "Hutu" for Rwandans. There is no information on the ethnicity of Ugandan refugees in Kenya, though it is certain they do not share a kinship with any of Kenya's major ethnic groups.

statements included a reference to foreign policy, compared to 75% of MP statements. In other words, MPs were more likely than FP personnel to cite ethnicity and less likely than FP personnel to cite foreign policy.

For example, FP personnel explained Kenya's receptivity to Namibian and South African refugees in the context of stressing its support for anticolonial liberation movements. Assistant Minister for Foreign Affairs Kamwithi Munyi (KANU-Embu East Constituency) was asked about government support for liberation movements on October 13, 1981. He noted: "Kenya supports the liberation movements in South Africa and in Namibia . . . Kenya also accommodates and employs a number of refugees from Namibia and South Africa."[180]

In fact, Kenya had long been concerned about refugees from African liberation struggles. In 1971, it was decided on a "high up level" that Namibians would not be given refugee status because "Kenya has been attacked . . . for having enticed such persons to betray the African cause."[181] Similarly, Mozambicans "belonging to the wrong, or having deserted from the right parties" were barred from receiving any documentation or assistance from the Kenyan government.[182] Only those who were fleeing colonial rule were recognized as refugees. Mozambicans who were dissenters from the Mozambican Liberation Front could not be accepted, particularly after it came to rule Mozambique. There were, according to Ministry of Home Affairs officials, "political considerations vis-à-vis the new Mozambican authorities which have to be taken into account by Kenya."[183] After the country's independence, asylum-seekers were "flatly refused recognition."[184] Kenya was unwilling to accept Mozambican refugees "as a matter of policy."[185]

In contrast, MP David Ekwee Ethuro (NARC-Turkana Central Constituency), speaking on November 20, 2003, expressed concern about refugees shifting the ethnic balance in his district. He complained that the "Kakuma area has a population of about 30,000 people, but the refugee population is about 90,000. So,

[180] Kenya 1981, 437.

[181] Carsten Brink-Peterson to UNHCR Headquarters in Geneva, 15 February 1971, "Eligibility—Kenya," UNHCR Archives, Fonds 11, Series 2, Box 1197, 630 KEN Protection and General Legal Matters—Eligibility—Kenya [Volume 1], Folio 5.

[182] Otto Bayer to UNHCR Headquarters in Geneva, 24 March 1972, "Resettlement of Mozambican Refugees," UNHCR Archives, Fonds 11, Series 2, Box 1197, 630 KEN Protection and General Legal Matters—Eligibility—Kenya [Volume 1], Folio 17.

[183] Usamah T. Kadry [UNHCR Representative in Kenya] to UNHCR Headquarters in Geneva, 15 June 1976, "Memorandum: Mozambican 'Appeals' for Continuing Refugee Status in Kenya," UNHCR Archives, Fonds 11, Series 2, Box 1197, 630 KEN Protection and General Legal Matters—Eligibility—Kenya [Volume 1], Folio 60.

[184] Eberhard Jahn, 7 April 1978, "Report on Dr. Jahn's Mission to the Sudan, Kenya, and Uganda, 4–18 March 1978," UNHCR Archives, Fonds 11, Series 2, Box 1198, 630 KEN Protection and General Legal Matters—Eligibility—Kenya [Volume 2], Folio 94.

[185] Eberhard Jahn to UNHCR Branch Office in Kenya, 28 June 1978, "Mozambicans in Kenya," UNHCR Archives, Fonds 11, Series 2, Box 1198, 630 KEN Protection and General Legal Matters—Eligibility—Kenya [Volume 2], Folio 103.

you have one local person to three refugees. We are reduced to a minority and those people can easily run over us . . . If we are going to integrate 90 people with 30 people, is that integration or assimilation? Very soon, you may never get an ethnic group in this country known as Turkana or Somali."[186]

To summarize, a simple tally of statements shows that MPs were more likely than FP personnel to cite ethnicity, while FP personnel were more likely than MPs to cite foreign policy. Examples drawn from the parliamentary record feature FP personnel emphasizing Kenya's support for liberation struggles abroad, while MPs stressed the effect refugee groups would have on their districts' ethnic balance. Thus, even though politicians are likely to be more sincere about their motivations in private, the public record still provides some evidence in support of my theoretical expectations.

## Divergence among Legislators

The final observable implication deals with divergence among legislators. When a legislator's constituents share an ethnic affinity with a refugee group, I expect her to demand inclusive asylum policies for that group. Conversely, she should call for restrictive policies toward groups seen by her constituents as ethnic others.

One way to assess whether these patterns hold is to focus on districts in which refugee camps are located. Figure 6.4 shows the geographic location of refugee camps in Kenya, along with the settlement patterns of the country's main ethnic groups. Both Kakuma and Dadaab are located in remote, sparsely populated, and underdeveloped areas that have long been neglected by the central government. In deciding to consolidate refugees in those two camps, the government was effectively containing them on the periphery of the state.[187]

In general, we should expect legislators from the NEP to advocate for more inclusive policies compared to legislators from the Rift Valley Province. The NEP borders Somalia and has a significant Kenyan Somali population. The majority of refugees encamped in the Dadaab complex in the NEP are Somali. These refugees share the language, religion, and ethnicity of Kenyan Somalis in that province, as well as a common nomadic pastoralist background. The Kakuma camps, meanwhile, are located in Turkana district of the Rift Valley Province in the northwest. The Kakuma complex hosted refugees from at least 9 countries and 18

---

[186] Kenya 2003, 3998–99.

[187] Milner 2009, 90; Campbell, Crisp, and Kiragu 2011, 6; Wagacha and Guiney 2008, 93; Hyndman and Nylund 1998, 41; Verdirame 1999, 61; Veney 2007, 113; Pérouse de Montclos and Kagwanja 2000, 207; Kagwanja and Juma 2008, 221; Verdirame and Harrell-Bond 2005, 33; Veney 2007, 97, 100; Kagwanja and Juma 2008, 224.

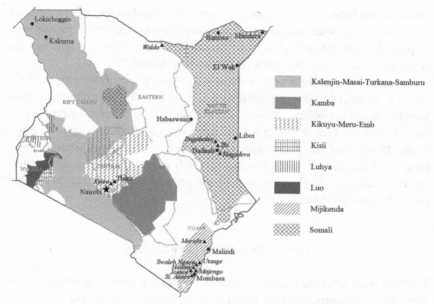

**Figure 6.4** Ethnic geography and refugee camp locations in Kenya

Note: Data on settlement patterns of politically relevant ethnic groups obtained from the GeoEPR Dataset. Approximate camp locations (marked by triangles) are from Pérouse de Montclos 1998a, 158; Pérouse de Montclos 1999, 29; Veney 2007, 112.

ethnic groups; roughly two-thirds were Sudanese, with Somalis and Ethiopians forming large groups as well. Unlike Somalis in Dadaab, the Sudanese refugees in Kakuma did not share the ethnicity of their Turkana hosts.[188]

My theoretical expectations are largely borne out by Figure 6.5: 60% of statements made by NEP MPs called for inclusive refugee policies, compared to 32% of statements by Rift Valley MPs. Conversely, 36% of statements made by Rift Valley MPs advocated for restrictive refugee policies, compared to just 13% of statements by NEP MPs.

At a more fine-grained level, comparing statements by MPs representing Lagdera constituency (where Dadaab is located) with those made by MPs representing Turkana North constituency (where Kakuma is located) is informative. In Somali-majority Lagdera, constituents shared an ethnic kinship with the predominantly Somali refugees in Dadaab camp. In contrast, constituents in Turkana North did not share an ethnic tie with the refugees residing in Kakuma camp.

---

[188] Verdirame 1999, 62; Jamal 2000, 37; Veney 2007, 100; Aukot 2003, 74; Pérouse de Montclos 2008, 201; Aukot 2003, 74.

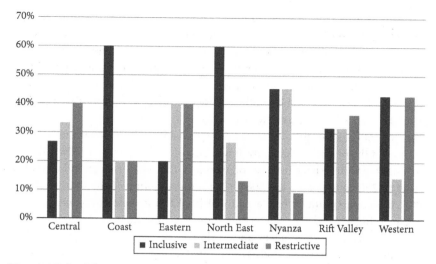

**Figure 6.5** Legislator statements on refugee policies post-1991, by province

Note: Each bar represents the percentage of statements on refugee policy made by MPs from that district that can be characterized as inclusive, intermediate, or restrictive. The graph covers 90 statements in total, distributed as follows: Central 15, Coast 10, Eastern 10, North Eastern 15, Nyanza 11, Rift Valley 22, and Western 7. I exclude Nairobi because it was only represented in one statement.

Indeed, Maalim Mohamed Farah (KANU-Lagdera Constituency) objected to a statement by the vice-president on October 24, 1996, saying: "Prof. Saitoti is making a very serious and misleading allegation in this House by saying that Somalia refugees are involved in activities that cause insecurity in the country when we know that not a single refugee has either been killed or caught by the Kenya police . . . Somali refugees should not be used as a scapegoat here. They are people."[189] He returned to the same theme some years later, on July 13, 2010, saying, "To profile Somalis and create a form of xenophobia emanating from our own House is a very bad precedent."[190]

Meanwhile, on April 15, 1998, John Munyes Kiyong'a (FORD-K, Turkana North Constituency) was concerned about what he called "the refugee influx in Turkana." He protested, "This Government is dumping all the refugees in Kakuma, in my constituency . . . We cannot allow Turkana to be a dumping ground for refugees from all countries, like Somalia and Ethiopia. Why can they not be taken to the Coast or some other places in this country? Why are they being dumped there?"[191]

[189] Kenya 1996, 2334.
[190] Kenya, 2010, 36.
[191] Kenya 1998, 223.

Finally, if we look at the parliamentary debate around the 2006 Refugee Act, we find a pattern consistent with my argument. As far as I can tell, this debate took place on November 20 and 25, 2003, on a draft bill and then on November 14 and 15, 2006, on an amended bill. The statements do not follow party lines, nor are all parliamentarians whose districts already hosted refugees similar compared to all those who did not. Rather, there is a difference in tone depending on the ethnic majority of each electoral district.

By way of background, Kenya had no national legislation governing refugees for most of the period under study. It was only after the election of Mwai Kibaki, and possibly to draw back international donors, that a new refugee bill was introduced in 2003 and passed in 2006.[192] With the adoption of the Refugee Act in 2006, the country finally had a national legal framework governing asylum-seekers, refugees, and status determination. The 2006 Refugee Act defined statutory and prima facie refugees and outlined criteria for disqualification and cessation of refugee status. It also established a Department of Refugee Affairs to be "responsible for all administrative matters concerning refugees in Kenya" and to "coordinate activities and programs relating to refugees." As head of this department, the commissioner of refugee affairs was tasked with formulating policy, coordinating refugee protection and assistance measures, managing refugee camps and facilities, registering refugees and issuing them documents, and promoting durable solutions.[193]

In debating this bill, David Ekwee Ethuro (NARC-Turkana Central Constituency), whose constituents did not share an ethnic tie with refugees, complained that host communities were not consulted when the government appropriated land for refugee camps and asked "Why can we not establish refugee camps in Thika, Tetu or other nice places in the Central Province?" Refugees were receiving food and water, with local communities "looking across the fence." Comparing the local Somali and Turkana communities, he stressed: "At least, the Somali have an entire province whereas we only have one district, and these refugees could easily overrun us." Though he supported the adoption of legislation to manage refugees in principle, he opposed the draft provisions in this bill.[194]

Compare this statement with those of parliamentarians from Somali-majority Garissa County who shared an ethnic tie with Somali refugees. Aden A. Sugow (KANU-Fafi Constituency) also acknowledged that hosting refugees entailed problems with insecurity, economic disparities, and environmental degradation. However, he felt that freedom of movement would solve many of these problems.

[192]  Milner 2009, 89.
[193]  Kenya 2007.
[194]  Kenya 2003, 3997–99.

The bill would help refugees as well as host communities, and would enhance Kenya's image "as a very hospitable state."[195] Mohamed Yussuf Haji (KANU-Ijara Constituency) emphasized "the plight of refugees," saying that "[t]hey need sympathy," even as he recognized that local communities do not benefit from hosting refugees. He also defended Somali refugees in Eastleigh, noting that remittances were contributing to the Kenyan economy and that they employed Kenyans. Kenya could benefit from allowing refugees to get legitimate employment, he argued.[196]

This debate suggests that legislators were demanding inclusive (or restrictive) policies depending on whether their constituencies shared (or lacked) an ethnic affinity with the refugee group they host. In Garissa County, the majority of voters are Kenyan Somalis who share an ethnic affinity with Somali refugees. Accordingly, parliamentarians representing that district seem generally supportive of refugees. Meanwhile, in Turkana County, the majority of voters are Turkana who regard Sudanese refugees as ethnic others.

In short, legislators demanded more inclusive asylum policies when their constituents shared an ethnic affinity with the refugees encamped there and more restrictive policies otherwise. NEP MPs, whose constituents shared an ethnic tie with the Somali refugees living in Dadaab, were more likely to call for inclusive refugee policies percentage-wise. Meanwhile, Rift Valley MPs, whose constituents regarded the inhabitants of Kakuma camp as ethnic others, called for restrictive policies at a higher rate. Moving from the province to the constituency level, by comparing Lagdera and Turkana North constituencies, reveals a similar trend. Finally, during discussions about the 2006 Refugee Act, there were stark differences between representatives from Garissa County and Turkana County.

## References to UNHCR

A final implication of my argument involves examining references to UNHCR. On the one hand, cabinet officials should attribute responsibility to the Agency. On the other, legislators should be persuaded by these claims, referring to UNHCR's influence and its impartiality. The evidence presented next aligns with these expectations.

Discussions surrounding the 2006 Refugee Act, which would ostensibly transfer responsibility from UNHCR to the government, are especially illuminating here. Expressing his support for the bill, the assistant minister for agriculture noted that "[I]n the past . . . it was the responsibility" of UNHCR and NGOs

---

[195] Ibid., 4043–45.
[196] Kenya 2006, 3705–07.

"to look after refugees." He welcomed the government stepping in "instead of us being dependent on the UNHCR."[197] Likewise, the minister of state for immigration and registration of persons decried the status quo, explaining that "Kenya is the only country in the world that has abrogated its national sovereignty to the United Nations agencies through the lack of a law to manage refugees."[198]

Legislators echoed these claims numerous times across the years. For example, in 1993, Eliud Matu Wamae (Democratic Party-Mathira Constituency) noted that UNHCR "takes care of the refugees in Kenya . . . not the Kenya Government."[199] Three years later, Maalim Mohamed Farah (KANU-Lagdera Constituency) complained that "[w]e have tried to talk to the Government on numerous occasions to own up to its own responsibility and negotiate firmly with UNHCR."[200] And in 2002, David Musila (NARC-Mwingi South Constituency) referred to UNHCR "under whose jurisdiction these refugees . . . fall."[201]

Like the cabinet officials quoted above, legislators also applauded the 2006 Refugee Act for ostensibly bringing refugee affairs under the government's control. Abdi Tari Sasura (KANU-Saku Constituency) noted that there was "very little participation from Kenyan officials" in refugee affairs, leaving refugees "at the mercy of international organizations" like UNHCR.[202]

Aden A. Sugow (KANU-Fafi Constituency) described the status quo, whereby UN agencies and NGOs "have been running the affairs of refugees." The new bill would allow the Kenyan government to "take the bull by the horns and take responsibility for its guests."[203] Similarly, Mohamed Yussuf Haji (KANU-Ijara Constituency) said it was "unfortunate" that Kenya had "almost abdicated its responsibility" to UNHCR. He disclosed that when he was provincial commissioner for Rift Valley Province, he "had to ask permission to visit Kakuma Refugee Camp" which ought to have fallen under his jurisdiction.[204]

Legislators also stressed UNHCR's stature as an international organization. Joseph Lagat Kipchumba (KANU-Eldoret East) expressed his concern in 2003 that the government would be able to take responsibility for refugees via the Refugee Act. He noted that UNHCR "is a very old arm of the [UN] which has dealt with refugees for a very long time and, therefore, it is very experienced in terms of handling the refugees."[205]

---

[197] Kenya 2003, 4032.
[198] Kenya 2006, 3711.
[199] Kenya 1993, 65.
[200] Kenya 1996, 484.
[201] Kenya 2002, 2584.
[202] Kenya 2003, 3986.
[203] Ibid., 4044.
[204] Kenya 2006, 3705–06.
[205] Kenya 2003, 3993.

Years later, in 2010, Adnan Keynan Wehliye (KANU-Wajir West) also stressed that the UN is "an international organization" and "not a government." Accordingly, "UNHCR has international recognition because it is one of the arms of the UN." Kenya ought to rely on "international accepted organizations" like UNHCR in order to register refugees and "allow them the necessary decorum."[206]

The examples cited here show a cabinet official attributing responsibility for asylum policy to UNHCR. Various legislators appeared to believe such a claim, referring to the Agency's influence and its prominence. These statements were especially prevalent during debates regarding the 2006 Refugee Act, which would purportedly shift responsibility for refugees from UNHCR to the Kenyan government.

## Summary of Findings

This chapter presented analyses covering discrimination and delegation. Then, it used parliamentary debates to compare statements by Kenyan diplomats and legislators. This section presents a summary of my findings and assesses their fit with my theoretical expectations. Overall, the trends in discrimination and delegation are consistent with my argument. Evidence from the within-country level also aligns with my expectations. These findings demonstrate that Kenyan policies were more complex than conventional accounts, which emphasize a wholesale shift in the 1990s, suppose.

Up until the fall of the Barre regime, and despite significant donor pressure, Somali refugees who attempted to enter Kenya encountered closed borders, pushbacks, and expulsions. Meanwhile, officials loyal to Barre did not face barriers to entry. Unrelenting pressure from foreign donors notwithstanding, Kenya only opened the border with the fall of the Barre regime in 1991, even though refugee numbers had swelled by that point. Settlements of Somali refugees which posed no discernible economic or security threat (like Marafa) were closed, and the refugees were confined in harsh conditions at the Dadaab complex in the marginalized NEP. Government policies remained consistent, moreover, even as the numbers of Somali refugees stabilized or declined.

After the arrival of thousands of Sudanese refugees in 1991, Kakuma refugee camp was established to house them in the poor and marginalized Turkana district. SPLA fighters fleeing Sudan's government were admitted and received support from the Kenyan government. SPLA commanders became active in Kakuma, sometimes taking leadership positions or engaging in forcible

---

[206] Kenya, 2010, 43, 35.

recruitment within the camp. In contrast, refugees who attempted to flee the SPLA into Kenya were turned back or experienced violence.

There is not much information available about the experience of Ethiopian refugees. However, it appears that they were denied refugee status by Kenyan authorities and barred from receiving UNHCR assistance. Moreover, they reportedly faced harassment by agents of the Ethiopian government, likely with the tacit approval of the Kenyan government. Ethiopian refugees also sought help from NGOs to avoid abduction and forcible repatriation by their home government.

Ugandan refugees, meanwhile, experienced several shifts in treatment. In the early 1970s, when relations between Kenya and Uganda were cordial, they faced expulsions and were unable to set up organizations to resist Amin's government. However, in the mid-1970s, amid tensions between Kenya and Uganda, the Kenyan government permitted the establishment of resistance organizations, so long as these were discreet. Experiencing the most inclusive treatment by the Kenyan government, Ugandans enjoyed freedom of movement, as well as access to social services and the labor market. With Obote's assumption of power in 1980, relations between the two countries thawed again, and Kenya once again began deporting politically-active exiles. For the first time, Ugandans were required to acquire a permit in order to work in Kenya. Nevertheless, after Museveni came to power and bilateral relations soured, the Kenyan government actively sponsored Ugandan exiles. In a final shift, in 1990, Ugandans were the target of police sweeps and were ordered to leave the country.

Rwandan refugees witnessed a dramatic shift in 1997. After Habyarimana was killed, Rwandan refugees were well treated, despite allegations that some were *génocidaires*. Following a rapprochement between the Kenyan and Rwandan governments in 1997, however, there was a police sweep targeting Rwandans. Kenya reversed its earlier position and agreed to transfer some of the Rwandans who had been rounded up to the ICTR.

With regard to delegation, the Kenyan government scrapped its own RSD mechanisms in 1991 and turned over refugee recognition along with camp management to UNHCR. Overburdened as it was, and especially as funds began drying up, the Agency may have deliberately kept its recognition rates low and encouraged the rapid repatriation of refugees. When the government decided to close and consolidate camps, UNHCR went along with this scheme and helped relocate refugees, perhaps because this helped reduce its own burden. In general, UNHCR has been criticized for prioritizing good relations with the Kenyan government over condemning abuses or advocating for refugees. In fact, UNHCR would not be able to operate in Kenya without the government's consent and support. Far from being weak or powerless, the Kenyan government decided where camps would be located and which ones would remain open. Moreover, the large screening exercises in the NEP demonstrate that the Kenyan government can employ significant resources and capacity.[207] Notably, the Kenyan government at times described refugees as UNHCR's responsibility, and at other times disregarded the Agency's status determinations.

Finally, parliamentarians and diplomats in Kenya expressed divergent sentiments regarding refugees in that country. While the policies pushed by diplomats seemed to be associated with foreign policy, legislators' statements appeared linked to ethnicity. Indeed, each legislator's position toward each refugee group seemed to align with whether they were co-ethnics of her constituents. In the Kenyan parliament, the UN Refugee Agency was consistently described as neutral and cast as largely in charge of asylum policymaking.

My theoretical predictions match up well with observed patterns in Kenya's inclusiveness and restrictiveness. However, the government transferred responsibility for all refugees to UNHCR in the early 1990s, rather than varying this delegation across groups and time periods. Still, my analysis of parliamentary debates lends additional support to the relevance of sending country relations and ethnic affinity in shaping group-specific asylum policies.

At the same time, there is little evidence that refugee flows from Somalia, Sudan, Ethiopia, Uganda, and Rwanda shaped relations between Kenya and these sending countries. Moreover, patterns of hostility or friendship with these countries have not been shaped by Kenya's reaction to refugee flows. Indeed, Kenya's support for the SPLA, Ugandan rebels, and Rwandan *génocidaires* appeared to result from, rather than cause, hostile relations with Sudan, Uganda, and Rwanda respectively.

It seems likely that Somali refugees, in particular, were singled out because they share an affinity with an excluded minority in Kenya. As ethnic "others," Somali refugees and Kenyan Somalis alike were the target of substantial government discrimination and repression, including screenings, expulsions, and violence. Though the Kenyan government frequently cited security concerns with regard to Somali refugees, these were inextricable from the exclusionary politics directed at Kenyan Somalis.

In short, this chapter's discussion points to the relevance of sending country relations and ethnic affinity in shaping group-specific asylum policies. The following section reviews possible alternative explanations that might explain the patterns in Kenya's asylum policies, including economic motivations, security considerations, and humanitarianism.

---

[207] As Veney puts it: "The screening of Kenyan-Somalis demonstrated how Kenyan sovereignty trumped the UNHCR's mandate." Veney 2007, 171.

## Alternative Explanations

This section considers various alternative explanations, demonstrating that these do not persuasively and fully explain trends in Kenyan asylum policies. First, far from being arbitrary, Kenyan asylum policy followed highly defined patterns and sometimes featured high-level involvement by political officials.

Moreover, shifts in policy do not seem to match changes in economic performance. Throughout the period under study, Kenya's real GDP per capita remained fairly steady, growing from about US$1,150 in 1966 to over US$1,250 in 2010.[208] The treatment of refugees did not become more restrictive across the board with the adoption of economic liberalization and structural adjustment policies in the 1980s and 1990s. Nor did policies become more restrictive across the board as the size of the refugee "burden" grew.

Though Kenya is heavily reliant on international assistance, most pressure from donors focused on democratization and domestic human rights abuses, rather than refugee policy.[209] As mentioned above, the government also saw fit to crack down on the most highly skilled refugees (Ugandans). Furthermore, Kenya's resource capacity cannot explain the divergences in treatment across refugee groups described in this chapter.

National security concerns, meanwhile, likely influenced the Kenyan government's response to Somali refugees. As I argued above, these concerns are tied up with domestic ethnic politics, particularly the history of repression in the NEP and the government's tendency to regard Kenyan Somalis with suspicion. Further, militant Islamist groups based in Somalia have been involved in terrorist attacks throughout East Africa.[210] Especially following the 1998 US embassy bombing in Nairobi, Kenya feared that radical Islamist organizations were using refugee camps as recruiting and training grounds.[211] While these security concerns may have shaped Kenya's restrictive responses to Somali refugees, they cannot explain why Kenya only admitted Somali refugees after the fall of the Barre regime nor can they explain differences in the treatment of other refugee groups.

---

[208] GDP per capita is reported at 2005 constant prices. Heston, Summers, and Aten 2012.

[209] According to Milner, however, some Kenyan officials were concerned about how the refugee question could affect Kenya's relationship with donor countries. Milner 2009, 106–07.

[210] During the 1990s, al-Ittihaad al-Islami engaged in recruitment and fundraising among ethnic Somalis in the NEP, Nairobi, and Mombasa. Al-Qaeda in East Africa attacked the US embassy in Nairobi in 1998 and the Israeli-owned Paradise Hotel in Mombasa in 2002. By the late 2000s, small-scale attacks on Kenyan territory were being attributed to al-Shabaab. International Crisis Group 2012.

[211] Kagwanja and Juma 2008, 222.

The numerical size of the Somali refugee flow may have played a role in Kenya's decision-making, but it is difficult to gauge the extent to which it was influential. Somali refugees numbered in the hundreds of thousands, but they were also ethnic others who shared an identity with a marginalized domestic minority. That said, the Kenyan government's varied treatment of other refugee groups cannot be attributed to their respective sizes. Moreover, there is no evidence that Kenya adapted its asylum policies in line with the responses of other host countries in the region.

Though Kenya held its first multiparty elections in 1992, this does not coincide with a major observed shift for any of the refugee groups. Refugee policies have not become uniformly more restrictive (or, alternatively, uniformly more inclusive) as publics gained power at the polls. In any case, insofar as ethnic mobilization around the issue of refugees was part of the electoral strategy of elites, this would be consistent with my argument. Legislators' party affiliation, moreover, does not explain the patterns observed in this chapter. However, the country's delegation pattern may be explained by path dependence.

Finally, there is no evidence that policies were shaped by humanitarian concerns. For example, there were stark differences in the treatment of Somali and Sudanese refugees fleeing civil war and in the treatment of Ethiopian and Ugandan refugees fleeing repression. Furthermore, all groups were not initially welcomed and then gradually shunned as the compassion fatigue argument would expect. Thus, these alternative explanations cannot fully account for the variation in Kenya's asylum policies.

## Conclusion

This analysis demonstrates that the common account of refugees in Kenya, which emphasizes a shift in 1991, masks important differences in the ways different refugee groups were viewed. It is true that Kenya shifted responsibility to UNHCR and adopted an encampment policy in the early 1990s. However, it was not uniformly generous to refugee groups prior to that period nor uniformly restrictive afterwards. For example, the Kenyan government's treatment of Ugandan refugees shifted multiple times. Even after 1991, Sudanese refugees experienced more inclusive treatment than Ethiopians. Further, Rwandans fleeing the aftermath of the genocide starting in 1994 were initially welcomed.

In chapter 2, I laid out the argument that, in selecting their asylum policy, policymakers weigh concerns related to foreign policy and ethnic politics. On the one hand, there are advantages to treating refugees from rivals well and those fleeing friendly states poorly. On the other, policymakers have incentives to be accepting of ethnic kin, but not of refugees with whom they lack an ethnic tie. In some cases, these domestic and international incentives will align. In other cases, domestic and international pressures will push in opposite directions, and the government will shift responsibility for unpopular decisions to UNHCR.

The variation in Kenyan responses to refugee groups is well explained by this theoretical framework. Foreign policy and ethnic politics together seem to have shaped Kenya's generosity and restrictiveness. Although there were few shifts in delegation, UNHCR's relationship with the Kenyan government functioned as expected. Moreover, existing explanations that attempt to account for the evolution of Kenya's refugee policies are insufficient.

This chapter also showed that asylum policy is shaped by two sets of domestic actors with divergent incentives: legislators and diplomats. Parliamentarians who represent domestic constituencies are most concerned about ethnic affinity with refugees. Members of the foreign policy establishment are more attuned to relations with the refugee-sending country. There is evidence that ethnic identity and sending country relations figure into the calculations of Kenyan legislators and diplomats, respectively.

Together with the previous three chapters, this analysis of Kenya's asylum policies offers persuasive support for my theoretical argument. Using quantitative analysis of a global dataset, chapter 3 demonstrated that my claims regarding foreign policy and ethnic politics may generally apply across countries and over time. Chapters 4 and 5 analyzed discrimination and delegation in a typical refugee recipient (Egypt) and an outlier (Turkey), again demonstrating the influence of ethnic identity and bilateral relations. The discussion in this chapter tackled the important case of Kenya, supplementing my examination of discrimination and delegation with an investigation of cross-cutting pressures in the Kenyan parliament. The next chapter elaborates on the implications of these findings for state sovereignty and refugee rights.

# 7

# The Implications of Selective Sovereignty for Refugee Rights

"The decisions we make to grant or refuse citizenship or refugee status are fundamental to our sovereignty," explained prominent Canadian politician and academic Michael Ignatieff in 2011.[1] Policymakers in developing countries have echoed this sentiment. In 2004, the Ugandan minister for disaster preparedness and refugees asserted: "I will not accept our sovereignty to be compromised by softness to refugees."[2] And in the early years of the Syrian refugee crisis, a Turkish official clarified: "we obviously will not allow [Syrian refugee] camps to be under the control of UNHCR. We will not give up our sovereign rights."[3] These statements, and numerous other examples like them, suggest that states are intent on asserting their sovereignty in regards to refugees.

But there are countries around the world where asylum applications are adjudicated, in whole or in part, by UNHCR. In effect, a number of governments have granted UNHCR authority to determine who is granted or denied refugee status and the privileges associated with that status (such as the right to remain in the country and to access assistance and social services). Moreover, countries have not adopted uniform border control measures, nor do they implement exclusionary policies across the board. Existing academic literature demonstrates that oftentimes a single country will treat different refugee groups differently.

We—scholars, practitioners, concerned citizens—need to better understand why countries treat refugees the way they do. So far, we have tended to focus on developed countries, which collectively host only 15% of the world's refugees. We have fixated on whether a country admits refugees at the border, largely overlooking how it deals with them after they enter. We have labeled countries with across-the-board adjectives, like generous or restrictive. But every government sifts refugees. And sometimes, instead of welcoming or rejecting refugees, governments outsource them to the UN.

This book argues that states' approaches to refugees are shaped by foreign policy and ethnic politics. These two factors explain the selective exercise of

---

[1] Ignatieff 2011.
[2] Olupot 2004.
[3] Yinanç 2012.

*Discrimination and Delegation*. Lamis Elmy Abdelaaty, Oxford University Press (2021). © Oxford University Press.
DOI: 10.1093/oso/9780197530061.003.0007

sovereignty, that is, when countries will welcome refugees, restrict them, or shift the burden to the UN. Internationally, leaders use refugees in order to reassure allies and exert pressure on rivals. And domestically, policymakers have incentives to favor those refugee groups with whom they share an ethnic identity. When these incentives point in opposite directions, policymakers are more likely to turn over refugee affairs to the UN. My argument is corroborated by evidence from cross-national statistical analysis, qualitative case studies of Egypt and Turkey, and content analysis of Kenyan parliamentary debates.

The following discussion uses the empirical evidence presented in previous chapters to reflect on the influence of foreign policy and ethnic politics on countries' approaches to refugees. This chapter considers the implications of these findings for a reconceptualization of the relationship between sovereignty and rights. It also addresses the consequences of selective sovereignty for the international refugee regime. In so doing, it suggests some policy implications, such as attempting to identify when and where the international community can fruitfully exert pressure on states to welcome refugees. Selective sovereignty shapes the experiences of growing numbers of refugees around the world and, as a result, has consequences for long-term processes related to conflict, peacebuilding, and post-conflict reconstruction. Recent events underscore the importance of understanding why states sometimes assert their sovereignty and at other times uphold refugee rights.

## Explaining State Responses to Refugees

This book is motivated by the discrimination and delegation puzzles: Why do countries welcome some refugees and treat others poorly? And when do governments willingly hand asylum policy over to the UN? In this section, I briefly review my theoretical answers to these questions and summarize my findings, before comparing policies relating to specific refugee groups across country cases. These cross-country comparisons include Iraqi refugees in Egypt and Turkey as well as Sudanese, Somali, Ethiopian, and Eritrean refugees in Egypt and Kenya.

### Foreign Policy, Ethnic Politics, and the Decision to Delegate

Research on refugees has often been more concerned with their admission at the border than their treatment within a country's territory. The question of whether borders are open or closed, or whether individuals are granted refugee status, is certainly crucial. But examining the treatment of individuals, whether their asylum applications are accepted or not, is also important. For these reasons, my research understands asylum policy to encompass more than just the decision to grant entry to asylum-seekers. To compare asylum policy across countries and refugee groups, chapter 2 introduced a set of indicators that assess the gap between international standards and a given country's law and practices. Are refugees permitted to move around freely? Are they allowed to work? Are they able to send their children to school? How are repatriation or integration handled? A country's asylum policies can thereby vary both over time and by refugee group.

I define asylum policy to include both de jure laws and de facto practices. Sometimes de jure laws on the books differ from the de facto practices implemented on the ground. This distinction certainly matters for the daily lives of refugees. For instance, their decisions to remain or move on are likely to be shaped by de facto experiences rather than de jure protections. And the distinction matters if scholars want to explain patterns of state compliance or noncompliance with their commitments under international refugee and human rights law.

This book argues that a two-level dynamic shapes whether state responses to refugees will involve inclusion, exclusion, or delegation. At the international level, refugee treatment can pressure rivals and reassure allies. By encouraging refugee flight, inclusive policies can have consequences for the sending government's stability. Refugee movements can also be used to impose reputational costs on a hostile sending country. In addition, refugees may be permitted to engage in cross-border activities that oppose a rival sending government. Policymakers will not want to destabilize or embarrass friendly sending countries, however.

At the same time, policymakers heed domestic political incentives to favor refugees with whom they share an ethnic (i.e., linguistic, racial, and/or religious) identity. Constituents generally prefer to welcome ethnic kin and to treat ethnic others poorly. Inclusive policies toward ethnic kin can also enlarge the policymaker's constituency, while exclusionary policies toward ethnic others can safeguard his constituency's relative size. Finally, asylum policies can be used to cultivate in-group favoritism and encourage mobilization along ethnic lines.

As a result, policymakers will adopt inclusive policies toward refugees who hail from a rival state and share their ethnic identity. Meanwhile, refugees who are fleeing a friendly sending state and lack an ethnic tie will be treated restrictively. Policymakers shift responsibility to the UN when incentives and pressures at the international and domestic levels point in opposite directions. Claiming that a neutral international organization is in charge of refugee affairs allows policymakers to avoid alienating refugee sending countries and domestic constituencies. At the same time, the UN Refugee Agency is easily punished and may self-censor to preserve its continued presence in the country.

## Discrimination and Delegation across and within Countries

The previous chapters substantiated my argument using a three-stage, multilevel research design that includes evidence from a quantitative dataset, elite interviews, special collections, archival research, and parliamentary records. The first stage involved statistical analysis of asylum admissions worldwide. The second stage considered refugee treatment, more broadly conceived, through qualitative case studies of Egypt and Turkey. The third stage zoomed in on parliamentary debates in Kenya, presenting a content analysis of individual statements about refugees.

In chapter 3, I used a global dataset to answer two questions relating to RSD. First, when are countries likely to delegate decision-making on asylum applications to the UN Refugee Agency? And second, when they retain these decision-making functions themselves, why do countries accept or reject asylum applications? Using a double-hurdle model, the first step estimates delegation and the second estimates acceptance rates given no delegation. Among the factors included in the model, in addition to foreign policy and ethnic politics, are the distance between the two countries, economic factors in each country, and whether the sending country is experiencing domestic violence. This chapter indicated that the theory may apply broadly across countries and over time, setting the stage for subsequent chapters to add detailed evidence.

Chapter 4 considers the case of Egypt, a "typical" refugee recipient in several respects: it is a developing country that has signed on to the 1951 Refugee Convention and hosts a relatively small number of refugees per capita. This chapter begins by reviewing the conventional wisdom about Egypt's asylum policy, that is, that it has no policy. And indeed, Egypt does not have domestic refugee legislation or a single, clearly articulated official asylum policy. However, as chapter 4 demonstrates, there are clear patterns in Egypt's responses to refugees. Drawing on elite interviews as well as archival sources and unpublished materials, I analyze and compare Egypt's post-WWII policies toward six refugee groups: Palestinians, Sudanese, Iraqis, Somalis, Eritreans, and Ethiopians. The fluctuation in Egyptian policies over time and their variation by refugee group is shown to be consistent with my argument about foreign policy and ethnic politics.

By analyzing the case of Turkey as a refugee-receiving country, chapter 5 enables a side-by-side comparison with the more typical Egyptian case laid out in chapter 4. One of only a handful of countries that retains a geographical limitation to the 1951 Refugee Convention (in effect, recognizing only Europeans as refugees), Turkey has experienced several mass refugee influxes and boasts one of the largest refugee resettlement programs in the world. The conventional wisdom in this "extreme" case emphasizes a dichotomy between European and non-European refugees. Chapter 5 establishes that Turkish policies are more nuanced than the conventional wisdom expects. Once again, I draw on a range of sources to examine how Turkey responded to Bulgarians, Iraqis, Iranians, refugees from the former Yugoslavia, and refugees from Soviet and post-Soviet states. This analysis reveals that even seemingly general policies that exist on the books were applied selectively, a pattern that betrays the influence of foreign policy and ethnic politics on Turkey's asylum policies.

To examine the mechanisms that shape asylum policy at a more fine-grained level, a final empirical chapter (chapter 6) concentrates on cross-cutting pressures within the Kenyan parliament. Kenya is often considered a "crucial" case: it hosts one of the largest refugee populations in the world, is home to one of the largest refugee camps in the world, and is the site of a grave, protracted refugee situation. Unlike previous work on refugees in Kenya, this chapter zooms in on parliamentary debates. It shows that statements about refugees vary depending on whether they are delivered by members of the foreign policy bureaucracy or by parliamentarians who represent domestic constituencies. This evidence further bolsters the argument that foreign policy and ethnic politics shape asylum policy.

There are considerable differences between Egypt, Turkey, and Kenya regarding their adoption of domestic legislation, their use of refugee camps, their relations with UNHCR, and their domestic conditions. Yet, the findings are consistent with my argument in all three cases, suggesting that my results are generalizable. Taken together, the evidence suggests that my argument is more convincing than alternative explanations that stress humanitarian ideals, refugee skills, the magnitude of refugee flows, and the arbitrariness of asylum decisions made by low-level bureaucrats.

## Shared Refugee Groups in Egypt, Turkey, and Kenya

The three countries that I focus on in this book share some of the same refugee groups. Both Egypt and Turkey host Iraqi refugees, and there are Sudanese, Somali, Ethiopian, and Eritrean refugees in Egypt and Kenya. This section briefly compares the treatment of each refugee group across countries.

Chapter 4 details the experience of Sudanese refugees in Egypt, and Kenya's policies toward the group are examined in chapter 6. Sudanese refugees began arriving in both countries in the early 1990s and lacked an ethnic tie with the group in power in each country. In Egypt, Sudanese refugees initially had access to a wide range of rights and were able to escape restrictions imposed on labor migrants from Sudan in the mid-1990s. But they began experiencing crackdowns in the late 1990s, corresponding with a normalization in Egypt's bilateral relations with Sudan. Refugees fleeing Sudan's government were also admitted to Kenya, in line with that country's allegiances during the Sudanese civil war, and the SPLA was able to recruit fighters and receive support. Of course, there was no encampment in Egypt, while Kenya restricted Sudanese refugees to Kakuma refugee camp. Still, comparing the treatment of Sudanese refugees in Egypt and Kenya seems to underscore the role of sending country relations in shaping asylum policy.

The Iraqis who sought refuge in Egypt and Turkey were fleeing different events and had different ethnic compositions. As described in chapter 4, Iraqi refugees flowing into Egypt were fleeing the wave of violence sparked by the 2006 al-Askari Mosque bombing. As Arab Sunnis, they shared an ethnic affinity with Egyptians. Meanwhile, Iraqi refugees who went to Turkey in 1998 and 1991 were ethnic Kurds fleeing Saddam's military campaigns. While Turkey restricted Iraqi Kurds to camps and repatriated them as soon as possible, Egypt simply denied Iraqis access to public services and the formal labor market. In short, Iraqis' experiences were markedly better in Egypt (where they were ethnic kin of the group in power) compared to Turkey (where they shared an affinity with Turkey's persecuted Kurdish minority). Thus, this comparison highlights the influence of ethnic identity.

Somalis fleeing the civil war entered Egypt and Kenya, both countries where they lacked an ethnic tie. In Egypt, Somalis experienced few detentions and deportations. In contrast, Somali refugees in Kenya faced encampment as well as extensive screenings, expulsions, and violence. It is likely that Somali refugees in Kenya, because they share an affinity with Kenya's own ethnic Somali minority, have been targeted for increased discrimination. The sheer magnitude of these refugee populations might explain the divergence between the two countries, at least in part, since the relatively small number of Somalis in Egypt could have escaped the attention of the authorities.

There is limited information about the experience of Eritrean and Ethiopian refugees in Egypt and Kenya. However, these refugees appear to have been treated restrictively in both countries. In Egypt, Eritreans and Ethiopians were detained and deported. In Kenya, the government was reluctant to recognize Ethiopians as refugees or allow them access to UNHCR assistance. The Ethiopian government was supportive of Egypt's border shootings policy, and it engaged in harassment of Ethiopian refugees on Kenyan soil. This treatment is broadly consistent with my theoretical expectations for ethnic others from friendly sending countries.

## Scholarly Contributions

This book explores state responses to refugees by weaving three thematic threads related to sovereignty and human rights, the politics of refugee migration, and delegation to international organizations. The argument that states are selective in their appeals to, and exercise of, sovereignty calls for a rethinking of the relationship between sovereignty and human rights. In addition, this book elaborates on and combines international and domestic political considerations into a two-level framework that is then tested across countries and regions. Finally, the book contributes to the literature on delegation by examining cases in which a country shifts responsibility for domestic asylum policies to the UN. This section details these scholarly contributions.

## Sovereignty, Human Rights, and Refugees

Global refugee movements have obvious consequences for sovereignty and the nation-state. To use Krasner's terms, asylum policy involves three kinds of sovereignty: interdependence sovereignty (the ability to regulate transborder flows), domestic sovereignty (the ability to exercise control within borders), and Westphalian sovereignty (the ability to exclude external actors).[4]

Refugee movements also invoke compliance with, and differential application of, international law as well as domestic contention over human rights and the involvement of international organizations. Though largely absent from the literature on the politics of human rights, displaced individuals may be mistreated at their destination, despite being entitled to certain universal rights and freedoms.

Examining whether refugees are included, restricted, or delegated can illuminate current debates about the relationship between sovereignty and rights. Refugee rights are similar to other human rights, in that they evoke some of the same questions related to commitment to international treaties, compliance with treaty obligations, and enforcement. At the same time, the international refugee regime is arguably more institutionalized, in terms of conventions and organizations, than the regimes relating to many other human rights. The 1951 Refugee Convention is subject to daily interpretation by judges and other officials, making it one of the most applied treaties in the world. On the other hand, refugee rights are distinct because they deal with how a government treats non-citizens rather than its own people. In a sense, then, the study of refugee rights can bridge the gap between scholarship on human rights and on humanitarianism.

---

[4] Krasner 1999.

Existing scholarship has considered how concerns about sovereignty and the development of the international human rights regime shape state responses to refugees. Some authors argue that we are witnessing the "end of asylum" or suggest that regulating migration is "the last bastion of sovereignty."[5] Others have suggested that states are "losing control" of their borders due to the forces of globalization and transnational networks.[6]

These accounts tend to disregard the fact that the desire for control and the exercise of sovereignty are not uniform, even for a single state. Clearly countries are not simply clamping down on population flows because they are besieged by the forces of globalization. Instead, countries have been selective in their appeals to, and exercise of, sovereignty in response to refugee flows. A country may assert its sovereign prerogative to control borders, turning away refugees and restricting their rights. Or it may relax it to welcome displacees and extend to them hospitable treatment. Finally, a government could cede decision-making to international organizations, empowering them to admit and assist refugees.

Thus, the relationship between refugee rights and sovereignty is more complex than one trumping the other. States may sometimes assert control to deny refugee rights, they may exercise their sovereignty to ensure that refugees are protected, or they may cede refugee protection to an international organization altogether.

This study also has implications for our understanding of the category of "the refugee," itself defined by sovereignty and its linkage of the state with citizenship and territory. The analysis in this book underlines the fact that the conferral of the refugee label is itself a political act. As shown in chapter 5, for example, Turkey has designated certain populations as guests rather than asylum-seekers or refugees. In doing so, Turkey was able to discriminate among groups who would otherwise belong under the same legal status, treating some better than others in line with considerations related to foreign policy and ethnic politics.[7] These findings call into question the assumption that the category of the refugee, on which the international refugee regime rests, is stable.

## Discrimination and the Politics of Asylum

This book also puts two growing bodies of research into conversation: the literature on the politics of migration and asylum and research on the international sources of domestic politics. For scholars from refugee studies, it is important to

[5] Rutinwa 1999; Dauvergne 2008, 47.
[6] Sassen 1996.
[7] Abdelaaty 2019.

recognize how much of the refugee experience is shaped by government policy and international politics. For scholars of international relations, refugees bring to the fore questions about sovereignty and border control, the effects of globalization, the role of international organizations, and the influence of human rights ideals.

The determinants of states' refugee policies remain understudied. Many studies of refugees in international relations have instead focused on conflict as a cause or consequence of refugee flows, while others have sought to analyze international cooperation in the global refugee regime. Meanwhile, the far smaller literature on asylum policymaking by receiving countries has tended to be narrow in geographic scope, descriptive (rather than theoretical), or otherwise limited analytically and empirically.

To be sure, a number of scholars have examined asylum policy in the United States; an important case of course, though hardly representative of refugee-receiving countries. Many of these studies emphasize what Zolberg, Suhrke, and Aguayo have termed the "Haitian-Cuban syndrome."[8] During the 1980s, the United States was willing to define Cuban asylum-seekers as refugees since they were coming from an unfriendly communist country. However, similar treatment was not extended to Haitian asylum-seekers. It is not clear how and whether these international dynamics interact with domestic identity politics. Moreover, whether these strategic dynamics are widely generalizable beyond the United States has not heretofore been established.

Indeed, much of the existing scholarship on states' refugee policies has been narrow in geographic scope. The prevailing focus on Western countries in the literature, even while most of the world's refugees reside elsewhere, limits our ability to draw generalizable conclusions about refugee treatment. Meanwhile, research on asylum policies outside Western countries has tended to be descriptive rather than theoretical. Though this work provides a rich descriptive account of asylum politics, it has not developed generalizable theoretical explanations.

This book provides a theoretically grounded set of hypotheses regarding refugee responses that are tested more broadly and systematically across multiple countries and regions. Unlike previous work that has hinted at these dynamics, the analysis in this book combines foreign policy and ethnic identity in a two-part framework. Moreover, it identifies the specific incentives that operate at international and domestic levels. Namely, refugees fleeing a rival country offer an opportunity to undermine that country's stability, saddle it with reputation costs, and engage in guerrilla-style, cross-border attacks. Welcoming refugees who are ethnic kin can please domestic constituencies, expand the policymaker's support group, and foster mobilization along ethnic lines.

---

[8] Zolberg, Suhrke, and Aguayo 1989, 273.

In addition, this book goes beyond existing research by widening its empirical scope beyond the United States and other Western countries. Some 85% of refugees reside in developing countries. Turkey had the world's largest refugee population in 2019, and Lebanon ranked first in number of refugees hosted per capita. Not only are these countries more resource-constrained, but some developing countries have experienced successive refugee movements from multiple crises. And some have been hosting long-standing refugee populations for years or even decades. Accordingly, this book's case selection emphasizes asylum policies in developing countries, specifically Egypt, Turkey, and Kenya.

In doing so, this book reveals a key shortcoming of conventional explanations that emphasize resources, security concerns, regional dynamics, and democratization: these predict a "one size fits all" policy and therefore cannot explain discrimination between refugee groups. If access to material resources determines refugee policy, then poorer countries might adopt more exclusionary policies across the board. Countries that have previously experienced civil violence or terrorist incidents might shut out refugees altogether. We might observe a "race to the bottom" for all refugees if each state fears becoming an attractive regional destination. Or all refugee groups might experience increased restrictiveness in democratizing states. These factors may influence asylum policy, but they cannot explain differences in the treatment of refugee groups.

While other alternative explanations may appear more promising, they remain unsatisfactory. For instance, the existing literature suggests that humanitarianism might influence asylum policies, or that states might be more welcoming of refugees with particular attributes, or that countries fashion their responses depending on the magnitude of the refugee flow. Alternatively, asylum policies might simply stem from idiosyncratic decisions made by low-level government employees. The analysis in this book indicates that these alternative explanations do not adequately explain the variation in asylum policies across and within countries.

## Delegation to the UN Refugee Agency

The delegation puzzle has not been systematically studied. Moreover, the existing literature on delegation cannot account for the fact that various countries have given the UN control of asylum procedures on their territory. As I note in chapter 2, research in international relations has focused on interstate cooperation, whereby two or more states delegate to a third party. Meanwhile, scholarship on American politics has looked at delegation to domestic actors rather than international organizations. Part of this book's contribution, therefore, is examining situations in which a single government delegates domestic activities to an international organization.

Of the potential explanations offered by principal-agent theory for delegation to international organizations, three may appear to apply to delegation to UNHCR: specialization gains, managing collaboration, and ensuring lock-in of policy bias.[9] However, it is not obvious that delegating asylum policy functions to UNHCR fits any of these accounts squarely. While UNHCR certainly has expertise in conducting RSD and managing refugee camps, viewing it as a "specialized agent" does not explain why some governments have switched delegation on and off over the years and why several countries have parallel RSD procedures. Moreover, if UNHCR is acting as a "collaboration agent" and providing a public good by taking on RSD, then it is puzzling that some countries delegate and others do not. Finally, delegation to UNHCR is easy to undo, making it unlikely that governments are locking in desired preferences by having UNHCR function as a "policy-biased agent."

In contrast, this book argues that policymakers shift responsibility to UNHCR when international and domestic pressures push in opposite directions. By claiming that a neutral international organization is in charge, policymakers can avoid antagonizing refugee-sending countries and/or domestic constituencies. At the same time, UNHCR suffers from serious limitations and is fairly easy to sanction. Even while delegating, the policymaker retains control of a range of other policy measures.

## Policy Implications

If we understand why governments treat refugees as they do, then we will be on more solid ground to advocate for policy change to protect their rights. This book shows how foreign policy and ethnic identity shape reactions to refugee flows. These insights can inform the activities of UN agencies and NGOs and can assist the international community in forecasting when exerting pressure will bear fruit. Selective sovereignty also has consequences for long-term processes related to conflict, peacebuilding, and post-conflict reconstruction.

My analysis demonstrates that treating countries as though each had a single blanket asylum policy masks important disparities in treatment between refugee groups. Foreign policy and ethnic identity lead some refugee groups to be treated inclusively, while others will experience exclusionary policies. As a result, the UN and NGOs may need to target their advocacy and assistance toward particular refugee groups.

---

[9] Hawkins et al. 2006, 13–20.

These findings also extend to concerned states and the international community, which might exert pressure to try to improve a country's treatment of refugees. When exclusionary treatment is expected for a refugee group, shifting the receiving country's calculus will require significant material punishments and incentives. In some cases, other tools must be used instead. For example, resettlement programs can be designed to assist those refugees who would otherwise experience particularly restrictive policies.

In addition, this book's research improves our understanding of when host countries pursue policies that can have implications for conflict, peacebuilding, and post-conflict reconstruction in the country of origin. The screening of asylum-seekers to determine if they are "genuine" refugees can prevent armed elements from residing in the host country or infiltrating refugee communities. If host countries restrict refugees to camps or segregated settlements, the possibility of radicalization or infiltration seems compounded. Moreover, when host countries engage in early and coerced mass returns of refugees, this can undermine peacebuilding efforts in the country of origin by straining fragile institutions or even sparking conflict anew. In contrast, where host countries allow refugees access to social services and employment, refugees may be able to acquire transferable skills or generate remittances that can contribute to state-building and post-conflict reconstruction in their country of origin. These long-term consequences make it all the more important that UNHCR, NGOs, and the international community work toward inclusionary treatment for all refugees.

## Conclusions

At the time of writing, there were 26 million refugees around the world, and one out of every three was Syrian. Nearly four-fifths of the world's refugees had been in exile for five years or more; millions of Afghan and other refugees had been displaced for decades. Over four million asylum-seekers, including many Venezuelans, were waiting for their applications to be adjudicated. And there were ongoing refugee crises in South Sudan, Myanmar, and elsewhere. This book seeks to understand the factors underlying these refugees' experiences. What circumstances lead to discrimination between refugee groups, whereby some are treated well while others are treated poorly? What explains countries' delegation decisions, such that refugee affairs are sometimes turned over to UNHCR?

The previous chapters demonstrated that foreign policy and ethnic politics shape state responses to refugees. Policymakers in the host country consider bilateral relations with the refugees' home country: hostile relations create incentives to welcome refugees, while friendly ties may result in them being shunned. At the domestic level, it matters whether there is a shared ethnic identity between refugees and the group in power in the host country: ethnic affinity incentivizes inclusive treatment, while the lack of ethnic kinship may result in exclusionary policies. When these two factors point in opposite directions, policymakers delegate in order to shift blame to the UN.

The discrimination and delegation puzzles not only point to gaps in the academic literature, they also have significance for the lives of tens of millions of refugees around the world. Yet, the scholarly and policy communities lack a coherent and clearly articulated account of how and why countries respond to refugee movements. This book provides a plausible account that emphasizes foreign policy and ethnic politics, one that can inform our responses to new and continuing refugee situations around the world.

# Appendix 1: Supplementary Data

For each country of asylum, Table AI.1 summarizes the type of RSD procedure, the number of asylum applications filed, and the size of the refugee population in 2011.

Table AI.1  RSD, asylum applications, and refugee population in 2011, by country of asylum

| Country of Asylum | RSD Type | Asylum Applications Filed | Refugees and People in Refugee-Like Situations |
|---|---|---|---|
| Afghanistan | U | 58 | 3009 |
| Albania | G | 19 | 82 |
| Algeria | U | 1038 | 94148 |
| Angola | G | 542 | 16223 |
| Argentina | G | 871 | 3361 |
| Armenia | J | 89 | 2918 |
| Aruba | G | 3 | — |
| Australia | G | 15441 | 23434 |
| Austria | G | 14416 | 47073 |
| Azerbaijan | J | 158 | 1730 |
| Bahamas | G | 9 | 28 |
| Bahrain | U | 138 | 199 |
| Bangladesh | U | 7 | 229669 |
| Belarus | J | 144 | 595 |
| Belgium | G | 41152 | 22402 |
| Belize | G | 32 | 78 |
| Benin | G | 464 | 7217 |
| Bolivia | G | 32 | 716 |
| Bosnia and Herzegovina | G | 44 | 6933 |
| Botswana | G | 219 | 3312 |
| Brazil | G | 4980 | 4477 |

*Continued*

**Table AI.1** *Continued*

| Country of Asylum | RSD Type | Asylum Applications Filed | Refugees and People in Refugee-Like Situations |
|---|---|---|---|
| British Virgin Islands | U | 1 | 2 |
| Bulgaria | G | 893 | 5688 |
| Burkina Faso | G | 179 | 546 |
| Burundi | G | 3638 | 35659 |
| Cambodia | G | 19 | 64 |
| Cameroon | U | 3215 | 100373 |
| Canada | G | 24985 | 164883 |
| Cayman Islands | J | 1 | 3 |
| Central African Rep. | G | 1292 | 16730 |
| Chad | J | 5914 | 366494 |
| Chile | G | 305 | 1674 |
| China | U | 52 | 301018 |
| - Hong Kong | U | 1066 | 152 |
| - Macao | G | 8 | 1 |
| Colombia | G | 109 | 219 |
| Congo | G | 640 | 141232 |
| Costa Rica | G | 964 | 20057 |
| Croatia | G | 858 | 824 |
| Cuba | U | 6 | 384 |
| Curacao | U | 8 | 6 |
| Cyprus | J | 4167 | 3503 |
| Czech Rep. | G | 756 | 2449 |
| Côte d'Ivoire | J | 646 | 24221 |
| Dem. Rep. of the Congo | U | 225 | 152749 |
| Denmark | G | 3811 | 13399 |
| Djibouti | U | 1382 | 20340 |
| Dominica | U | 1 | — |
| Dominican Rep. | G | 28 | 595 |
| Ecuador | G | 14171 | 123436 |
| Egypt | U | 5499 | 95087 |
| El Salvador | G | 15 | 38 |
| Eritrea | U | 5 | 4719 |

Table AI.1  *Continued*

| Country of Asylum | RSD Type | Asylum Applications Filed | Refugees and People in Refugee-Like Situations |
|---|---|---|---|
| Estonia | G | 67 | 50 |
| Ethiopia | J | 839 | 288844 |
| Fiji | J | 5 | 7 |
| Finland | G | 3086 | 9175 |
| France | G | 89320 | 210207 |
| Gabon | G | 108 | 1773 |
| Gambia | G | 106 | 9528 |
| Georgia | G | 78 | 462 |
| Germany | G | 53347 | 571685 |
| Ghana | J | 20123 | 13588 |
| Greece | G | 15292 | 1573 |
| Grenada | U | 0 | 3 |
| Guatemala | G | 21 | 147 |
| Guinea | G | 367 | 16609 |
| Guinea-Bissau | G | 63 | 7800 |
| Guyana | U | 1 | 7 |
| Haiti | U | 2 | — |
| Honduras | U | 9 | 17 |
| Hungary | G | 1693 | 5106 |
| Iceland | G | 107 | 58 |
| India | U | 4775 | 185118 |
| Indonesia | U | 4052 | 1006 |
| Iran | U | 126 | 886468 |
| Iraq | U | 1161 | 35189 |
| Ireland | G | 3337 | 8249 |
| Israel | J | 5745 | 41235 |
| Italy | G | 34117 | 58060 |
| Japan | G | 3626 | 2649 |
| Jordan | U | 4579 | 451009 |
| Kazakhstan | J | 78 | 616 |
| Kenya | U | 15202 | 566487 |

*Continued*

**Table AI.1** *Continued*

| Country of Asylum | RSD Type | Asylum Applications Filed | Refugees and People in Refugee-Like Situations |
|---|---|---|---|
| Kuwait | U | 255 | 335 |
| Kyrgyzstan | J | 246 | 6095 |
| Latvia | G | 335 | 95 |
| Lebanon | U | 1687 | 8990 |
| Lesotho | G | 10 | 34 |
| Liberia | J | 573 | 128293 |
| Libya | U | 90 | 10130 |
| Liechtenstein | G | 75 | 94 |
| Lithuania | G | 406 | 821 |
| Luxembourg | G | 2375 | 2855 |
| Macedonia | G | 744 | 1130 |
| Madagascar | U | 1 | 9 |
| Malawi | G | 4498 | 6308 |
| Malaysia | U | 16964 | 86680 |
| Mali | G | 875 | 15624 |
| Malta | G | 2547 | 6952 |
| Mauritania | U | 378 | 26535 |
| Mexico | G | 753 | 1677 |
| Moldova | G | 72 | 146 |
| Mongolia | U | 6 | 1 |
| Montenegro | G | 235 | 12874 |
| Montserrat | U | 0 | — |
| Morocco | U | 1110 | 736 |
| Mozambique | G | 3905 | 4079 |
| Namibia | G | 267 | 6049 |
| Nepal | J | 44 | 72654 |
| Netherlands | G | 14631 | 74598 |
| New Zealand | G | 489 | 1934 |
| Nicaragua | G | 39 | 86 |
| Niger | G | 185 | 302 |
| Nigeria | G | 201 | 8806 |
| Norway | G | 18222 | 40691 |

**Table AI.1** *Continued*

| Country of Asylum | RSD Type | Asylum Applications Filed | Refugees and People in Refugee-Like Situations |
|---|---|---|---|
| Oman | U | 35 | 83 |
| Pakistan | U | 982 | 1702700 |
| Palau | U | 1 | 1 |
| Panama | G | 1396 | 17262 |
| Papua New Guinea | J | 3 | 9377 |
| Paraguay | G | 25 | 124 |
| Peru | G | 466 | 1144 |
| Philippines | G | 21 | 125 |
| Poland | G | 6887 | 15847 |
| Portugal | G | 275 | 408 |
| Qatar | U | 63 | 80 |
| Romania | G | 2061 | 1005 |
| Russia | G | 2292 | 3914 |
| Rwanda | G | 7 | 55325 |
| Saint Lucia | U | 2 | 2 |
| Saint Vincent and the Grenadines | U | 1 | — |
| Saudi Arabia | U | 22 | 599 |
| Senegal | G | 200 | 20644 |
| Serbia | J | 3320 | 70707 |
| Sierra Leone | J | 22 | 8092 |
| Slovakia | G | 491 | 546 |
| Slovenia | G | 373 | 142 |
| Somalia | U | 27 | 2099 |
| South Africa | G | 106904 | 57899 |
| South Korea | G | 1140 | 401 |
| South Sudan | U | 238 | 105023 |
| Spain | G | 3414 | 4228 |
| Sri Lanka | U | 165 | 188 |
| Sudan | J | 10591 | 139415 |
| Suriname | U | 4 | — |
| Sweden | G | 43759 | 86615 |

*Continued*

**Table AI.1** *Continued*

| Country of Asylum | RSD Type | Asylum Applications Filed | Refugees and People in Refugee-Like Situations |
|---|---|---|---|
| Switzerland | G | 19439 | 50416 |
| Syria | U | 3088 | 755445 |
| Tajikistan | J | 791 | 3323 |
| Thailand | J | 12958 | 89253 |
| Timor-Leste | G | 0 | — |
| Tanzania | J | 433 | 131243 |
| Togo | G | 5293 | 19270 |
| Tonga | U | 0 | 2 |
| Trinidad and Tobago | U | 29 | 22 |
| Tunisia | U | 4505 | 4097 |
| Turkey | U | 17854 | 14465 |
| Turkmenistan | G | 6 | 59 |
| Turks and Caicos | U | 3 | — |
| Uganda | G | 12704 | 139448 |
| Ukraine | J | 2228 | 3176 |
| United Arab Emirates | U | 216 | 677 |
| United Kingdom | G | 36429 | 193510 |
| United States | G | 60587 | 264763 |
| Uruguay | G | 20 | 174 |
| Vanuatu | U | 2 | — |
| Venezuela | G | 3176 | 202022 |
| Yemen | U | 5353 | 214740 |
| Zambia | G | 945 | 45632 |
| Zimbabwe | G | 1043 | 4561 |

Note: G=government, U=UNHCR, J=joint. Data is from UNHCR 2012.

# Appendix 2: Content Analysis Codebook

The proceedings of the Kenyan parliament were consulted using the online archive of the Kenya National Assembly Official Record (Hansard), compiled by the National Council for Law Reporting and Google, Inc.[1]

Research assistants assigned basic identifiers to each document (i.e., session date and agenda item and topic) and each statement within that document (i.e., speaker name, title, and district). They coded individual text segments to capture references to particular refugee groups, refugee-sending countries, refugee camps, and refugee-relevant actors. They also assigned codes to references to specific government policies that the Kenyan government has adopted/rejected or should adopt/reject, including policies related to the legal framework regulating refugee affairs, admission and status for asylum-seekers, protection and security of refugees, their basic needs, and durable solutions. Finally, they coded the reasons why the Kenyan government has adopted/rejected or should adopt/reject government policies, including foreign policy, ethnicity, and other justifications. There was substantial inter-coder agreement across three coders, with percent agreement at 97.3% (Krippendorff's alpha=0.74).

As a final step, I categorized each reference to government policies as inclusive, intermediate, or restrictive. For instance, references to the 1951 Refugee Convention or its 1967 Protocol were coded as: "inclusive" if the speaker was in favor of signing, ratifying, or implementing these international legal instruments; "intermediate" if they were in favor of acceding with reservations, or incomplete implementation; and "restrictive" if they were opposed to signing, ratifying, or implementing these treaties. Table AII.1 provides details for this refugee policy indicator.

---

[1] The online Parliament Hansard Archive can be found at http://books.google.co.ke/books/about/Kenya_National_Assembly_Official_Record.html?id=pvwVH2fQKWQC

Table AII.1  Coding details for asylum policies

| | | Inclusive | Intermediate | Restrictive |
|---|---|---|---|---|
| **Legal Framework** | International Treaties | In favor of signing, ratifying, or implementing the 1951 Refugee Convention or its 1967 Protocol | In favor of acceding with reservations, or incomplete implementation of the 1951 Refugee Convention or its 1967 Protocol | Opposed to signing, ratifying, or implementing the 1951 Refugee Convention or its 1967 Protocol |
| | National Legislation | In favor of drafting, passing, revising, or implementing national laws to regulate refugee affairs | In favor of utilizing or implementing ad hoc directives to regulate refugee affairs | Opposed to drafting, passing, revising, or implementing national laws or directives to regulate refugee affairs |
| **Admission and Status** | Entry | Opposed to border control or physical barriers to access; or in favor of facilitation of refugee arrival | In favor of border checks which may result in significant delays or restriction of entry; or in favor of requiring identity papers and visas which can be procured | In favor of border closure, non-entrée visa requirements, or turning back refugees |
| | Screening | In favor of screening by UNHCR or in accordance with UNHCR regulations for RSD | In favor of screening not in accordance with UNHCR regulations; or opposed to granting identity documents to recognized refugees | Opposed to asylum-seekers having access to a process for RSD; or in favor of ad hoc screening with no institutionalized procedures |
| **Protection and Security** | Movement | In favor of refugees enjoying full freedom of movement and residence | In favor of refugees residing in camps, segregated settlements, or a location not of their choosing, though they may leave them temporarily; or in favor of tying aid to encampment | In favor of full containment of refugees in camps or segregated settlements |
| | Physical Safety | In favor of permitting refugees to settle at a safe distance from the border and protecting them from agents of the receiving country | In favor of refugees being settled close to border such that they are at risk of attacks from country of origin; or in favor of refugees facing limited threats to their physical safety from agents of the receiving country | Not opposed to refugees and asylum-seekers being subjected to arbitrary detention, torture, or executions by agents of the receiving country; or in favor of asylum-seekers being detained for illegal entry without adequate screening for refugees |

| | | | | |
|---|---|---|---|---|
| | Refoulement | In favor of strictly voluntary repatriation of refugees to their country of origins | In favor of limited forcible expulsion of recognized refugees to their country of origin on an individual basis | In favor of mass expulsion of recognized refugees; or in favor of mass return of asylum-seekers or migrants without adequate screening for refugees |
| *Basic Needs* | Services | In favor of refugees having access to public health services and primary and secondary education | In favor of unequal or low-quality access to public health services and primary and secondary education, or in favor of cumbersome procedures for access to these services | Opposed to refugees having access to public health services and primary and secondary education |
| | Employment | In favor of refugees being permitted to work in the formal market with no legal barriers | In favor of work authorizations that are difficult or expensive to obtain, or are restricted in time, activity, or place of employment | In favor of refugees being banned from the formal labor market |
| *Durable Solutions* | Integration | In favor of institutionalized and facilitated procedures for naturalization | In favor of cumbersome procedures for naturalization | Opposed to naturalization, or to existence of institutionalized procedures |

# References

## Selected Personal Interviews

Gasser Abdel-Razek (Country Director, Africa and Middle East Refugee Assistance-Egypt). AMERA-Egypt Office, Cairo, Egypt, June 7, 2010.

Aydoğan Asar (Chief Superintendent, Migration and Asylum Bureau, Ministry of Interior). Ministry of Interior, Ankara, Turkey, February 23, 2012.

Lina Attalah (Managing Editor, *Al-Masry Al-Youm* English Edition). *Al-Masry Al-Youm* Office, Cairo, Egypt, June 30, 2010.

Ahmed Badawy (Chairman, Egyptian Foundation for Refugee Rights). EFRR Office, Cairo, Egypt, August 3, 2010.

Fiona Cameron (Assistant Director, St. Andrew's Refugee Services Children's Education Programme). St. Andrew's Church, Cairo, Egypt, August 25, 2010.

Roel Debruyne (Regional Protection and Migration Adviser, Danish Refugee Council—Horn of Africa & Yemen). Danish Refugee Council Office, Nairobi, Kenya, May 10, 2012.

Expert. Migration and Asylum Bureau, Ministry of Interior. Ankara, Turkey, February 21, 2012.

Volkan Görendağ (Refugee Affairs Coordinator, Amnesty International). Amnesty International Office, Ankara, Turkey, February 24, 2012.

Barbara Harrell-Bond (Founder, Center for Migration and Refugee Studies). American University in Cairo, Cairo, Egypt, June 16, 2010.

Martin Jones (Vice Chairman, Egyptian Foundation for Refugee Rights). American University in Cairo, Cairo, Egypt, June 22, 2010.

Ray Jureidini (Director, Center for Migration and Refugee Studies). American University in Cairo, Cairo, Egypt, June 15, 2010.

NGO worker. Istanbul, Turkey, February 2, 2012.

NGO worker. Nairobi, Kenya, May 4, 2012.

NGO worker. Nairobi, Kenya, May 10, 2012.

Official. Ministry of Foreign Affairs, Cairo, Egypt, September 4, 2010.

Grace Omweri (Legal Program Officer, Kituo Cha Sheria). Kituo Cha Sheria Branch Office—Eastleigh, Nairobi, Kenya, May 11, 2012.

Sara Sadek (Outreach Coordinator, Center for Migration and Refugee Studies). American University in Cairo, Cairo, Egypt, June 9, 2010.

Hania Sholkamy (Assistant Professor, Social Research Center). American University in Cairo, New Cairo, Egypt, June 20, 2010.

Elçin Türkdoğan (Refugee Project Coordinator, Human Rights Foundation of Turkey). Human Rights Foundation of Turkey Office, Ankara, Turkey, February 20, 2012.

UNHCR Turkey official. Istanbul, Turkey, February 10, 2012.

# UNHCR Archives

Fonds 11, Series 1, Box 76, 2/3/20 UAR Administration and Finance—Staff Privileges and Immunities—UAR.

Fonds 11, Series 1, Box 76, 2/5/1/1 ACC/KEN Branch Offices—Accreditation—Kenya.

Fonds 11, Series 1, Box 77, 2/5/1/1 ACC/TUR Branch Offices—Accreditation—Turkey.

Fonds 11, Series 1, Box 348, 22/1 TUR Eligibility—Turkey.

Fonds 11, Series 1, Box 354, 22/2 Eligibility—Refugees from Bulgaria in Turkey 22-2-I & II.

Fonds 11, Series 2, Box 11, 10 TUR Relations with Governments—Turkey.

Fonds 11, Series 2, Box 400, 203 KEN Privileges, Immunities and Accreditations—Kenya.

Fonds 11, Series 2, Box 403, 203 TUR Privileges, Immunities and Accreditations—Turkey.

Fonds 11, Series 2, Box 1197, 630 KEN Protection and General Legal Matters—Eligibility—Kenya [Volumes 1 & 2].

Fonds 11, Series 2, Box 1206, 630 TUR Protection and General Legal Matters—Eligibility—Turkey.

Fonds 11, Series 3, 10 ARE External Relations—Relations with Governments—Egypt [Volumes A & B].

Fonds 11, Series 3, 10 KEN External Relations—Relations with Governments—Kenya [Volumes A–C].

Fonds 11, Series 3, 10 TUR External Relations—Relations with Governments—Turkey [Volumes A & B].

Fonds 11, Series 3, 100 ARE ETH Refugee Situations—Special Groups of Refugees—Ethiopian Refugees in Egypt.

Fonds 11, Series 3, 100 ARE SOM Refugee Situations—Special Groups of Refugees—Refugees from Somalia in Egypt.

Fonds 11, Series 3, 100 ARE SUD Refugee Situations—Special Groups of Refugees—Sudanese Refugees in Egypt.

Fonds 11, Series 3, 100 KEN GEN Refugee Situations—Special Groups of Refugees—Refugees in Kenya [Volumes A & B].

Fonds 11, Series 3, 100 KEN RWA Refugee Situations—Special Groups of Refugees—Rwandan Refugees in Kenya.

Fonds 11, Series 3, 100 KEN SOM Refugee Situations—Special Groups of Refugees—Somalian Refugees in Kenya [Volumes A & B].

Fonds 11, Series 3, 100 KEN UGA Refugee Situations—Special Groups of Refugees—Ugandan Refugees in Kenya.

Fonds 11, Series 3, 100 TUR BSN Refugee Situations—Special Groups of Refugees—Refugees from Bosnia in Turkey.

Fonds 11, Series 3, 100 TUR BUL Refugee Situations—Special Groups of Refugees—Refugees from Bulgaria in Turkey [Volume A].

Fonds 11, Series 3, 100 TUR GEN Refugee Situations—Special Groups of Refugees—Refugees in Turkey—General.

Fonds 11, Series 3, 100 TUR IRAQ Refugee Situations—Special Groups of Refugees—Refugees from Iraq in Turkey [Volumes A–F & H].

Fonds 11, Series 3, 100 TUR KURD Refugee Situations—Special Groups of Refugees—Kurdish Refugees in Turkey.

Fonds 11, Series 3, 100 TUR LKA Refugee Situations—Special Groups of Refugees—Sri Lankan Refugees in Turkey.

Fonds 11, Series 3, 203 TUR Administration and Finance—Privileges, Immunities and Accreditations—Turkey.

## Published Scholarship and Reports

Abdelaaty, Lamis. 2019. Refugees and Guesthood in Turkey. *Journal of Refugee Studies*. Advance online publication. doi: 10.1093/jrs/fez097.

Adida, Claire L. 2014. *Coethnic Strangers: Immigrant Exclusion and Insecurity in Africa*. Cambridge: Cambridge University Press.

Africa Watch. 1991. *Kenya: Taking Liberties*. New York, NY: Human Rights Watch.

African Rights. 1993. *The Nightmare Continues . . . Abuses against Somali Refugees in Kenya*. London: African Rights.

Alexander, Michael. 1999. Refugee Status Determination Conducted by UNHCR. *International Journal of Refugee Law* 11(2): 251–89.

Al-Sharmani, Mulki. 2003. Livelihood and Identity Constructions of Somali Refugees in Cairo. Forced Migration and Refugee Studies Working Papers No. 2. Cairo: Forced Migration and Refugee Studies, American University in Cairo.

Al-Sharmani, Mulki. 2008. Refugees in Egypt: Transit Migrants? Paper presented at the Imiscoe Conference on (Irregular) Transit Migration the European Space: Theory, Politics, and Research Methodology, Koç University, Istanbul, Turkey.

Amnesty International. 1994. *Turkey: Selective Protection—Discriminatory Treatment of Non-European Refugees and Asylum-Seekers*. London: Amnesty International.

Amnesty International. 1997. *Turkey: Refoulement of Non-European Refugees—A Protection Crisis*. London: Amnesty International.

Amnesty International. 2007. *Denied Refuge: The Effect of the Closure of the Kenya/Somalia Border on Thousands of Somali Asylum-Seekers and Refugees*. London: Amnesty International.

Amnesty International. 2008. *Egypt: Deadly Journeys through the Desert*. London: Amnesty International.

Anteby-Yemini, Lisa. 2008. Migrations Africaines Et Nouveaux Enjeux De La Frontière Israélo-Égyptienne. *Cultures & Conflits* 72: 77–99.

Aras, Bülent. 2003. Turkey's Relations with Iran in the Post-Cold War Era. In *Turkey's Foreign Policy in the 21st Century: A Changing Role in World Politics*, edited by Tareq Y. Ismael and Mustafa Aydın, 181–98. Burlington, VT: Ashgate.

Aukot, Ekuru. 2003. "It Is Better to Be a Refugee Than a Turkana in Kakuma": Revisiting the Relationship between Hosts and Refugees in Kenya. *Refugee Survey Quarterly* 21(3): 73–83.

Azzam, Fateh, ed. 2006. *A Tragedy of Failures and False Expectations: Report on the Events Surrounding the Three Month Sit-in and Forced Removal of Sudanese Refugees in Cairo, September–December 2005*. Cairo: Forced Migration and Refugee Studies Program, American University in Cairo.

Badawy, Tarek. 2009. Iraqi Refugees in Egypt. CARIM Analytic and Synthetic Notes 2009/23. Florence: Robert Schuman Centre for Advanced Studies, European University Institute.

Badawy, Tarek. 2010. The Memorandum of Understanding between Egypt and the Office of the United Nations High Commissioner for Refugees: Problems and Recommendations. CARIM Analytic and Synthetic Notes 2010/07. Florence: Robert Schuman Centre for Advanced Studies, European University Institute.

Badawy, Tarek, and Abdallah Khalil. 2005. Rights of Foreigners and Access to Citizenship. In *Africa Citizenship and Discrimination Audit: The Case Study of Egypt*, edited by Kasia Grabska, 4–33. Cairo: Center for Migration and Refugee Studies, American University in Cairo.

Barnett, Michael, and Martha Finnemore. 2004. *Rules for the World: International Organizations in Global Politics*. Ithaca, NY: Cornell University Press.

Barth, Fredrik. 1969. *Ethnic Groups and Boundaries: The Social Organisation of Culture Difference*. Boston: Little and Brown.

Bartholomeusz, Lance. 2009. The Mandate of UNRWA at Sixty. *Refugee Survey Quarterly* 28(2–3): 452–74.

Basok, Tanya. 1990. Welcome Some and Reject Others: Constraints and Interests Influencing Costa Rican Policies on Refugees. *International Migration Review* 24(4): 722–47.

Bates, Robert H. 1983. Modernization, Ethnic Competition, and the Rationality of Politics in Contemporary Africa. In *State Versus Ethnic Claims: African Policy Dilemmas*, edited by Donald S. Rothchild, and Victor A. Olorunsola, 152–71. Boulder, CO: Westview Press.

Beals, Greg. 2013. Syria: The Journey to Safety Gets More Dangerous by the Day, but Refugees Keep Coming. *UNHCR News and Stories*. September 3.

Bélanger, Danièle, and Cenk Saraçoğlu. 2019. Syrian Refugees and Turkey: Whose "Crisis"? In *The Oxford Handbook of Migration Crises*, edited by Cecilia Menjívar, Marie Ruiz, and Immanuel Ness, 279–95. Oxford: Oxford University Press.

Bendor, Jonathan, Amihai Glazer, and Thomas H. Hammond. 2001. Theories of Delegation. *Annual Review of Political Science* 4(1): 235–69.

Benhabib, Seyla. 2004. *The Rights of Others: Aliens, Residents and Citizens*. Cambridge, UK: Cambridge University Press.

Birnir, Jóhanna K., Jonathan Wilkenfeld, James D. Fearon, David Laitin, Ted Robert Gurr, Dawn Brancati, Stephen Saideman, Amy Pate, and Agatha S. Hultquist. 2015. Socially Relevant Ethnic Groups, Ethnic Structure and Amar. *Journal of Peace Research* 52(1): 110–15.

Borjas, George J. 1989. Economic Theory and International Migration. *The International Migration Review* 23(3): 457–85.

Borjas, George J. 2014. *Immigration Economics*. Cambridge, MA: Harvard University Press.

Bradley, Curtis A., and Judith G. Kelley. 2008. The Concept of International Delegation. *Law and Contemporary Problems* 71(1): 1–36.

Brand, Laurie A. 1991. *Palestinians in the Arab World*. New York: Columbia University Press.

Brecher, Michael, and Jonathan Wilkenfeld. 1997. *A Study of Crisis*. Ann Arbor: University of Michigan Press.

Burns, Avery. 2010. Feeling the Pinch: Kenya, Al-Shabaab, and East Africa's Refugee Crisis. *Refuge* 27(1): 5–15.

Calabrese, John. 1998. Turkey and Iran: Limits of a Stable Relationship. *British Journal of Middle Eastern Studies* 25(1): 75–94.

Campbell, Elizabeth. 2006. Urban Refugees in Nairobi: Problems of Protection, Mechanisms of Survival, and Possibilities for Integration. *Journal of Refugee Studies* 19(3): 396–413.

Campbell, Elizabeth, Jeff Crisp, and Esther Kiragu. 2011. *Navigating Nairobi: A Review of the Implementation of Unhcr's Urban Refugee Policy in Kenya's Capital City.* Geneva: UNHCR Policy Development and Evaluation Service.

Cederman, Lars-Erik, Brian Min, and Andreas Wimmer. 2009. Ethnic Power Relations Dataset. Available from http://www.epr.ucla.edu/.

CEPII. n.d. Distances Dataset. Available from http://www.cepii.fr/anglaisgraph/bdd/distances.htm.

Chau, Donovan C. 2010. At the Crossroads of Cultures? A Historic and Strategic Examination of Kenya-Somalia Relations. *Journal of the Middle East and Africa* 1(1): 67–83.

Chimni, B. S. 1994. The Legal Condition of Refugees in India. *Journal of Refugee Studies* 7(4): 378–401.

Convention Relating to the Status of Refugees. United Nations Treaty Series 189, 137. Geneva: July 28, 1951.

Cooper, Dereck. 1992. *Urban Refugees: Ethiopians and Eritreans in Cairo, Cairo Papers in Social Science* Vol. 15, Mono. 2. Cairo: American University in Cairo Press.

Cragg, John G. 1971. Some Statistical Models for Limited Dependent Variables with Application to the Demand for Durable Goods. *Econometrica* 39(5): 829–44.

Crisp, Jeff. 2000. A. State of Insecurity: The Political Economy of Violence in Kenya's Refugee Camps. *African Affairs* 99(397): 601–32.

Dauvergne, Catherine. 2008. *Making People Illegal: What Globalization Means for Migration and Law.* Cambridge: Cambridge University Press.

Doyle, Chris. 2012. The Syrian Refugee Crisis Is Aggravating Old Tensions in Lebanon. *The Guardian.* March 7.

Dumper, Michael. 2006. Introduction: The Comparative Study of Refugee Repatriation Programmes and the Palestinian Case. In *Palestinian Refugee Repatriation: Global Perspectives*, edited by Michael Dumper, 1–19. London: Routledge.

Edwards, Sebastian,. and Julia A. Santaella. 1993. Devaluation Controversies in the Developing Countries: Lessons from the Bretton Woods Era. In *A Retrospective on the Bretton Woods System*, edited by Michael D. Bordo and Barry Eichengreen, 405–55. Chicago, IL: University of Chicago Press.

Egypt, Arab Republic of. 1984. Presidential Decree No. 188 of 1984. KE-44 EGY: Refugee Studies Centre Grey Literature Collection, University of Oxford.

El-Abed, Oroub. 2009. *Unprotected: Palestinians in Egypt since 1948.* Beirut, Lebanon: Institute for Palestine Studies.

Erlikh, Ḥagai. 2002. *The Cross and the River: Ethiopia, Egypt, and the Nile.* Boulder, CO: Lynne Rienner.

Evans, Peter B., Harold K. Jacobson, and Robert D. Putnam, eds. 1993. *Double-Edged Diplomacy: International Bargaining and Domestic Politics.* Berkeley: University of California Press.

Fargues, Philippe, Saeed El-Masry, Sara Sadek, and Azza Shaban. 2008. Iraqis in Egypt: A Statistical Survey in 2008. Cairo: Centre for Migration and Refugee Studies, American University in Cairo and Information and Decision Support Centre.

Fearon, James D., and David D. Laitin. 1996. Explaining Interethnic Cooperation. *American Political Science Review* 90(4): 715–35.

Ferris, Elizabeth G. 1985. Regional Responses to Central American Refugees: Policymaking in Nicaragua, Honduras, and Mexico. In *Refugees and World Politics*, edited by Elizabeth G. Ferris, 187–211. New York: Praeger.

Finnemore, Martha, and Kathryn Sikkink. 1998. International Norm Dynamics and Political Change. *International Organization* 52(4): 887–917.

FitzGerald, David Scott, and Rawan Arar. 2018. The Sociology of Refugee Migration. *Annual Review of Sociology* 44: 387–406.

Frantz, Elizabeth. 2003. *Report on the Situation of Refugees in Turkey: Findings of a Five-Week Exploratory Study, December 2002–January 2003*. Cairo: Forced Migration and Refugee Studies Program, American University in Cairo.

Freedom House. 2011. *Freedom in the World*. New York: Freedom House.

Freeman, Gary P. 2006. National Models, Policy Types, and the Politics of Immigration in Liberal Democracies. *West European Politics* 29(2): 227–47.

Frelick, Bill. 1997. Barriers to Protection: Turkey's Asylum Regulations. *International Journal of Refugee Law* 9(1): 8–34.

Gailmard, Sean, and John W. Patty. 2012. Formal Models of Bureaucracy. *Annual Review of Political Science* 15(1): 353–77.

Gartzke, Erik. 2010. The Affinity of Nations: Similarity of State Voting Positions in the UNGA. Available from http://dss.ucsd.edu/~egartzke/htmlpages/data.html.

Gibney, Mark, Linda Cornett, and Reed M. Wood. 2010. Political Terror Scale 1976–2009. Available from http://www.politicalterrorscale.org/.

Gleditsch, Nils Petter, Peter Wallensteen, Mikael Eriksson, Margareta Sollenberg, and Håvard Strand. 2002. Armed Conflict 1946–2001: A New Dataset. *Journal of Peace Research* 39(5): 615–37.

Goldstein, Judith, and Robert O. Keohane. 1993. Ideas and Foreign Policy: An Analytical Framework. In *Ideas and Foreign Policy: Beliefs, Institutions, and Political Change*, edited by Judith Goldstein and Robert O. Keohane, 3–30. Ithaca, NY: Cornell University Press.

Grabska, Katarzyna. 2006. *Who Asked Them Anyway? Rights, Policies and Wellbeing of Refugees in Egypt*. Cairo: Forced Migration and Refugee Studies Program, American University in Cairo.

Grabska, Katarzyna. 2008. Brothers or Poor Cousins? Rights, Policies and the Well-Being of Refugees in Egypt. In *Forced Displacement: Why Rights Matter*, edited by Katarzyna Grabska and Lyla Mehta, 71–92. Basingstoke, UK: Palgrave Macmillan.

Hale, William. 2000. *Turkish Foreign Policy, 1774–2000*. London: Frank Cass.

Hamdallah, Gomaa. 2010. قنصل السودان فى القاهرة: إسرائيل تستغل الظاهرة سياسياً .. لكننا نثق فى مواطنينا [Sudan's Consul in Cairo: Israel Is Exploiting the Phenomenon Politically . . . But We Trust Our Citizens]. *Al-Masry Al-Youm*. March 24.

Hamlin, Rebecca. 2014. *Let Me Be a Refugee: Administrative Justice and the Politics of Asylum in the United States, Canada, and Australia*. Oxford: Oxford University Press.

Hardin, Russell. 1995. *One for All: The Logic of Group Conflict*. Princeton, NJ: Princeton University Press.

Hathaway, James C. 1992. The Emerging Politics of Non-Entrée. *Refugees* 91: 40–41.

Hathaway, James C. 2005. *The Rights of Refugees under International Law*. Cambridge, UK: Cambridge University Press.

Hawkins, Darren G., David A. Lake, Daniel L. Nielson, and Michael J. Tierney. 2006. Delegation under Anarchy: States, International Organizations, and Principal-Agent Theory. In *Delegation and Agency in International Organizations*, edited by Darren G. Hawkins, David A. Lake, Daniel L. Nielson and Michael J. Tierney, 3–38. Cambridge, UK: Cambridge University Press.

Helsinki Citizens' Assembly. 2011. *Unsafe Haven: The Security Challenges Facing Lesbian, Gay, Bisexual and Transgender Asylum Seekers and Refugees in Turkey.* Istanbul: Helsinki Citizens' Assembly.

Heston, Alan, Robert Summers, and Bettina Aten. 2009. Penn World Table Version 6.3. Center for International Comparisons of Production, Income and Prices at the University of Pennsylvania. Available from http://pwt.econ.upenn.edu/.

Heston, Alan, Robert Summers, and Bettina Aten. 2012. Penn World Table Version 7.1. Center for International Comparisons of Production, Income and Prices at the University of Pennsylvania. Available from http://pwt.econ.upenn.edu/.

Hilal, Leila, and Shahira Samy. 2008a. *Asylum and Migration Country Fact Sheet: Egypt.* Copenhagen: Euro-Mediterranean Human Rights Network.

Hilal, Leila, and Shahira Samy. 2008b. *Asylum and Migration in the Mashrek.* Copenhagen: Euro-Mediterranean Human Rights Network.

Hirschman, Albert O. 1993. Exit, Voice, and the Fate of the German Democratic Republic: An Essay in Conceptual History. *World Politics* 45(2): 173–202.

Hornsby, Charles. 2012. *Kenya: A History since Independence.* London: I.B. Tauris.

Human Rights Watch. 1990. *Screening of Ethnic Somalis: The Cruel Consequences of Kenya's Passbook System.* New York: Human Rights Watch.

Human Rights Watch. 2002. *Hidden in Plain View: Refugees Living without Protection in Nairobi and Kampala.* New York: Human Rights Watch.

Human Rights Watch. 2003. *Egypt: Mass Arrests of Foreigners, African Refugees Targeted in Cairo.* New York: Human Rights Watch.

Human Rights Watch. 2008. *Sinai Perils: Risks to Migrants, Refugees, and Asylum Seekers in Egypt and Israel.* New York: Human Rights Watch.

Human Rights Watch. 2012. *Criminal Reprisals: Kenyan Police and Military Abuses against Ethnic Somalis.* New York: Human Rights Watch.

Human Rights Watch. 2014. *Not Welcome: Jordan's Treatment of Palestinians Escaping Syria.* New York: Human Rights Watch.

Hurrell, Andrew. 2011. Refugees, International Society, and Global Order. In *Refugees in International Relations*, edited by Alexander Betts and Gil Loescher, 85–104. Oxford: Oxford University Press.

Hyndman, Jennifer. 1997. Border Crossings. *Antipode* 29(2): 149–76.

Hyndman, Jennifer. 2003. Preventive, Palliative, or Punitive? Safe Spaces in Bosnia-Herzegovina, Somalia, and Sri Lanka. *Journal of Refugee Studies* 16(2): 167–85.

Hyndman, Jennifer, and Bo Viktor Nylund. 1998. UNHCR and the Status of Prima Facie Refugees in Kenya. *International Journal of Refugee Law* 10(1/2): 21–48.

Ignatieff, Michael. 2011. Don't Deal Away Our Sovereignty. *The Globe and Mail.* February 10.

International Commission of Jurists (Kenya Section). 1998. *Protecting Refugee Rights in Kenya.* Kenya: International Commission of Jurists (Kenya Section).

International Crisis Group. 2012. *Kenyan Somali Islamist Radicalisation.* Africa Briefing No. 85. Brussels: International Crisis Group.

Jacobsen, Karen. 1996. Factors Influencing the Policy Responses of Host Governments to Mass Refugee Influxes. *International Migration Review* 30(3): 655–78.

Jacobson, David. 1996. *Rights across Borders: Immigration and the Decline of Citizenship.* Baltimore, MD: Johns Hopkins University Press.

Jamal, Arafat. 2000. *Minimum Standards and Essential Needs in a Protracted Refugee Situation: A Review of the UNHCR Programme in Kakuma, Kenya.* Geneva: UNHCR Evaluation and Policy Analysis Unit.

Jordan-Syria. Refugees Say It Is Becoming Harder to Leave. 2012. *IRIN News*. March 21.

JRS, Jesuit Refugee Service. 1993. Wood Avenue Referral and Information Center for Refugees. Kenya Refugee Notes 4. Nairobi: JRS. (LK-3: Refugee Studies Centre Grey Literature Collection, University of Oxford).

Kagan, Michael. 2006. The Beleaguered Gatekeeper: Protection Challenges Posed by UNHCR Refugee Status Determination. *International Journal of Refugee Law* 18(1): 1–29.

Kagan, Michael. 2009. The (Relative) Decline of Palestinian Exceptionalism and Its Consequences for Refugee Studies in the Middle East. *Journal of Refugee Studies* 22(4): 417–38.

Kagan, Michael. 2011. "We Live in a Country of UNHCR": The UN Surrogate State and Refugee Policy in the Middle East. New Issues in Refugee Research No. 201. Geneva: UNHCR Policy Development and Evaluation Service.

Kagan, Michael. 2016. RSD Watch. Available from https://rsdwatch.com/.

Kagwanja, Peter. 1998. Investing in Asylum: Ethiopian Forced Migrants and the Matatu Industry in Nairobi. In *Réfugiés Urbains À Nairobi (Les Cahiers De L'IFRA N° 10)*, 51–69. Nairobi: Institut Français de Recherche en Afrique.

Kagwanja, Peter. 2002. Strengthening Local Relief Capacity in Kenya: Challenges and Prospects. In *Eroding Local Capacity: International Humanitarian Capacity in Africa*, edited by Monica Juma and Astri Suhrke, 94–115. Uppsala, Sweden: Nordiska Afrikainstitutet.

Kagwanja, Peter, and Monica Juma. 2008. Somali Refugees: Protracted Exile and Shifting Security Frontiers. In *Protracted Refugee Situations: Political, Human Rights, and Security Implications*, edited by Gil Loescher, James Milner, Edward Newman, and Gary Troeller, 214–47. Tokyo: United Nations University Press.

Kaiser, Tania. 2008. Sudanese Refugees in Uganda and Kenya. In *Protracted Refugee Situations: Political, Human Rights, and Security Implications*, edited by Gil Loescher, James Milner, Edward Newman, and Gary Troeller, 248–76. Tokyo: United Nations University Press.

Kaşlı, Zeynep, and Ayşe Parla. 2009. Broken Lines of Il/Legality and the Reproduction of State Sovereignty: The Impact of Visa Policies on Immigrants to Turkey from Bulgaria. *Alternatives* 34: 203–27.

Kaya, İbrahim. 2009. The Iraqi Refugee Crisis and Turkey: A Legal Outlook. CARIM Analytic and Synthetic Notes 2009/20. Florence: Robert Schuman Centre for Advanced Studies, European University Institute.

Kaynak, Muhteşem, ed. 1992. *The Iraqi Asylum Seekers and Türkiye, 1988–1991*. Ankara: Tanmak Publications.

Keely, Charles B. 1996. How Nation-States Create and Respond to Refugee Flows. *International Migration Review* 30(4): 1046–66.

Kenya. 2010. In *Europa World Online Archive*, 2571–94. London: Routledge.

Kenya, Republic of. 1980. *Kenya National Assembly Official Record (Hansard)*. 4th Parliament, 2nd Session.

Kenya, Republic of. 1981. *Kenya National Assembly Official Record (Hansard)*. 4th Parliament, 3rd Session.

Kenya, Republic of. 1987. *Kenya National Assembly Official Record (Hansard)*. 5th Parliament, 5th Session.

Kenya, Republic of. 1991. *Kenya National Assembly Official Record (Hansard)*. 6th Parliament, 4th Session.

Kenya, Republic of. 1993. *Kenya National Assembly Official Record (Hansard)*. 7th Parliament, 2nd Session.

Kenya, Republic of. 1995. *Kenya National Assembly Official Record (Hansard)*. 7th Parliament, 4th Session.

Kenya, Republic of. 1996. *Kenya National Assembly Official Record (Hansard)*. 7th Parliament, 5th Session.

Kenya, Republic of. 1998. *Kenya National Assembly Official Record (Hansard)*. 8th Parliament, 1st Session.

Kenya, Republic of. 2002. *Kenya National Assembly Official Record (Hansard)*. 8th Parliament, 4th Session.

Kenya, Republic of. 2003. *Kenya National Assembly Official Record (Hansard)*. 9th Parliament, 2nd Session.

Kenya, Republic of. 2006. *Kenya National Assembly Official Record (Hansard)*. 9th Parliament, 5th Session.

Kenya, Republic of. 2007. The Refugees Act 2006. *Kenya Gazette Supplement No. 97*. Acts No.13, 2 January.

Kenya, Republic of. 2009. *The Refugees (Reception, Registration and Adjudication) Regulations, 2009*. 27 February.

Kenya, Republic of. 2010. *Kenya National Assembly Official Record (Hansard)*. 10th Parliament, 4th Session.

Kenyan Ministry of State for Immigration and Registration of Persons. 2009. *Strategic Plan 2008–2012*. Nairobi: Kenya National Bureau of Statistics.

Kirişci, Kemal. 1991a. The Legal Status of Asylum Seekers in Turkey: Problems and Prospects. *International Journal of Refugee Law* 3(3): 510–28.

Kirişci, Kemal. 1991b. Refugee Movements and Turkey. *International Migration* 29(4): 545–60.

Kirişci, Kemal. 1996a. Is Turkey Lifting the "Geographical Limitation"? The November 1994 Regulation on Asylum in Turkey. *International Journal of Refugee Law* 8(3): 293–317.

Kirişci, Kemal. 1996b. Refugees of Turkish Origin: "Coerced Immigrants" to Turkey since 1945. *International Migration* 34(3): 385–412.

Kirişci, Kemal. 2000. Disaggregating Turkish Citizenship and Immigration Practices. *Middle Eastern Studies* 36(3): 1–22.

Kirişci, Kemal. 2001. UNHCR and Turkey: Cooperating for Improved Implementation of the 1951 Convention Relating to the Status of Refugees. *International Journal of Refugee Law* 13(1/2): 71–97.

Kirkby, John, Ted Kliest, Georg Frerks, Wiert Flikkema, and Phil O'Keefe. 1997. Unhcr's Cross Border Operation in Somalia: The Value of Quick Impact Projects for Refugee Resettlement. *Journal of Refugee Studies* 10(2): 181–98.

Klotz, Audie. 2013. *Migration and National Identity in South Africa, 1860–2010*. New York: Cambridge University Press.

Krajeski, Jenna. 2013. The Accidental Victims of Morsi's Fall. *The New Yorker*. September 8.

Krasner, Stephen D. 1999. *Sovereignty: Organized Hypocrisy*. Princeton, NJ: Princeton University Press.

Kressler, Iren. 2017. Egypt Picks Sides in the Syrian War: How Sisi Learned to Love Asad. *Foreign Affairs*. February 12.

Lancaster, Tony. 2000. The Incidental Parameter Problem since 1948. *Journal of Econometrics* 95(2): 391–413.

Latif, Dilek. 2002. Refugee Policy of the Turkish Republic. *Milletlerarası Münasebetler Türk Yıllığı [The Turkish Yearbook of International Relations]* 33: 1–29.

Lawyers Committee for Human Rights. 1995. *African Exodus: Refugee Crisis, Human Rights, and the 1969 OAU Convention.* New York: Lawyers Committee for Human Rights.

Lindley, Anna. 2011. Between a Protracted and a Crisis Situation: Policy Responses to Somali Refugees in Kenya. *Refugee Survey Quarterly* 30(4): 14–49.

Loescher, Gil. 1989. Introduction: Refugee Issues in International Relations. In *Refugees and International Relations*, edited by Gil Loescher and Laila Monahan, 1–33. Oxford: Oxford University Press.

Loescher, Gil. 2001. *The UNHCR and World Politics: A Perilous Path.* Oxford: Oxford University Press.

Loescher, Gil, and John A. Scanlan. 1986. *Calculated Kindness: Refugees and America's Half-Open Door, 1945 to the Present.* New York: Free Press.

Lomongin, Augustine. 2001. Policy Overview: Kenya Experience. Presentation at the second Workshop of the Refugee Policy Review Project, Dar es Salaam, Tanzania, 30 Mar., LT-40 CONF REFPOL 2001: Refugee Studies Centre Grey Literature Collection, University of Oxford.

Maigua, Patrick. 2010. Human Rights Chief Decries Egypt's Use of Lethal Force against Migrants. *UN Radio.* March 2.

Makinda, Samuel. 1985. Shifting Alliances in the Horn of Africa. *Survival: Global Politics and Strategy* 27(1): 11–19.

Marshall, Monty G. 1999. *Third World War: System, Process, and Conflict Dynamics.* Boulder, CO: Rowman & Littlefield.

Marshall, Monty G., and Keith Jaggers. 2002. Polity IV Dataset. Center for International Development and Conflict Management, University of Maryland. Available from http://www.systemicpeace.org/polityproject.html.

Marshall, Monty G., Ted Robert Gurr, and Barbara Harff. 2010. Political Instability Task Force, State Failure Problem Set, 1955–2009. Center for Systemic Peace. Available from http://www.systemicpeace.org/inscrdata.html.

Metz, Helen Chapin. 1992. *Sudan: A Country Study.* Washington, DC: Federal Research Division, Library of Congress.

Miller, Banks, Linda Camp Keith, and Jennifer S. Holmes. 2015. *Immigration Judges and US Asylum Policy.* Philadelphia: University of Pennsylvania Press.

Milner, James. 2009. *Refugees, the State, and the Politics of Asylum in Africa.* Basingstoke, UK: Palgrave Macmillan.

Minorities at Risk Project. 2009. Minorities at Risk Dataset. Center for International Development and Conflict Management, College Park, MD. Available from http://www.mar.umd.edu/.

Mogire, Edward. 2009. Refugee Realities: Refugee Rights versus State Security in Kenya and Tanzania. *Transformation: An International Journal of Holistic Mission Studies* 26(1): 15–29.

Mogire, Edward. 2011. *Victims as Security Threats: Refugee Impact on Host State Security in Africa.* Burlington, VT: Ashgate.

Moore, Will H., and Stephen M. Shellman. 2007. Whither Will They Go? A Global Study of Refugees' Destinations, 1965–1995. *International Studies Quarterly* 51(4): 811–34.

Moorthy, Shweta, and Robert Brathwaite. 2016. Refugees and Rivals: The International Dynamics of Refugee Flows. *Conflict Management and Peace Science*. Advance online publication. doi: 10.1177/0738894216657047.

Moravcsik, Andrew. 2000. The Origins of Human Rights Regimes: Democratic Delegation in Postwar Europe. *International Organization* 54(2): 217–52.

Moret, Joëlle, Simone Baglioni, and Denise Efionayi-Mäder. 2006. *The Path of Somali Refugees into Exile: A Comparative Analysis of Secondary Movements and Policy Responses*. Sfm Studies 46. Neuchâtel, Switzerland: Swiss Forum for Migration and Population Studies.

Mueller, Carol. 1999. Escape from the GDR, 1961–1989: Hybrid Exit Repertoires in a Disintegrating Leninist Regime. *American Journal of Sociology* 105(3): 697–735.

Müftüler-Bac, Meltem. 1997. *Turkey's Relations with a Changing Europe*. New York: St. Martin's Press.

Naimark, Norman M. 1992. "Ich Will Hier Raus": Emigration and the Collapse of the German Democratic Republic. In *Eastern Europe in Revolution*, edited by Ivo Banac, 72–95. Ithaca, NY: Cornell University Press.

Ndege, Peter O., Peter Kagwanja, and Edward O. Odiyo. 2002. *Refugees in Law and in Fact: A Review of the Literature and Research Agenda in Kenya*. Eldoret, Kenya: Moi University Press.

Neumayer, Eric. 2004. Asylum Destination Choice: What Makes Some European Countries More Attractive Than Others? *European Union Politics* 5(2): 155–80.

Neumayer, Eric. 2005. Asylum Recognition Rates in Western Europe: Their Determinants, Variation, and Lack of Convergence. *Journal of Conflict Resolution* 49(1): 43–66.

Neyman, J., and Elizabeth L. Scott. 1948. Consistent Estimates Based on Partially Consistent Observations. *Econometrica* 16(1): 1–32.

O'Neill, William, Bonaventure Rutinwa, and Guglielmo Verdirame. 2000. The Great Lakes: A Survey of the Application of the Exclusion Clauses in the Central African Republic, Kenya, and Tanzania. *International Journal of Refugee Law* 12(Suppl. 1): 135–70.

OAU Convention Governing the Specific Aspects of Refugee Problems in Africa. 1969. United Nations Treaty Series 1001. Addis Ababa.

Odhiambo-Abuya, E. 2004. United Nations High Commissioner for Refugees and Status Determination Imtaxaan in Kenya: An Empirical Survey. *Journal of African Law* 48(2): 187–206.

Olupot, Milton. 2004. Uganda: Ali Warns on Refugee Law. *allAfrica.com*. February 18.

Othman, Dalia. 2010. سفير إريتريا فى القاهرة: الهارب ليس له أى حقوق فى أى دولة .. ونتفهم موقف مصر من المتسللين [Eritrea's Ambassador in Cairo: Fugitives Do Not Have Any Rights in Any Country . . . We Understand Egypt's Position on Infiltrators]. *Al-Masry Al-Youm*. March 24.

Otunnu, Ogenga. 1992. Factors Affecting the Treatment of Kenyan-Somalis and Somali Refugees in Kenya: A Historical Overview. *Refuge* 12(5): 21–26.

Paoletti, Emanuela. 2011. *The Migration of Power and North-South Inequalities: The Case of Italy and Libya*. Basingstoke, UK: Palgrave Macmillan.

Papke, Leslie E., and Jeffrey M. Wooldridge. 1996. Econometric Methods for Fractional Response Variables with an Application to 401(K) Plan Participation Rates. *Journal of Applied Econometrics* 11(6): 619–32.

Papke, Leslie E., and Jeffrey M. Wooldridge. 2008. Panel Data Methods for Fractional Response Variables with an Application to Test Pass Rates. *Journal of Econometrics* 145(1–2): 121–33.

Pavanello, Sara, Samir Elhawary, and Sara Pantuliano. 2010. Hidden and Exposed: Urban Refugees in Nairobi, Kenya. Humanitarian Policy Group Working Paper. London: Overseas Development Institute.

Pérouse de Montclos, Marc-Antoine. 1998a. Le Poids De L'histoire Et Le Choc Des Cultures: Les Réfugiés Somaliens Du Kenya Confrontés À La Raison D'état. In *Communautés Déracinées Dans Les Pays Du Sud (Autrepart / Les Cahiers Des Sciences Humaines N° 5)*, edited by Véronique Lassailly-Jacob, 155–71. Bondy, France: ORSTOM.

Pérouse de Montclos, Marc-Antoine. 1998b. Nairobi: Des Étrangers En La Ville. Quelle Assimilation Urbaine Pour Les Réfugiés Immigrés En Afrique? *Réfugiés Urbains À Nairobi (Les Cahiers De L'ifra N° 10)*, 7–40. Nairobi: Institut Français de Recherche en Afrique.

Pérouse de Montclos, Marc-Antoine. 1999. Les Reconstructions Identitaires De L'exode: Les Réfugiés Somaliens À Montbassa, Kenya. In *Variations (Autrepart N° 11)*, 27–46. Bondy: ORSTOM.

Pérouse de Montclos, Marc-Antoine. 2008. Marges Urbaines Et Migrations Forcées: Les Réfugiés À L'épreuve Des Camps En Afrique De L'est. In *La Ville Face À Ses Marges (Autrepart / Revue De Sciences Sociales Au Sud N° 45)*, edited by Alexis Sierra and Jérôme Tadié, 191–205. Bondy, France: L'Institut de Recherche pour le Développement (IRD).

Pérouse de Montclos, Marc-Antoine, and Peter Kagwanja. 2000. Refugee Camps or Cities? The Socio-Economic Dynamics of the Dadaab and Kakuma Camps in Northern Kenya. *Journal of Refugee Studies* 13(2): 205–22.

Petkova, Lilia. 2002. The Ethnic Turks in Bulgaria: Social Integration and Impact on Bulgarian-Turkish Relations, 1947–2000. *Global Review of Ethnopolitics* 1(4): 42–59.

Pfaff, Steven. 2006. *Exit-Voice Dynamics and the Collapse of East Germany: The Crisis of Leninism and the Revolution of 1989*. Durham, NC: Duke University Press.

Polat, Rabia Karakaya. 2018. Religious Solidarity, Historical Mission and Moral Superiority: Construction of External and Internal "Others" in AKP's Discourses on Syrian Refugees in Turkey. *Critical Discourse Studies* 15(5): 500–16.

Protocol Relating to the Status of Refugees. 1967. *United Nations Treaty Series 606, 267*. New York.

Putnam, Robert D. 1988. Diplomacy and Domestic Politics: The Logic of Two-Level Games. *International Organization* 42(3): 427–60.

Ramji-Nogales, Jaya, Andrew I. Schoenholtz, and Philip G. Schrag. 2009. *Refugee Roulette: Disparities in Asylum Adjudication and Proposals for Reform*. New York: New York University Press.

RCK, Refugee Consortium of Kenya. 2003. Refugee Management in Kenya. *Forced Migration Review* 16: 17–19.

RCK, Refugee Consortium of Kenya. 2012. *Asylum under Threat: Assessing the Protection of Somali Refugees in Dadaab Refugee Camps and Along the Migration Corridor*. Nairobi: RCK.

Refugees International. 2007. *Egypt: Respond to the Needs of Iraqi Refugees*. Washington, DC: Refugees International.

Refugees International. 2007. *Iraqi Refugees: A Lot of Talk, Little Action*. Washington, DC: Refugees International.

Remmer, Karen L. 1986. The Politics of Economic Stabilization: IMF Standby Programs in Latin America, 1954–1984. *Comparative Politics* 19(1): 1–24.

Riddle, Liesl A., and Cynthia Buckley. 1998. Forced Migration and Destination Choice: Armenian Forced Settlers and Refugees in the Russian Federation. *International Migration* 36(2): 235–53.

Risse, Thomas, Stephen C. Ropp, and Kathryn Sikkink. 1999. *The Power of Human Rights: International Norms and Domestic Change*. New York: Cambridge University Press.

Roman, Howaida. 2009. Iraqi Refugees in Egypt. CARIM Research Reports 2009/06. Florence: Robert Schuman Centre for Advanced Studies, European University Institute.

Rosen, Nir. 2007. The Flight from Iraq. *New York Times*. May 13.

Rosenblum, Marc. 2004. *The Transnational Politics of US Immigration Policy*. La Jolla, CA: Center for Comparative Immigration Studies, University of California, San Diego.

Rosenblum, Marc R., and Idean Salehyan. 2004. Norms and Interests in US Asylum Enforcement. *Journal of Peace Research* 41(6): 677–97.

Rüegger, Seraina, and Heidrun Bohnet. 2018. The Ethnicity of Refugees (ER): A New Dataset for Understanding Flight Patterns. *Conflict Management and Peace Science* 35(1): 65–88.

Rutinwa, Bonaventure. 1999. *The End of Asylum? The Changing Nature of Refugee Policies in Africa*. Geneva: Centre for Documentation and Research, United Nations High Commissioner for Refugees.

Sadek, Sara. 2010. Iraqi "Temporary Guests" in Neighboring Countries. In *On the Move: Migration Challenges in the Indian Ocean Littoral*, edited by Ellen Laipson and Amit Pandya, 43–54. Washington, DC: Henry L. Stimson Center.

Sadiq, Kamal. 2009. *Paper Citizens: How Illegal Immigrants Acquire Citizenship in Developing Countries*. Oxford: Oxford University Press.

Sakataka, William. 1992. Kenya's Experience in Refugee Administration. Paper presented at the National Seminar on Refugee Rights and Law, Eldoret, Kenya, LK-44 CONF MOI 1992: Refugee Studies Centre Grey Literature Collection, University of Oxford.

Salehyan, Idean, and Kristian Gleditsch. 2006. Refugees and the Spread of Civil War. *International Organization* 60(2): 335–66.

Samy, Shahira. 2009. The Impact of Civil Society on Refugee Politics in Egypt. CARIM Research Reports 2009/07. Florence: Robert Schuman Centre for Advanced Studies, European University Institute.

Saraçoğlu, Cenk, and Özhan Demirkol. 2015. Nationalism and Foreign Policy Discourse in Turkey under the AKP Rule: Geography, History and National Identity. *British Journal of Middle Eastern Studies* 42(3): 301–19.

Sarkees, Meredith Reid. 2000. The Correlates of War Data on War: An Update to 1997. *Conflict Management and Peace Science* 18(1): 123–44.

Sarkees, Meredith Reid, and Frank Wayman. 2010. *Resort to War: A Data Guide to Inter-State, Extra-State, Intra-State and Non-State Wars, 1816–2007*. Washington, DC: CQ Press.

Sassen, Saskia. 1996. *Losing Control? Sovereignty in an Age of Globalization*. New York: Columbia University Press.

Shanks, Cheryl. 2001. *Immigration and the Politics of American Sovereignty, 1890–1990*. Ann Arbor: University of Michigan Press.

Slaughter, Amy, and Jeff Crisp. 2008. A Surrogate State? The Role of UNHCR in Protracted Refugee Situations. In *Protracted Refugee Situations: Political, Human Rights and Security Implications*, edited by Gil Loescher, James Milner, Edward Newman, and Gary Troeller, 123–40. Tokyo: United Nations University Press.

Smrkolj, Maja. 2010. International Institutions and Individualized Decision-Making: An Example of Unhcr's Refugee Status Determination. In *The Exercise of Public Authority by International Institutions: Advancing International Institutional Law*, edited by Armin Bogdandy, Rüdiger Wolfrum, Jochen Bernstorff, Philipp Dann, and Matthias Goldmann, 165–93. Heidelberg: Springer.

Soysal, Yasemin Nuhoğlu. 1994. *Limits of Citizenship: Migrants and Postnational Membership in Europe*. Chicago, IL: University of Chicago.

Sperl, Stefan. 2001. *Evaluation of UNHCR's Policy on Refugees in Urban Areas: A Case Study Review of Cairo*. Geneva: UNHCR Evaluation and Policy Analysis Unit.

Stinnett, Douglas M., Jaroslav Tir, Philip Schafer, Paul F. Diehl, and Charles Gochman. 2002. The Correlates of War Project Direct Contiguity Data, Version 3. *Conflict Management and Peace Science* 19(2): 58–66.

Syria Laying Landmines along Border: Human Rights Watch. 2012. *BBC News*. March 13.

Tajfel, Henri. 1981. *Human Groups and Social Categories: Studies in Social Psychology*. Cambridge, UK: Cambridge University Press.

Tajfel, Henri, and John C. Turner. 1986. The Social Identity Theory of Intergroup Behavior. In *Psychology of Intergroup Relations*, edited by Stephen Worchel and William G. Austin, 7–24. Chicago, IL: Nelson-Hall.

Tanrısever, Oktay F. 2003. Turkey and the Russian Federation: Towards a Mutual Understanding? In *Turkey's Foreign Policy in the 21st Century: A Changing Role in World Politics*, edited by Tareq Y. Ismael and Mustafa Aydın, 121–38. Burlington, VT: Ashgate.

Tekle, Amare. 1996. International Relations in the Horn of Africa (1991–96). *Review of African Political Economy* 23(70): 499–509.

Thielemann, Eiko R. 2018. Why Refugee Burden-Sharing Initiatives Fail: Public Goods, Free-Riding and Symbolic Solidarity in the EU. *Journal of Common Market Studies* 56(1): 63–82.

Torpey, John. 1992. Two Movements, Not a Revolution: Exodus and Opposition in the East German Transformation, 1989–1990. *German Politics and Society* 26: 21–42.

Tóth, Miklós. 2011. African Refugees and the Challenges to UNHCR. In *The African State in a Changing Global Context*, edited by István Tarrósy, Loránd Szabó and Goran Hyden, 173–88. Berlin: Lit.

Trapped between Egypt and Iraq. 2008. *Al-Ahram Weekly*. April 10–16.

Tschirgi, Dan. 2003. Turkey and the Arab World in the New Millennium. In *Turkey's Foreign Policy in the 21st Century: A Changing Role in World Politics*, edited by Tareq Y. Ismael and Mustafa Aydın, 103–20. Burlington, VT: Ashgate.

Turkey. 2010. In *Europa World Online Archive*, 4460–96. London: Routledge.

Turkey, Republic of. 1953. *Türkiye Büyük Millet Meclisi—Genel Kurul Tutanağı [Grand National Assembly of Turkey—Minutes of the General Assembly]*. 9. Dönem, 3.Yasama Yılı.

Turkey, Republic of. 1988. *Türkiye Büyük Millet Meclisi—Genel Kurul Tutanağı [Grand National Assembly of Turkey—Minutes of the General Assembly]*. 18. Dönem, 2. Yasama Yılı.

Turkey, Republic of. 1990. *Türkiye Büyük Millet Meclisi—Genel Kurul Tutanağı [Grand National Assembly of Turkey—Minutes of the General Assembly]*. 18. Dönem, 3. Yasama Yılı.

Turkey, Republic of. 1992. *Türkiye Büyük Millet Meclisi—Genel Kurul Tutanağı [Grand National Assembly of Turkey—Minutes of the General Assembly].* 19. Dönem, 1. Yasama Yılı.

Turkey, Republic of. 1995. *Türkiye Büyük Millet Meclisi—Genel Kurul Tutanağı [Grand National Assembly of Turkey—Minutes of the General Assembly].* 19. Dönem, 5. Yasama Yılı.

Turkish Ministry for EU Affairs. 2001. *National Program for the Adoption of the EU Acquis.* Available from https://www.ab.gov.tr/_195_en.html.

UNHCR, United Nations High Commissioner for Refugees. n.d. UNHCR Statistical Online Population Database. Available from http://popstats.unhcr.org/.

UNHCR, United Nations High Commissioner for Refugees. 1977. Conclusion Adopted by the Executive Committee on the International Protection of Refugees No. 8 (Xxviii): Determination of Refugee Status. Geneva: UNHCR.

UNHCR, United Nations High Commissioner for Refugees. 2004. *Country Operations Plan 2005—Arab Republic of Egypt.* Geneva: UNHCR.

UNHCR, United Nations High Commissioner for Refugees. 2005. *Analysis of Refugee Protection Capacity, Kenya.* Geneva: UNHCR.

UNHCR, United Nations High Commissioner for Refugees. 2009. Egypt. Global Report 2008. Geneva: UNHCR.

UNHCR, United Nations High Commissioner for Refugees. 2009. *Global Appeal 2010– 2011.* Geneva: UNHCR.

UNHCR, United Nations High Commissioner for Refugees. 2011a. *Global Report 2010.* Geneva: UNHCR.

UNHCR, United Nations High Commissioner for Refugees. 2011b. *Statistical Yearbook 2010.* Geneva: UNHCR.

UNHCR, United Nations High Commissioner for Refugees. 2011c. *UNHCR Global Trends 2010: 60 Years and Still Counting.* Geneva: UNHCR.

UNHCR, United Nations High Commissioner for Refugees. 2012. *UNHCR Global Trends 2011: A Year of Crises.* Geneva: UNHCR.

UNHCR, United Nations High Commissioner for Refugees. 2013. Episode 1: Welcome to Za'atari. *A Day in the Life: Za'atari.* YouTube.

UNHCR, United Nations High Commissioner for Refugees. 2014. *Providing for Protection: Assisting States with the Assumption of Responsibility for Refugee Status Determination.* Geneva: UNHCR.

UNHCR, United Nations High Commissioner for Refugees. 2015. *Guidelines on International Protection No. 11: Prima Facie Recognition of Refugee Status.* Geneva: UNHCR.

UNHCR, United Nations High Commissioner for Refugees. 2019. *UNHCR Global Trends: Forced Displacement in 2018.* Geneva: UNHCR.

UNHCR, United Nations High Commissioner for Refugees. 2020a. *Global Report 2019.* Geneva: UNHCR.

UNHCR, United Nations High Commissioner for Refugees. 2020b. *UNHCR Global Trends: Forced Displacement in 2019.* Geneva: UNHCR.

UNRWA, United Nations Relief and Works Agency for Palestine Refugees in the Near East. 1955. Special Report of the Director Concerning Other Claimants for Relief. UN Doc. A/2978/Add.1. New York: United Nations.

US Department of Justice. 2017. Office of the Chief Immigration Judge. Available from https://www.justice.gov/eoir/office-of-the-chief-immigration-judge.

US Department of State. 2006. 2005 Human Rights Report: Egypt. In *2005 County Reports on Human Rights Practices*. Washington, DC: US G.P.O.

US Department of State. 2009. 2008 Human Rights Report: Egypt. In *2008 Country Reports on Human Rights Practices*. Washington, DC: US G.P.O.

USCRI, US Committee for Refugees and Immigrants. 1997. *World Refugee Survey 1997*. Washington, DC: USCRI.

USCRI, US Committee for Refugees and Immigrants. 1998. *World Refugee Survey 1998*. Washington, DC: USCRI.

USCRI, US Committee for Refugees and Immigrants. 2009. *World Refugee Survey 2009*. Washington, DC: USCRI.

Vaubel, Roland. 1986. A Public Choice Approach to International Organization. *Public Choice* 51(1): 39–57.

Veney, Cassandra. 2007. *Forced Migration in East Africa: Democratization, Structural Adjustment, and Refugees*. New York: Palgrave Macmillan.

Verdirame, Guglielmo. 1999. Human Rights and Refugees: The Case of Kenya. *Journal of Refugee Studies* 12(1): 54–77.

Verdirame, Guglielmo, and Barbara Harrell-Bond. 2005. *Rights in Exile: Janus-Faced Humanitarianism*. New York: Berghahn Books.

Vogt, Manuel, Nils-Christian Bormann, Seraina Rüegger, Lars-Erik Cederman, Philipp Hunziker, and Luc Girardin. 2015. Integrating Data on Ethnicity, Geography, and Conflict: The Ethnic Power Relations Dataset Family. *Journal of Conflict Resolution* 59(7): 1327–42.

Volkens, Andrea, Pola Lehmann, Theres Matthieß, Nicolas Merz, Sven Regel, and Annika Werner. 2016. The Manifesto Data Collection: Manifesto Project (MRG/CMP/MARPOR) Version 2016a. Wissenschaftszentrum Berlin für Sozialforschung (WZB). Available from https://manifesto-project.wzb.eu/.

Vreeland, James Raymond. 2003. *The IMF and Economic Development*. Cambridge: Cambridge University Press.

Wagacha, John Burton, and John Guiney. 2008. The Plight of Urban Refugees in Nairobi, Kenya. In *Refugee Rights: Ethics, Advocacy, and Africa*, edited by David Hollenbach, 91–101. Washington, DC: Georgetown University Press.

Waters, Mary C. 1990. *Ethnic Options: Choosing Identities in America*. Berkeley: University of California Press.

Weiner, Myron. 1992. Security, Stability and International Migration. *International Security* 17(3): 91–126.

Weiner, Myron. 1993. Security, Stability and International Migration. In *International Migration and Security*, edited by Myron Weiner, 1–35. Boulder, CO: Westview Press.

Weiner, Myron. 1996. Bad Neighbors, Bad Neighborhoods: An Inquiry into the Causes of Refugee Flows. *International Security* 21(1): 5–42.

Whitaker, Beth Elise. 2008. Funding the International Refugee Regime: Implications for Protection. *Global Governance* 14(2): 241–58.

Williams, John H. P., and Lester A. Zeager. 2004. Macedonian Border Closings in the Kosovo Refugee Crisis: A Game-Theoretic Perspective. *Conflict Management and Peace Science* 21: 233–54.

Wimmer, Andreas. 2008. The Making and Unmaking of Ethnic Boundaries: A Multilevel Process Theory. *American Journal of Sociology* 113(4): 970–1022.

Wooldridge, Jeffrey M. 2010. *Econometric Analysis of Cross Section and Panel Data*. 2nd ed. Cambridge: Massachusetts Institute of Technology Press.

World Bank. 2019. World Development Indicators. Available from http://www.world-bank.org/data.

Yinanç, Barçın. 2012. West, Turkey Split over Aid for Syrians. *Hürriyet Daily News.* September 25.

Yoshikawa, Lynn. 2007. Iraqi Refugees in Egypt. *Forced Migration Review* 29: 54.

Zaiotti, Ruben. 2006. Dealing with Non-Palestinian Refugees in the Middle East: Policies and Practices in an Uncertain Environment. *International Journal of Refugee Law* 18(2): 333–53.

Zieck, Marjoleine. 2010. UNHCR and Turkey, and Beyond: Of Parallel Tracks and Symptomatic Cracks. *International Journal of Refugee Law* 22(4): 593–622.

Zohry, Ayman, and Barbara Harrell-Bond. 2003. *Contemporary Egyptian Migration: An Overview of Voluntary and Forced Migration.* Cairo: Forced Migration and Refugee Studies Program, American University in Cairo.

Zolberg, Aristide R., Astri Suhrke, and Sergio Aguayo. 1986. International Factors in the Formation of Refugee Movements. *International Migration Review* 20(2): 151–69.

Zolberg, Aristide R., Astri Suhrke, and Sergio Aguayo. 1989. *Escape from Violence: Conflict and the Refugee Crisis in the Developing World.* New York: Oxford University Press.

Zucker, Norman L., and Naomi Flink Zucker. 1987. *The Guarded Gate: The Reality of American Refugee Policy.* San Diego: Harcourt Brace Jovanovich.

# Index

Tables, figures and map are indicated by *t, f* and *m* following the page number